· Dr Hubertus F. Jahn
  ↳ Cambridge
      ↳ Russia, Poverty,
      Social and cultural
      History, Popular
      Culture.

· David Moon
  ↳ York
      ↳ Russia, Peasantry,
      Agrarian History,
      Poverty and
      Land.

Peasants in Russia
from Serfdom to Stalin

The Bloomsbury History of Modern Russia Series

This ambitious and unique series offers readers the latest views on aspects of the modern history of what has been and remains one of the most powerful and important countries in the world. In a series of books aimed at students, leading academics and experts from across the world portray, in a thematic manner, a broad variety of aspects of the Russian experience, over extended periods of time, from the reign of Peter the Great in the early eighteenth century to the Putin era at the beginning of the twenty-first.

Available:

Crime and Punishment in Russia: A Comparative History from Peter the Great to Vladimir Putin, Jonathan Daly

Forthcoming:

The History of the Russian Worker: Life and Change from Peter the Great to Vladimir Putin, Alice Pate (2018)

Law and the Russian State: Russia's Legal Evolution from Peter the Great to Vladimir Putin, William Pomeranz (2018)

Marx and Russia: A History of Marxist Thought in Russia, James D. White (2018)

A Modern History of Russian Childhood: From Imperialism to the End of the Soviet Era, Elizabeth White (2018)

Peasants in Russia
from Serfdom to Stalin

Accommodation, Survival, Resistance

Boris B. Gorshkov

Bloomsbury Academic
An imprint of Bloomsbury Publishing Plc

BLOOMSBURY
LONDON · OXFORD · NEW YORK · NEW DELHI · SYDNEY

Bloomsbury Academic

An imprint of Bloomsbury Publishing Plc

50 Bedford Square	1385 Broadway
London	New York
WC1B 3DP	NY 10018
UK	USA

www.bloomsbury.com

BLOOMSBURY and the Diana logo are trademarks of Bloomsbury Publishing Plc

First published 2018

British Library Cataloguing-in-Publication Data
A catalogue record for this book is available from the British Library.

ISBN: HB: 978-1-4742-5481-6
ePDF: 978-1-4742-5482-3
eBook: 978-1-4742-5483-0

Library of Congress Cataloging-in-Publication Data
A catalog record for this book is available from the Library of Congress.

Series: The Bloomsbury History of Modern Russia Series

Cover image: 'Peaceful Fields', 1950. Found in the collection of the State Russian Museum, St Petersburg. (© Fine Art Images/Heritage Images/Getty Images)

Typeset by Integra Software Services Pvt. Ltd.
Printed and bound in Great Britain

To find out more about our authors and books visit www.bloomsbury.com. Here you will find extracts, author interviews, details of forthcoming events and the option to sign up for our newsletters.

In memory of millions of Russian peasants.
To all my students and teachers.

Contents

Figures

Tables

Acknowledgments

The author is highly indebted to all with whom he had the chance and pleasure to study and work. He is grateful to his colleagues at the University of Tennessee at Chattanooga and his former colleagues at Kennesaw State University and Auburn University. He is especially thankful to his Russian History students at the University of Tennessee at Chattanooga.

Preface

Scholarship on the Russian peasantry has been experiencing a period of testing in both manner and matter. In recent years, popular culture, identities, and memories have become innovative areas of peasant studies. This book offers a combination of social, economic, political, and cultural history of the Russian peasantry with a slight emphasis on peasant ecology in order to accommodate the environmental diversity of Russia. This book is directed at students of Russian history or peasant studies, as well as at general readers and scholars interested in Russian history. Wherever possible I have tried to avoid excessive citations. Footnotes contain references to historiography and primary sources, as well as basic facts regarding events, places, or people in order to help the general reader with the historical setting. Bibliographic notes and suggested readings will help the reader with further inquiries and additional historical investigation about the subject. The author assumes that most readers do not read Russian. In most instances I have therefore used the English equivalents for Russian terms, which follow immediately in parentheses. In most cases I have used the standard U.S. Library of Congress method for the transliteration of the Russian spellings of Russian given names, patronymics (middle names), and surnames. Customarily, in Russia people have three names: the given (first) name, the middle name (patronymic), and the surname (family name). The Russian middle name (patronymic) is derived from the father's given name. Along with the person's given name, the patronymic is used as a polite or formal form of address. The names of certain historical figures, such as Alexander I or Nicholas II, are given in an anglicized spelling form. Names of cities, places, and rivers are given in a manner familiar to those who read English. Direct transliteration is used for the titles of Russian-language publications in those notes that contain suggested further reading. I am assuming that the further reading suggestions will be taken up mostly by specialists in Russian studies who are familiar with Russian. For those with no knowledge of Russian, I have provided titles of some pertinent English-language studies. All dates are given in the Russian (pre-1917) and post-1917 calendars of the periods, which were used in original texts. The pre-1917 calendar was thirteen days behind the post-1917, Western, and modern Russian calendar.

GEOGRAPHIC ZONES OF MUSCOVY

Legend:

- Central black earth
- Central non-black earth
- Lower-Volga and Don
- Mid-Volga
- North-western
- Northern
- Northern Urals
- Siberia
- Southern Urals

Arkhangelsk
Olonets
Vologda
Great Novgorod
Perm
Viatka
Pskov
Penza
Saratov
Astrakhan
Caucasus
Georgia
Tobolsk
Enisej
Iakutsk
Okhotsk
Tomsk
Irkutsk
Omsk

500 km
200 mi
1 : 17471330

ENVIRONMENTAL ZONES OF MUSCOVY

Legend:

- Forest-heartland
- Open steppe belt
- Siberia
- Transitional forested steppe belt

Arkhangelsk
Olonets
Vologda
Great Novgorod
Pskov
Perm
Viatka
Smolensk
Vladimir
Penza
Orenburg
Saratov
Astrakhan
Caucasus
Georgia
Tobolsk
Enisej
Iakutsk
Okhotsk
Tomsk
Irkutsk
Omsk

500 km
200 mi
1 : 17471330

REGIONS OF IMPERIAL RUSSIA, ca1820

1 : 17471330

Introduction: Institutional, Historiographical, and Conceptual Framework

The reader is the co-author

—*Marina Tsvetaeva*

Perhaps the social issue of utmost importance throughout the long course of imperial and early Soviet history of Russia was the peasant question. The peasantry accounted for the majority of the population. According to the 1897 census, the peasant population was almost 97 million, or 77 percent of the total population. This book offers a history of the Russian peasantry during the imperial and early Soviet eras in light of the most recent research. Its interpretative stance stresses ecology and environment, with emphasis on the dynamic nature of peasant life and work rather than the changeless paradigm that formerly dominated peasant studies. It addresses (a) the rise, evolution, decline, and demise of serfdom; (b) the relationship among the state, lord, and peasant, peasant communal and social institutions (the family and commune); (c) state peasant and rural policies; (d) agrarian reforms; and (e) the rural economy as a complex ecological entity, which included peasant agriculture, land usage, livestock rearing, and nonagricultural endeavors and their evolution over the time period covered. The book also explores revolutionary and early Soviet times, focusing on peasant experiences and activities, agrarian programs, government policies, and peasant strategies to survive and maintain their well-being. The book aims to familiarize students with a way of life that has now largely passed away but which, in one form or another, once characterized rural life throughout much of the world.

Traditionally, the term "peasantry" defined rural inhabitants who engaged in agricultural activities and in raising livestock. In imperial Russia, the peasantry was a legally defined social estate within a broader category called "rural inhabitants." The Russian peasantry represents something of a puzzle, because the Russian term for it, *krest'ianstvo* (peasantry) or *krest'ianin* (male peasant) and *krest'ianka* (female peasant), derives from the word "Christian" and originally referred to Russian Orthodox peasants. The broader social estate "rural inhabitants" includes all imperial peasants, Christian and non-Christian alike. Consequently, total accuracy would require us to call *Russian* peasants "the Russian Orthodox peasantry"; even so, the accustomed term "Russian peasants" will suffice here to signify all such persons. In Russian primary sources, the term "peasants" was first mentioned in the fourteenth century. Even then, rural residents were often called by the traditional older name *liudi*, meaning people or men and women. Another conundrum as regards the Russian peasantry is that the term did not exhaustively reflect its economic activities. It would be a rude, although common, mistake to ascribe to it only activities associated with agriculture and animal husbandry. The Russian peasantry was always multi-occupational, depending on time, place, and season. Russian peasants combined various economic activities needed to sustain their livelihood: from tilling land and raising crops to manufacturing cloth and making tools or working in factories. Some peasants were actors and performers at local marketplaces or noble theatres, or produced arts. Many peasants also engaged in commercial and entrepreneurial activities and were the predominant group at local and national markets. In addition, peasants were the largest subordinate social segment. They were exploited by landlords and by the state (both the imperial and Soviet); they paid state taxes and peasant communes were required to send recruits to the military; and, albeit unequally, they were represented in the elected representative institutions at the local and national levels established in 1864 and 1905. The first and second Dumas gave peasants considerable electoral weight (a majority), whereas the third and fourth drastically lessened that weight. Yet, with their diverse and multifaceted social and economic roles, peasants were important and numerous agents in society rather than the passive ciphers often portrayed in histories.

The Russian peasantry was a subject of the crown (the imperial government) and, later, of the Soviet state. Therefore the state regulated lives of peasants through various laws and reforms. There were numerous kinds of peasants, as defined by the law. During the centuries of serfdom, the majority of them belonged to the state or to individual owners or institutions, including the church and the imperial family. The peasants who belonged to the state were known as state peasants, and those who belonged to landlords were serfs. In addition to these broad classifications, there were numerous subcategories and groups of peasants. These categories derived from the state's policies and the laws or from types of land tenure. Most peasants were multi-occupational, while some worked full-time in imperial and noble factories as workers. Until the abolition of serfdom, the latter were known as "bound peasants" (*posessionnye krest'ane*). Numbers of state peasants and serfs varied, depending on the period under discussion. During the half-century prior to the 1861 reform, the number of serfs gradually decreased. According to the Tenth Imperial Census (1857), male serfs made up about 42 percent of all male peasants and 37 percent of the empire's male population. After the emancipation reforms of 1861–1864, the Russian peasantry obtained legal freedom from the landlord, but the state continued to regulate it through laws and reforms, most notably the Stolypin land reform. Even so, they still were exclusive subjects to the draft (until 1874, when a new law made men from all social strata subject to military service), and they alone paid the poll tax until 1883, when it was abolished. Under the Soviet government, peasants witnessed sweeping and dramatic institutional transformations, originating from the early Bolshevik reforms and culminating in the Stalinist collectivization of agriculture.

Nevertheless, in addition to these characterizations of the Russian peasantry, which are official and scholarly, peasants had their own ways of self-perception and of perceiving other peasants. Perhaps the most fascinating question about peasant identity is how they identified themselves. In contrast to official and scholarly identities, these identities, by nature, were not ascribed. Although peasants were predominantly illiterate and rarely left diaries or memoires, a few pleasant memories are available and offer insights into this matter. From these and other sources, it is clear that peasants thought about themselves in multiple ways. Their self-identity was flexible, multiple, and diverse. It depended on the relation to their immediate environment and on circumstances capable of fostering a feeling of belonging to something or someone. Usually they identified themselves according to their occupation, socioeconomic standing, and place of origin. Serfs might also affiliate themselves with their landlord. For example, trading peasants from Vladimir province would identify themselves as such, if they were trading in other provinces of the Russian Empire. Peasants from other provinces identified the trading peasants from the Vladimir province as *ofeni* (petty traders), whereas trading peasants from other regions were called, variously, *khodebshiki, korobeiniki, kantiuzhniki, shchepetil'shchiki*, etc. (all local variants signifying traders of certain goods). When travelling within their own province, peasants usually identified themselves as peasants of a certain landlord or village. Russian Orthodox peasants identified themselves and others as "Orthodox" when they visited a "non-Orthodox" environment, for example, among Old Believers (a sect within Orthodoxy) or non-Christians. Peasants identified themselves with their villages, districts, provinces, and the country. The affiliation with the country often resulted from events that involved the Russian Empire and gave them a sense of belonging to it. For example, the 1812 war with France, which Russians called the "Great Patriotic War," cultivated solidarity among peasants and made them think as residents (if not citizens) of the country. In this regard, perhaps in contrast with the predominant view, one may assume that peasants did possess a sense of nationality and had a definite concept of their own identity. A sense of ethnic, national, and religious affiliation was particularly common among travelling peasants, who engaged in commercial activities and came into contact with other ethnic, religious, linguistic, or national groups. One serf peasant from Yaroslavl' province, who was literate and accustomed to traveling, visiting Moscow after the 1812 fire, clearly expressed in his memoir a sense of belonging as regards Moscow, the old Russian capital and symbol of Russia. His "heart was beating loud," when he saw the burnt city and the Kremlin.[1] Within Russia, Russian peasants identified themselves and others according to their place of origin and immediate environment. Lastly, peasants possessed personal characteristics and for the most part they acted as individuals; therefore, it is better to view and identify peasants, and analyze their actions as individuals or subgroups rather than en masse as a collective. They acted primarily as individuals, in pursuit of their individual interests and, at the same time, when necessary, as a group (Figure I.1).

Figure I.1 Party by a tavern.

As an important category of analysis, this book utilizes peasant ecology, defined here as the interdependence between peasants, considered as a group and as individuals, and their natural, geographical, and social environments. With its focus on these pertinent factors, this approach helps better understand the vast diversity and complex dynamics of Russia's rural life. Many studies of Russia's rural economy and peasantry have concentrated on state agrarian policies and reforms, and on policymakers' and elites' views about the rural economy and life. Until recently, scholars of the Russian peasantry concentrated too little attention on the peasants' own aptitudes and efforts to develop and carry out their rural economic strategies. Obviously, peasants produced limited records about their lives and therefore finding paths to approach peasant behavior from their point of view is an arduous task for any scholar. The chief primary source that historians use to write peasant history is the record left by the state and by educated elites. Answering questions about peasant economic or social behavior through the eyes of elites and reformers is a tempting and necessary strategy, but it is by no means a sufficiently inclusive or exhaustive one. Furthermore, by definition all existing categories and concepts we habitually use to analyze peasant behavior are scholarly inventions, with all attendant drawbacks.

Over the past century, peasant studies in general (that is, not restricted to Russia) have been dominated by the class and market-relations paradigms. Both paradigms have roots in modernist and later Marxist premises, yet both approach village life from one of two diverse perspectives—moral economy and rational choice—and, it follows, offer contradictory versions of peasant economic behavior. The peasant commune and household traditionally serve as the categories of analysis and models for analyzing the rural economy. Peasant economic activity—within the commune and in the household—has been approached, as noted, from two distinct viewpoints: moral economy, suggested by James Scott, which stresses peasant *communitarianism*,[2] and the rational choice perspective, proposed by Samuel Popkin, which underlines peasant individualist motivations.[3] According to the moral economy perspective, Russia's peasants, who possessed a sense of *communitarianism* rooted in the traditional peasant commune, were driven into collective action, protest, and rebellion by exploitation and oppression. In this light, peasants eventually form a revolutionary class. The peasant commune emerges as the pivotal economic and social organization of peasants. Contrarily, the rational choice school highlights peasants' individualism and tends to portray peasants as rational actors driven by market motivations and profit. In this approach, peasants emerge as counterrevolutionary and even reactionary. Pursued generally from the state and elite perspectives, both approaches have generated many unresolved problems. For example, the dynamics and alterations in the peasant commune and in individual households and the implications of these changes for the rural economy and peasant economic conditions remain unclear. Even the meaning of the commune for the rural economy and peasants remains vague. Nevertheless, the evidence and statistical data that historians provide in support of these disparate approaches actually suggest the existence of *both* communalist and individualist tendencies. Historians of the peasantry tend to accentuate one or the other tendency, without allowing the possibility of their coexistence. Therefore this model of analysis—commune versus individual household—falls short in explaining the dynamics and variations in peasant communal and individual economic activities. Standing alone, each paradigm fails to accommodate contradictory sources, let alone the complexity, regional diversity, and dynamics of the rural economy and society.

Traditionally, historians have viewed tsarist Russia as an exclusively agricultural, non-dynamic, highly structured, rigid, and hierarchical society with an "omnipotent" autocratic aristocracy on the top and, on the bottom, a weak and amorphous, overwhelmingly peasant population, helpless before the power of the state. Historians who utilize these still influential concepts emphasize the role of the state and focus on official state policy with the goal of understanding Russia's historical experience. For example, Richard Pipes stresses the "patrimonial" or "proprietary" nature of the Russian government and emphasizes the powerlessness of Russian society before the state. Thus, the relationship between the state and society was hierarchical and based on policies of coercion and force. The "backward peasant" remote from the outside world and immersed in timeless village customs stands out as one of the enduring images of Russian historiography.[4] Historian Orlando Figes, describing the historical background to the 1917 revolution, assumes "peasant isolation" from the rest of society "at almost every level—legal, political, economic, cultural, social, and geographic...." Figes concludes that peasants "rarely came across anything beyond the narrow confines of their own village and its fields ...."[5] Insofar as the peasantry has been explored from this viewpoint, it has not served as a discrete topic but as an aspect of late tsarist history and as the background to the Bolshevik revolution. In other words, no in-depth study of the peasantry and their way of life that fully utilizes available sources could defend such a position.

In order to understand Russian economic history, scholars concentrate on the economic policies of the state and top state officials or the peasant commune rather than on the efforts of the population, ecological factors, or access to resources. Exclusive focus on industrializing activities of the state has produced the single most influential concept of the industrial revolution in Russia, that of Gerschenkron. According to Gerschenkron's view, the Russian government compensated for the "missing" prerequisites for industrial development by promoting legislative, financial, and entrepreneurial support for industry.[6] Unfortunately, this interpretation provides no independent peasant role in Russia's economic and social development.

Later, as an alternative to Gerschenkron's influential viewpoints, a few historians have suggested the importance of industrialist forces other than those associated with the state. Arcadius Kahan, for example, challenged the notion of "missing" prerequisites by emphasizing the importance of the market, the efforts of the population, especially the peasantry, and the commercial interactions with other nations in Russia's economic development during the first half of the nineteenth century.[7] William Blackwell and Olga Crisp have argued that the early economic development that Gerschenkron thought was absent—in fact created one of the important foundations for the rapid industrial growth during the 1880s and 1890s. According to Crisp, the 1840s "marked the beginning" of Russian industrialization "based on modern technology."[8] Peasant involvement in the nonagricultural economy was not, however, a major concern of these historians.

Regardless, old—one might say outmoded—approaches to Russia's peasantry dominate in many general histories. Even addressing the industrial development of Russia, most historians still follow old interpretations. According to prevailing views, the peasantry constituted an obstacle to Russia's industrialization rather than played any positive role in it.[9] These views were often used and exploited by late imperial elites, who wanted Russia to follow a Western style modernization, and by Soviet scholars and state officials, in order to justify collectivization of agriculture. Among Western scholars, especially those who study the Stalinist period, the concept of the backward Russian peasant prevails. Despite the existence of a small specialized body of studies that point out (but do not explore) the multi-occupational character of the Russian peasant economy, most historians of Russia continue to treat Russian peasants as overwhelmingly medieval and rural and focus on their agricultural activities.[10]

The past two decades, however, have witnessed a significant proliferation of research on the history of the Russian peasantry and on the early Stalinist period in particular. Historians who absorbed the ideas of the "new social history," in contrast to the old school noted above, attempt to explain Russian history "from below," in E. P. Thompson's famous term. They explore various social, economic, and cultural issues, as well as diverse social groups and categories. Most histories, inspired by the promising idea of writing "history from below," deal with the revolutionary and the immediate prerevolutionary periods.[11]

Despite certain shortcomings, this tendency introduced several important new trends into peasant studies. A few social historians have found that within the context of local variations (which had usually been ignored), Russia's peasant society was more dynamic and flexible than previously noticed.[12] David Moon's seminal study of the persistence of serfdom in Russia, for example, suggests that Russian serfdom survived until the mid-nineteenth century because of its "coincidence of interests and compromise" rather than "conflict and crisis," as is traditionally argued.[13] Other studies point out that the peasantry, traditionally portrayed as amorphously homogeneous, "backward," "isolated," "insulated," and so forth, were, in fact, a diversified and versatile collection of groups and individuals. In her study on social identities in imperial Russia, historian Elise Kimerling Wirtschafter questions the widespread notion of peasant "isolation" and argues that a thorough exploration of peasants' activities within the broader economic, social, and political context would raise sharp questions about the idea of rural society as an isolated "little community."[14] These authors' approaches open the door to fresh viewpoints about the social and economic role of the peasantry in Russia's modernization. Influenced by these new tendencies of writing history from below, as well as postmodernist trends, my studies have explored the territorial mobility of serfs and peasants of the Russian central-industrial region, where the largest bulk of serfs lived and suggested the existence of a peasant public sphere, capable of contributing to the shaping of public opinion and state decisions.[15]

As mentioned, economic histories of the Russian peasantry have commonly prioritized agriculture and neglected other economic activities; in other words, they fail to portray the Russian rural economy as a multifaceted, multi-occupational entity. This delimited approach even neglects the raising of livestock, always a major peasant preoccupation. In part, this may result from insufficient statistics: the late imperial statisticians failed to give proper consideration to peasant nonagricultural activities. Meanwhile, the period's ethnographers also concentrated mostly on the agrarian modes of life. Thus, peasant cottage industry, which occupied most peasant households to one degree or another, has to this day escaped thorough research. The dominant image of the Russian "rural citizen" is still a peasant attached to and tilling his plot of land (Ivan with a hoe).

Viewing Russian peasants, as well as their economy and society, through the prism of agriculture alone is both restrictive and misleading. We will not have an accurate picture of the economic and social experiences of the bulk of the rural population while concentrating on agriculture and ignoring other important elements of rural life. Not only did nonagricultural rural activities exist, indeed prevail, in the so-called industrial provinces, but in the black-earth region these activities also constituted a vital part of the local economy. Therefore any analysis of the rural economy requires a multifaceted approach. Peasant economic policies and activities reflected not only the moral economy and rational choice but, notably, peasant economic ecology. The economic ecology of peasants rested upon very specific circumstances of peasant and community interactions. Keeping this in mind, one can analyze the rural economy from a microlevel perspective in order to create a more insightful and nuanced macroeconomic perspective.

Peasant ecological mentality determined their pursuits as well as the peasants' deployment of their social institutions, especially the commune, for their economic activities. Regardless of territory and climate, the rural economy everywhere combined work on the land or with livestock with various cottage industries, work outside the village locales, commerce, river transportation, fishing, hunting, and so on. Regional circumstances, such as climate and soil fertility, availability of natural resources, access to and availability of water, all, in one combination or another, determined the character of peasant economy. Local environmental conditions also affected cultivation, irrigation, and fertilization. In central Russia, clay and sandy soils prevailed and required intensive watering. In the north and central provinces, the soil required rigorous fertilizing. Peasants used the traditional three-field system for winter and spring sowing and fallow fields. The three-field system and crop rotation helped maintain stable productivity. In Tver and Kostroma provinces, peasants periodically used the clear and burn method; they set fire to woods and then cut down burned trees. In such newly developed fields, returns were particularly high during the first several years after clearing. The clear and burn practice prevailed in areas with a wide availability of forests.

The environment also influenced lord–peasant relations: in the areas which favored nonagricultural pursuits, landlords usually required their serfs to pay money rent (*obrok*). In these areas, peasant village communes had a significant degree of autonomy from the landlord, and peasants enjoyed some personal freedom from both the landlord and the village commune. As long as peasants paid the rent, landlords rarely intervened into communal or personal lives of their peasants. In contrast, in the black-earth regions where labor duties dominated, landlords and other authorities exercised much greater control over peasants than landlords and local authorities of peasants from the non-black-earth provinces, who paid rent. Still, readers should be aware that even in black-earth regions many landlords negotiated with village elders rather than simply imposed their will on them. Most Russian noble landlords were a vastly different type than, for instance, Southern plantation owners in the United States.

An environmentalist approach to analyze Russia's rural economy and politics is hardly novel. Complex interrelations between the environment and people have attracted imperial Russian and foreign scholars. Political and social thinkers attempted to provide an ecological analysis for explanation, justification, or rejection of Russian political and social institutions. For example, the German political economist August Haxthausen, writing during the first half of the nineteenth century, defended as a necessity the idea of preserving serfdom and autocracy. He viewed serfdom and autocracy as the only viable means to cope with Russian nature and geography.[16] In contrast to Haxthausen, by mid-nineteenth century, early socialists and populists, like N. G. Chernyshevsky and A. I. Herzen, tried to employ geography from the point of view of the peasantry, in order to justify the abolition of serfdom and the introduction of social and political reforms.[17]

N. A. Polevoi was perhaps the first Russian historian to use ecology for understanding history. He attempted to explain the influence of the environment on the course of Russian political history. His approach reflected the mechanistic materialism of the time.[18] Liberal historians, such as S. M. Soloviev, also considered the environment's impact on Russian history within the context of mid-nineteenth-century positivism. These scholars, however, related the environment to the history of political life and the mentality of the Russian people rather than to Russia's economic development. In fact, Soloviev believed that the environment's impact on the economy was irrelevant.[19] Later imperial historians, such as A. P. Shchapov and S. M. Kliuchevskii, suggested the influence of nature on the movements of populations and the peopling of the Russian Empire.[20] To the extent that these scholars explored the environment's influence on the economy and society, they were concerned primarily with the macroeconomic and wide-ranging social levels.

Among the recent studies of rural Russia, an environmentalist approach has been used in the studies of economic geographers and economic historians. For example, Judith Pallot's analysis suggests the multifaceted relationship of custom, faith, environment, and the influence of environment on resource organization, cottage industry, and family economy.[21] In his seminal study of the Russian economy, Arcadius Kahan stressed climate as one of the determining factors in agricultural development.[22] Regardless, as yet no study has deeply and consistently analyzed peasant ecological mentality in its relation to both the rural economy and society.

Outside of Russian scholarship, recent studies of the countryside attempt to reconcile this disparity and provide a more balanced understanding of peasant life. Among these are studies of peasant political ecology. They propose peasant political ecology as a category of analysis for understanding peasant politics, policies, and culture. For example, Leslie E. Anderson argues that peasants possessed a political ecological mentality shaped by their environment. Peasants existed within a mutually supporting network of relationships which included the environment, the family and community, and the state. Within this network, peasants balanced individual and communal interests because the community was necessary for their individual survival.[23] As a result, peasant rationality involved both individual and communal factors. For Anderson, this tactical aim of peasants and their fundamental institutional interdependencies are the core of any sufficient understanding of peasant politics.

This book offers an ecological approach as a category of analysis of the peasantry. Ecology is defined by the relationship between peasants and their natural, geographical, political, and social environments. The environment exerted a great influence on all spheres of peasant economic, social, and political activity. Peasants considered the environment in choosing specific types of activities. For example, they carefully observed the climatic changes, soil quality, and availability of natural resources and, on these bases, estimated their labor effort, assessed the amount of food necessary to sustain them in their labor, and accurately predicted the result of their work. Other links between peasant society and nature concerned peasant dealings with the environment and their social attitudes, which in turn determined the forms of utilization of natural resources and their labor productivity. This nuanced approach will help better understand the diversity and dynamics of Russian rural society.

The multifaceted approach I am suggesting can be best accomplished by deploying the concept of peasant ecology, defined as a reciprocal interrelationship between people and their environment. Although moral economy and rational choice provide pertinent insights, neither, as noted, fully accounts for all peasant economic and related activities. These are best analyzed from within the framework of peasant economic ecology, which in turn produced great regional variations. The economic ecology of peasants rested upon very specific circumstances of the peasant environment and community interactions. Keeping this in mind, one can analyze the rural economy from a microlevel perspective in order to create an insightful and nuanced macroeconomic perspective. This approach has the additional advantage that it avoids abstractions and deploys instead language and modes of analysis readily accessible to students.

The chapters describing the peasantry after the 1917 revolutions will deploy a second conceptual framework, *Realpolitik*, which, for reasons that will become clear, gradually supplants that of peasant ecology. The ecological approach rests on the assumption that peasants controlled their lives and work at least to some major extent. With the rise of Soviet Communist power, peasant independence suffered heavy blows during the War Communism era of 1918–1921 (see Chapter 12), revived to some degree during the New Economic Policy years of 1922–1928 (see Chapter 12), and then largely disappeared with Stalinist Collectivization beginning in 1928 (see Chapter 13). With the rise of Soviet-era absolutism, the ruling Communist Party, in order to control the peasantry and its produce, introduced policies of extreme force and even terror to bend the peasantry to its will. These policies supplemented and even supplanted Marxist-Leninist ideology, which, although it ideologically favored the proletariat, did not require anything like the degree of force the government employed. For this phenomenon, this book uses the term "Realpolitik," a term that signifies policies deployed outside the realm of ideology to achieve certain aims. The term implies a degree of immorality, which certainly applies to Soviet policies toward the peasantry between 1918 and 1934.

Depicting the history of Russia's peasantry, much of the largest population element in the Empire and in the Soviet era covered in this book, is a daunting task. By necessity, the analysis will focus mostly on European sectors of the empire: Russia's hundreds of ethnicities make complete coverage unfeasible. Likewise, even when one surveys only European areas of the Empire/Soviet Union, one finds a vast array of variations. A straightforward factual narrative would collapse either into meaningless detail or deceptive generalizations, whereas principal existing analytical modes (moral economy and rational choice) cannot account for the kaleidoscope of Russia's peasant economic, social, and political life. Although the primary purpose of this book is not to forge new analytical ground, it deploys ecology as a mode of summarizing an extraordinarily complex reality, in language accessible to advanced undergraduates and beginning graduates who have little previous background in this area of studies. Even here, for reasons of brevity and coherence, the focus will be on several widely dispersed areas.

Suggested readings

Burbank, Jane, Mark Von Hagen, Anatolii Remnyev, ed. *Russian Empire: Space, People, Power, 1700–1930*. Bloomington: Indiana University Press, 2007.

Kimerling Wirtschafter, Elise, *Social Identity in Imperial Russia*. Dekalb: University of Northern Illinois Press, 1997.

Pallot, Judith and Denis Shaw, *Landscape and Settlement in Romanov Russia*, 1613–1917. Oxford: Clarendon Press, 1990.

Life under Russian Serfdom: Peasant Society and Politics under Serfdom

Like American slavery, Russian serfdom was a "peculiar institution," which caused heated debates among contemporaries and continues to do so among present-day scholars. Although Russian serfdom has generated an enormous body of studies and, it would seem, has been thoroughly researched, it remains mysterious. This chapter will explore some of the mysteries, focusing on peasant agency, legal aspects, and the origins and decline of the institution.[1]

Traditionally, historians of serfdom have emphasized its political or economic aspects and have concentrated on the consolidation and centralization of state power or have focused on the development of master–serf economic and labor relations, analyzing labor obligations, taxes paid, and the degree of exploitation. Studies of this type invariably describe Russian peasants as slave-like, dark, passive, and isolated, or approach them from the "elitist" position displayed in some portrayals of the peasantry (by educated elites). This portrayal still dominates Russian, European, and world history textbook narratives, and alternative approaches have been hard to find. Only very recently has a new trend developed in the history of serfdom that devotes time to studying the serfs themselves and their everyday lives, and, in doing so, has advanced new interpretations and conclusions. In this regard, the British historian David Moon has made noteworthy contributions to the study of serfdom. Moon has produced several fundamental studies which view Russian peasants as rational actors.[2] While this chapter will not ignore traditional approaches to serfs, its narrative will emphasize their role as dynamic social and economic factors within the institution.

Perhaps of the utmost importance is that serfdom occurred in societies where peasants predominated demographically. In imperial and early Soviet Russia, the peasantry constituted a sizable majority of the population. During the centuries of serfdom, landlords' serfs and state peasants accounted for about 85 percent of the population. The category of state peasants hardly fits into the category of serfs. In Russian, state peasants were literally called *gosudarstvennye krest'iane* (i.e., state peasants), whereas serfs were called *krepostnye*, that is, "bound" peasants. The connotations were completely different. Serfs resided on individual landlords' land. The landlords themselves composed only about 1 percent of the population. The serf population varied from about 3 percent of the population in northern and southern provinces to as much as 70 percent in the central regions during the mid-nineteenth century. The overwhelming majority of serfs lived in the central Russian provinces. In addition, there were numerous other categories of peasants, who populated lands of various state institutions, the church, the imperial family, or who owned their own land. For example, the Fifth Imperial Census (1794) counted nineteen categories of peasants, including serfs and other types, who worked in state and private factories.[3]

Because of various military and political factors, during the fifteenth and sixteenth centuries, just when feudalism begun to decline in many parts of North Western Europe, a similar institution based on servility emerged in Russia. During the seventeenth and eighteenth centuries, Russian serfdom grew to its full-fledged status, approached its climax by the seventeenth century, and by the mid-nineteenth century had begun to decline. In 1861 it ended. Serfdom in Russia resulted from many political, economic, and cultural factors, including state centralization and territorial expansion. These developments, which also occurred throughout Europe and other parts of the world, also influenced the evolution and ultimate decline of serfdom in Russia. Although serfdom everywhere shared common features—such as the juridical rights lords enjoyed over peasants—the specifics of serfdom depended on place and time: Russian serfdom, for instance, was not monochromatic and differed from region to region. Regional variations of serfdom, such as the degree of exploitation of serfs and the degree of freedom they possessed to exercise their own economic and social needs, reflected Russia's varied geography, ecology, and climate. During the period of its existence, serfdom underwent important social changes. The relationship between a serf and the landowner was intertwined with many extremely complex factors.

In general, serfdom entailed a system of relations between serfs and their owners which was regulated by laws. The relations involved a range of legal, social, economic, and cultural characteristics, which together made serfdom a multifaceted institution. Laws passed over a hundred-year period, during the sixteenth and seventeenth centuries, entrenched Russia into serfdom, which in turn influenced many aspects of Russian life. At the very time North Western

Europe was moving away from feudalism (and serfdom), the Russian nobility and aristocracy were gradually stripping peasants of the small amount of rights and privileges they still possessed. Serfdom emerged in Russia in the sixteenth century. Beginning with a series of late sixteenth-century laws, the state step-by-step restricted the peasants' mobility and subjugated them to the authority of the landlords. The famous 1649 Law Code (*Ulozhenie*) capped the earlier legislation by attaching peasants to the land and the landlord by banning them from leaving their place of residence without permission. It must be pointed out, however, that all social estates in Russia, including the nobility (until 1762, when the decrees of Peter III emancipated the nobility from obligatory state and military service), were prohibited from moving their place of residence without special permission.

Russian peasants lived on the land in settlements known as communes or, in Russian, *mir*, a word which has other significant connotations, for instance, "peace" and "world." Although sometimes the land belonged to the peasants themselves, by the 1600s, the majority of communes were located on lands that belonged either to an individual landlord, to the church, or to the state. A peasant village and the landlord's lands on which it was settled constituted the landlord's estate, known as the manor or *pomest'e*. Before the sixteenth century, peasants enjoyed considerable autonomy from landlords. They possessed the legal freedom to move and, for the most part, to act subject to their own will. Peasants either worked the landlord's fields or paid annual fees for the land they utilized. In return, the landlord administered justice and provided his peasants with certain legal and military protections. Prior to serfdom, peasants also had the privileges of sharing communal pastures, owning their own homes, and having access to estate woodlands. Thus, a tradition of lord–peasant relations began to develop long before serfdom became institutionalized.

The process of binding the peasantry consisted of the gradual economic and legal subjugation of the peasant to the land where they resided and to the landlord, a very gradual process that lasted several centuries. This process resulted from a combination of many complex historical forces. Internal political, economic, and social developments within Russia and the general political and economic situation outside of it were perhaps the key factors in serfdom's development. In addition, the binding of the majority of Russia's population to the land was an outcome of the mentality of the early modern nobility of Russia, that is, the nobility became convinced that peasant subjugation was the only solution to the challenges it faced.

The decline of the position of free peasants, the earliest stage in peasant subjugation, began in Russia earlier, in the fifteenth century. The Russian nobility, as it gained political and economic strength, tried to impose more control over the peasant population. This was also encouraged by Russia's territorial growth. The state wanted to regulate and restrict peasant territorial mobility for a number of reasons (tying them down for tax and military purposes and so forth). In addition, many economic factors influenced the rise of serfdom. The expansion of markets and the sixteenth-century revolution in prices intensified peasant subjugation. The growth of cities and towns and the development of nonagricultural villages in Western Europe provided new demands for agricultural production. The export of cereals became a basic element of the Russian agricultural economy of noble estates in black-earth regions. Productivity of noble estates was low but the inexpensive labor of subjugated peasants nonetheless could keep grain prices low. Thus, to secure the necessary cheap labor force, the Russian landed nobility shifted their peasants from traditional rent in kind (usually agricultural commodities), called in Russian *obrok*, to labor duties—*barshchina*, or *corveé*. Labor obligation was typical in the black-earth regions. In the northern and central non-black-earth regions, where nonagricultural activities prevailed, peasants paid rent in kind (various products of cottage industry) and later on, as the money economy expanded, money replaced rent in kind. The nobility's desire for profit and boosts in production placed ever heavier economic burdens on the peasants. Peasants fell more and more into debt to the lords and, it follows, more and more economically dependent upon them.

All of this resulted in increasing peasant indebtedness to and economic dependence upon landlords. The debt resulted in fixing peasants for lengthy periods of time on landlords' estates since, obviously, they would not be allowed to move as long as the debt existed. Landlords began to view these longtime residents as bound to their manors. Others, the more active and energetic peasants, preferred simply to escape from the estates, leaving their debts behind and beginning their lives anew elsewhere. This growing peasant indebtedness, along with the destruction from wars, famine, epidemics, and pestilence that beset early modern Russia, caused mass peasant movement from the old settled areas to the peripheries. In order to prevent these movements, the emerging and consolidating Russian tsardom sought to eliminate the territorial mobility of peasants.

Political consolidation and centralization of Russia, as well as the integration of new conquered lands, further accelerated the process of peasant subjugation. The ties between the landlord and the peasant, with the latter's solidifying economic dependence upon the former, were reinforced by laws. During the years of the Muscovite state, more and more peasants became serfs. Serf labor ultimately maintained the entire structure of the state and was the backbone of

Muscovite agriculture. This reliance on serfs led to a rapid spread of bondage across the southern and western parts of Russia where it had not previously existed. With the implementations of the *Sudebniks* (Laws) of 1497 and 1550, Russian peasants became bound to feudal lords. During the 1580s and onward, a series of decrees heavily limited peasant movement in Russia. The 1649 *Sobornoye Ulozheniye* (Law Code) decreed that all landlords' peasants would be regarded as serfs. This set of laws finally tied millions of Russian peasants to the land, just when in Western Europe serfdom was dying out. Additionally, in order to provide financially for their bureaucratic and military needs, the state introduced various taxes and duties on the peasantry. Russia was not alone in this process. During this period, similar developments occurred in most parts of Eastern Europe. In Poland, a 1496 statute introduced, and later the 1501 law code reinforced, restrictions on peasant ability to move. By 1540 Polish peasants were tied to the land and could not migrate without authorization from landlords. In 1538 the Brandenburg Landtag prohibited unauthorized migration and bound thousands of Brandenburg peasants to the land. The laws not only constrained peasant mobility and amplified the economic burdens upon peasants but also gave landlords legal, judicial, executive, and police powers over them. On their manors, landlords became tax collectors, judges, and policemen, on behalf of the state. The state transformed the economic dependence of the peasant upon the landlord into the peasant's legal subordination, thus almost completely destroying peasant freedom. Another factor that stimulated the deterioration of the position of the Russian peasantry was slavery or *kholopstvo*. As the bondage of economically dependent peasants increased, their status gradually fused with that of the *kholops* (slaves), a subcategory that had survived from earlier times. At the same time, slaves were included in taxation, which eventually culminated in the elimination of their slave status. Consequently, as a result of all these factors, by the mid-seventeenth century, serfdom became a fully established institution in Russia. Legal limitations on their mobility reduced millions of peasants to the status of serfs tied to the soil and to the lord.

Arising from the economic needs of the lord and then strengthened by the politics of the state, Russian serfdom became a socioeconomic institution that survived over 200 years. Perhaps the most important social characteristic of Russian serfdom is that it happened in a society dominated by the peasantry, a matter which will receive further attention below. The peasantry dominated not only numerically, but also economically, especially, as regards the local market. At the time serfdom was established, the peasantry accounted for about 80–90 percent of the population. Approximately half of the peasants lived on individual

The Process of Enserfment of Russian Peasants

1. 1497—Restriction of the right to move from one landowner to another to St. George's Day (Yuryev Day) only
2. 1581—The abolition of St. George's Day
3. 1597—The introduction of the landlord's right to search for a runaway peasant for five years
4. 1607—The term for the search for fugitive peasants was increased to fifteen years
5. 1649—The abolition of the fifteen-year term search limit
6. 1718–1724—Tax reforms finally attached the peasants to the land
7. 1747—Landlords were given the right to sell their serfs as recruits to any person.
8. 1760—Landlords were given the right to exile peasants to Siberia.
9. 1765—Landlords received the right to exile the peasants to hard labor.
10. 1767—Banned peasants from submitting petitions (complaints) against their landowners personally to the empress or emperor.

landlords' lands and thus became serfs. Landlords constituted only about 1 percent of the population and owned lands populated with large numbers of peasants who performed labor obligations for the lord or paid rent in kind or in money. According to demographic studies, the proportion of landlords' serfs to the adult male population of the empire reached its height by the end of the reign of Peter the Great (55 percent); during the subsequent period of the eighteenth century it declined to about 50 percent and again grew by the beginning of the nineteenth century, reaching 57–58 percent in 1811–1817. For the first time a significant reduction in this ratio occurred under Nicholas I, by the end of whose reign, according to various estimates, it fell to 35–45 percent. According to the data of the 10th revision (1859–1860), there were 103,200 landlords in Russia who owned 10.7 million male serfs. Nobles who had no more than 100 serfs accounted for 41.6 percent of all landowners and 3.2 percent of serfs owned. The largest landowners, who possessed over 1,000 serfs, accounted for 3.8 percent and owned 43.7 percent of all serfs. Thus, an average estate held several hundred peasants, with individual estates running from a mere handful to tens of thousands of peasants. The Russian landed nobility in reality lived in a peasant society, a reality, which alters the way serfdom must be understood and interpreted. Most peasants and landlords were of the same ethnicity and religion, and shared common cultural roots (historical memory, language, and customs). This reality sharply distinguishes Russian (and general European) serfdom from New World slavery. In fact, peasants constituted the very essence of Russia, being, as they were, the major social element and the principal source of the national economy and culture.

There are further important intricacies and ambiguities of Russian serfdom that require attention. Despite the essential harshness of serfdom, the laws that enforced it also allowed peasants to sustain their basic economic and social needs. The very laws that tied millions of serfs to the land, at the same time gave them the right to engage in temporary employment outside their residence, as well as for various trading, commercial, and even entrepreneurial pursuits within and away from the village. Paradoxically, Russian serfs were sometimes bought, sold, or used as a loan bail by their lords while, simultaneously, the law protected them from personal insult and unreasonable corporal punishment. Despite the prohibition of serf complaints against their lords, the latter often sued the lords in state courts and sometimes succeeded in bringing to trial those who violated their rights. Serfs also frequently applied to legal institutions seeking emancipation. Having the goal of preserving hierarchy, serfdom concurrently, ironically, and, one assumes, unintentionally opened the door to a certain degree of social mobility for peasants. These legal dodges constituted a basis for maintaining a certain equilibrium between the interests of the state and the nobility on the one hand and those of the peasantry on the other.

Upon closer examination, one realizes that neither the state nor the landlord had an interest in completely restricting peasant freedom. For their economic needs, the state and the landlords had to provide the majority of the population with freedom to move. This freedom was particularly crucial in those areas where agriculture was not predominant or where nearby urban centers offered greater earning possibilities. Thus, the 1649 law indeed heavily restricted the peasant's ability to move and, at the same time, granted the peasant the right to migrate temporarily, with proper authorization, in order to seek employment away from the village.[4] No authorization was required for those peasants who temporarily migrated within 32 km of the estate, a legally sanctioned unofficial and uncounted migration. By the end of the eighteenth century, about a quarter of the serfs of Russia's central provinces officially temporarily migrated each year. Thus, Russian serfs and other categories of peasants were never totally attached to the land; they could be and in fact often were "on the move."

Consequently, serfs did not spend all of their time working on the landlord's estate. They sought employment or other opportunities elsewhere. This was particularly widespread in areas which paid money rent (*obrok*). Even in the areas where labor obligations (*barshchina*) prevailed, peasants spent about half of their time working on the land for the landlord and the other half of their time on other pursuits. As the social and economic climate changed through the years, the division of a serf's occupation would often change too. Depending on their geographic location, they might not be solely devoted to agriculture as commonly portrayed. Nonagricultural trades were particularly well developed in the non-black-earth region and where the local environment offered great opportunities for such trades. For example, in the south-western districts of the Yaroslavl' province, which were closely connected to the Volga and therefore to Moscow and St. Petersburg, peasants were nonagricultural. They engaged in a broad array of handicrafts, trades, and nonagricultural labor including seasonal labor migration, river faring, shipbuilding, the production of linen cloth and sheepskin coats, oil production, leather tanning, and horse breeding. Peasant activities outside the commune provided serfs with opportunities to establish a certain degree of independence from their lords and other authorities and controls. The social, economic, and cultural vitality of the peasants thus allowed them often to rise above the limitations of serfdom. Landlords allowed their peasants independence and a degree of personal freedom, as long as they paid rent.

In agricultural areas with labor obligations, landlords exercised greater power either themselves or via appointed estate managers and village communal elders. The degree of seigniorial control over peasants depended on the size of the manor and the landlords' own obligations in services to the state. About a half of landlords were nonresidents of their estates, while the other half lived on their manors. The nonresident lords were more likely the owners of several estates and performed state service. Even after Catherine the Great's Charter to the Nobility (1785), which gave them more power in local affairs, many lords remained in St. Petersburg or in provincial capitals. According to estimates, during the late eighteenth century, about 50 percent of landlords were nonresidents on manors they owned.[5] In these cases landlords appointed estate managers or regulated their estates through communal assemblies and elders.

Nonetheless, because the laws gave the lord authority over the peasantry, the lords sometimes came to view peasants as their private property. In estate appraisals, peasants were listed under the title of private property. Legal documents reveal that serfs were sold for various purposes, mortgaged, and given as gifts. For instance, Peter I authorized the sale of serfs as workers to encourage mining and other industries. The sale of peasants reached its apogee during the reign of Catherine the Great (1762–1796). In most cases, however, serfs were sold with the land they populated and farmed. In other words, this transaction simply indicated the transfer of entire villages to new owners. Incidents of sales of serfs without land, which did happen, often provoked criticism and condemnation as a most inhumane and brutal practice. In order to restrict such sales, the tsarist government implemented minute regulations into existing laws on the possession of serfs. Eventually, laws prohibited the sale and mortgage of peasants without land, as well as newspaper advertisements of such sales. Also laws restricted unreasonable punishment and mistreatment of peasants. Strict sanctions and penalties awaited lords who transgressed the new rules. During the reign of Catherine the Great, about twenty landowners were brought to trial for causing the deaths of their serfs. Two were exiled to Siberia for life and five were sentenced to hard labor for life. The most famous episode of abuse of power by a landlord was the atrocity committed by a noblewoman Daria Saltykova, nicknamed "Saltychikha," who married into a famous and influential family. Perhaps suffering a mental disorder, Saltykova tortured a number of peasants, mostly women, who died as a consequence. Peasants reported these abuses to the police and other local authorities on numerous occasions without any success. She always managed to use her connections or bribed authorities to escape the consequences of her actions. Finally, two of her peasants managed to send complaints against Saltykova to the newly crowned Empress Catherine II. Catherine ordered an investigation and Saltykova was taken into custody. The investigation found Saltykova guilty of the murder of 75 peasants, mostly women and teenage girls. She was stripped of her noble title and sent for life to a prison located within a women's monastery. In accordance with the sentence, Saltykova spent eleven years in a dark underground cell. She was allowed to see light only during the taking of meals and on major religious holidays. Thereafter, she spent the rest of her life in a cell with a window. Laws, introduced during the late eighteenth and early nineteenth century, increased state control of the lord–peasant relationship in such a way as to place sterner limits on the lord's power. This legislative tendency accelerated in the years prior to the final abolition of serfdom. Thus, clearly, the state, by regulating lord–peasant relations and restricting lords' power over them, considered serfs as imperial subjects and not as property of lords, who were themselves subjects of the imperial authority and had state obligations (Figure 1.1).

Figure 1.1 Saltychikha torturing peasants. Caricature.

As imperial subjects, all categories of peasants paid taxes to the state and provided conscripts for the military. Until the tax reform of Peter the Great, peasants paid a land tax. The size of their payments depended on the amount of land they cultivated. This was a household tax. Peasant households in non-black-earth areas paid fewer taxes than their black-earth region counterparts. This taxation method did not motivate peasants to cultivate more land and, at the same time, stimulated the tendency of peasants to hide some of their land or to look for other types of economic activities outside agriculture, if the local environment allowed. During the seventeenth century, the taxation methods changed and new specific taxes were added. After the 1718 census, completed in 1724, Peter the Great introduced a poll tax of 74 kopeks per male soul. Most historians assume that Peter increased the tax burden on the peasantry. Nevertheless, it is virtually impossible to reach a definite conclusion because of the absence of reliable data on the revenue gathered from taxes and on how peasants paid the poll tax. The size of the poll tax fluctuated during the reigns of Peter's successors, but, according to estimates, remained comparatively steady until the emancipation.[6]

Peasant villages also provided a number of conscripts annually to serve in the army. The Thirteen Years' war with Poland (1654–1667) marked the beginning of regular conscription. After the war, however, conscripted peasants mostly returned home. In 1699, the ambitious empire builder Peter the Great introduced military conscription for life at a rate of one male per every twenty households. In 1793 the life term was reduced to 25 years but, in general, Peter's system remained in place until the army reform of 1870.

Serfs also had their own social institutions which mitigated the harshness of serfdom and established a degree of autonomy and protection from the lord. These institutions included the extended family and the peasant commune. Family life for peasants was rooted in traditions. Most families were extended and could have several nuclear and generational units. The husband and wife with several children, grandparents, and their other unmarried or married sons with their wives and children all lived under one roof. The rationale of the extended family was an economic one. Extended families provided the household with much needed laboring hands. Additionally, married sons preferred to live together with their parents and other married siblings in order to avoid the extra costs of setting up their own homes and households. A larger family would have access to a larger plot of land, more animals and resources, and more opportunities. Nevertheless, regarding the institution of family, there was a considerable degree of diversity throughout Russia. In some areas of Russia, depending on the environment, nuclear families were not uncommon.

Most historians of Russian serfdom assume that a structurally complex family was the predominant type of family among Russian serfs as a direct by-product of serfdom. Structural complexity, however, was not peculiar to serf households in Russia. Family systems among serf and non-serf peasants throughout preindustrial Europe were widely diverse, depending upon local patterns of political and economic settlement, demography, culture, and ecological factors. For example, preindustrial France was characterized by a wide array of household systems, whereas extended family households characterized preindustrial Northern Swedish and Dutch peasant communities. Recent anthropological research illustrates that also in preindustrial Eastern Europe peasant household structures varied. For example, in Southern Estonia extended households were common, whereas nuclear family households prevailed in Northern Estonia. Nuclear families were not uncommon among the serfs of the northern provinces of Russia, whereas extended households dominated in the south. Extended families often reflected a certain stage of family development and were quite changeable. For example, young couples lived under the same roof with their parents until they had saved enough money to start their own households. Often married children lived in separate houses within the same structurally complex household. This was common for serfs of the northern and central provinces of Russia. Thus, family and household structures among Russian serfs witnessed significant variation, while usually fitting one or another definition of extended or complex family. Consequently, it is not clear that the structural complexity of the serf family resulted primarily from serfdom.

Peasant marriages were arranged strategically according to the size, status, and standing of each family. They were performed according to local tradition and custom, and received full legal sanction. Everyone had to abide by the laws from the tsar and the rules of the Russian Orthodox Church regarding marriage, which included bans for specific holidays. Married families had the same legal rights and protections for all classes. Women were expected to be good laborers and to bear many children, which was their primary obligation. Marriages began with "elaborate negotiations" between family members of the prospective bride and groom that included festive dinners, gift exchanges, and the presentation of the dowry. A marriage contract was usually agreed upon by the couple's parents. These dinners and gatherings continued even after the formal church wedding ceremony had ended. A serf from Vladimir province later recollected in his memoir that the arrangements for his marriage were made by his mother. He married at the age of eighteen, which, in his own words, "was nothing unusual."

The marriage age of male serfs of Russia's central provinces ranged from eighteen to twenty-five and of female serfs from seventeen to twenty-one, whereas in the southern regions the average marriage age for serfs was even lower. The marriage age of Russian serfs was relatively low in comparison to that of non-serf peasants and to West European peasants of that period. In the mid-nineteenth century the average marriage age for men was twenty-three and for women—nineteen. The pattern of low marriage age for serfs to a certain degree reflected economic pressures because the newly married couple constituted a work unit with its own share of communal land and property. Each couple had the legal and common law right to establish its own household with attendant benefits (and burdens). The landlord usually did not interfere or aid in marriage negotiations although occasionally marriage dues or taxes were paid to the landlord.[7] The marriage fees differed from place to place.

The peasant family acted as safety nets for family members, providing emotional comfort and material support. In most cases regarding family affairs and strategies, as well as actual decision making, the family enjoyed a significant degree of autonomy from the landlord. The family was headed by its eldest member, usually the grandfather, known as the patriarch. Patriarchs had a dominant role in making decisions about and supervising the daily activities of other family members and represented the family in communal institutions. Some historians argue that the position and authority of the patriarch in the family was unchallengeable and that this arrangement simultaneously contributed to the development of patriarchal culture among the Russian peasantry. In contrast, some anthropological researchers emphasize the patriarch's responsibility to the family and point out that all major family matters, such as the household economy, property, and the marriage of children, were usually settled in family meetings that consisted of all adult family members, males as well as females. In certain case the family meeting could displace an inept patriarch and appoint a new family head.[8] For these scholars, the authority of the patriarch was not unlimited; the process of decision making resulted from discussion and compromise among all concerned parties rather than exclusively from the authoritarian will of the patriarch.

Labor obligations in peasant families were shared according to the age, gender, and physical abilities of family members. The full working age depended on the life span and usually ranged from seventeen to sixty-five, a cluster that composed 60–64 percent of the peasant population. Children under the age of six, and people over sixty-five did not work.[9] In the village, the age of peasants when they received "full labor duty" (*tiaglo*) varied from province to province. Usually, starting from the age of seventeen, peasants carried full labor duty until sixty-five.

Living and social conditions of peasants varied and depended on local circumstances. In the nonagricultural areas with considerable seasonal migration peasants displayed greater awareness and developed better material culture than in the agrarian areas. Another complicating factor was that certain landlords (a minority) ran their estates like businesses: they used overseers and managers, applied strict rules that controlled the peasants' lives, and imposed harsh punishments, including the lash, for perceived violations. Landlords and estates of this type were atypical in Russia.

All peasants lived in villages of various sizes and with a range of communal facilities, such as shops, communal buildings, marketplaces, and church. The village is known in Russian as the *mir* (world) or the *obshchina*. Most Russian peasants, just like the majority of the peasantry of preindustrial Europe, belonged to communes. The peasant commune was the most important economic and social feature of serfdom. There are many theories surrounding the emergence of this institution and the issue of why the serfs grouped together. Certainly living and working together in a harsh elemental environment and society would provide an easier way of life. Everyone's success and destiny were linked to their neighbor's and there was a communal mind-set that permeated every facet of life. The peasant commune was essentially a democratic institution because the members of the commune, the villagers themselves, solved numerous issues and themselves made all decisions. The commune manifested peasants' ability to coalesce individual and public interests. Every manor was governed differently but in all cases serfs came together and voted as well as discussed various issues. They settled disputes in the village and maintained order, morality, and resource distribution as well. They were also responsible for electing their own officials to represent the commune. This showed that the serfs did have some authority and freedom to govern themselves. The legislation that established serfdom simultaneously empowered peasants to attain their rudimentary economic and social needs. Obviously, the commune's democracy was relative and had its own strengths and weaknesses. At times, the most prosperous peasants might take over the function of making the commune's decisions or, on the contrary, the village poor or middling levels could determine the solution. All this indicated a lively village life. In general, the commune maintained continuity and a functioning economy, and stimulated in people an active interest in communal, village, and parish affairs.

Through the commune's assembly, represented by the family heads (the patriarchs), the peasants managed village resources, directed economic and fiscal activities, and maintained internal order. The authority of the commune over the village varied, depending upon local custom and the degree to which the landlord restricted its autonomy. The serf commune was a site for interactions between the landlord and the village; the communal elders consulted the lord about appropriate taxes, duties, obligations, and recruitments into the military. The commune controlled land redistribution; coordinated agriculture (for example, made decisions about suitable crops and determined the dates of sowing and harvesting); sold, exchanged, or leased lands; and rented or bought additional land as needed. The custom law recognized and protected these interactions. The 1848 law allowed serfs to purchase lands in their own possession. The profit from the sale and lease of communal property was deposited in the communal treasury or divided directly among the households. The communes checked weights and measures, determined the quality of bread and beer, and set the wages of day laborers. Communes often supervised the moral behavior of its members and regulated the religious and social life of the village. Periodic redistribution of lands was also a vital function of the commune. Larger plots of land were given to larger families who were able to work the land and produce, whereas families that had lost members because of death, recruitment into the military, and so forth got smaller plots. This was in the interest of the serfs because it prevented them from falling into poverty and also the nobility because it ensured maximum agricultural productivity and yields.

The commune had some administrative power to perform certain essential functions, especially in the case of absent landlords who relied on their peasants to organize, run, and oversee their land and production. Community assemblies also had important juridical functions, such as resolving intra- and intervillage conflicts and representing the community's interests in all legal institutions. In pre-reform Russia, village commune representatives participated directly in the landlord's court. Additionally, communal assemblies filed suits in local or regional courts, seeking adjudication when deprived of their interests and rights by their own lords or anyone else. In some cases, serf communes even won their cases.

The quintessence of peasants' social experiences was the ability to regulate and coordinate, in the contest of economic activities, the interests of the individual with the interests of the family, and the interests of the family with the whole commune. The peasant village was a flexible organism, responsive to changes in sociopolitical conditions. On the one hand, it could not ignore state or landlord pressures; on the other—it constantly resolved issues in the interests of the peasants, distributing compulsory duties in a convenient way.

Communes often acted as safety nets for their members, providing assistance for poverty-stricken households. Certainly, this is not an indication of Russian peasant collectivism but rather their rationality and perhaps Christian culture. Collectivism was strongest when peasants faced outsiders or when they were working outside their villages. Peasant migrants from the same region usually grouped themselves into regional associations in order to facilitate labor protest and collective action, or to locate employment.

Peasant life was closely linked with faith. Russian Orthodox Christianity influenced the peasants' worldview and their way of life. Despite differences in the levels of personal piety, the collective spiritual experience of peasants helped determine their behavior. To some degree, the spread of atheism among the educated elites also eventually affected life in the village. In the moral ideals of peasants, the Christian interpretation of kindness, mercy, piety, and respect for the elders was closely intertwined with the concepts of diligence, mutual assistance, and conscientious fulfillment of duties. Moral concepts and corresponding norms of behavior were cultivated from early childhood. It was quite a conscious task of popular pedagogy. Outside the family, the public opinion of fellow villagers, which had a stable impact on children and adults, was no less significant.

Scholars debate the role of the commune in the agricultural economy, the degree of its autonomy from the landlord, and many other specific aspects that cannot be reasonably settled here. Some historians have viewed the commune as the bottom level of authority in a hierarchy of rule that linked the serf to the tsar. Older scholarship argued that the commune signified Russia's backwardness and was an obstacle to innovation, whereas recent studies suggest that the peasant communal system was suitably elastic and allowed for agricultural innovation and improvement. Indeed some communes were initiators of innovation. They encouraged the introduction of new crops and crop rotations, and organized communal drainage, irrigation, and land clearance systems.

Some specialists argue that serf communes carved out a certain degree of autonomy primarily because they served as instruments of the landlords. In this interpretation, the communes upheld the landlords' interests, ensuring that every household fulfilled its manorial and state obligations. In contrast, it may be argued, however, that the commune did not always act in the landlords' interests. Communal obligations were usually agreed upon with the lord in advance, with firm commitments from both sides. When lords unilaterally increased already negotiated and fixed duties, communes often protested vociferously and refused to comply. The commune's practice of periodic redistribution of arable land among households also remains a subject of scholarly controversy. Some historians claim that redistribution was largely a result of serfdom. In this interpretation, landlords required peasants to divide their lands in order to coordinate each household's landholdings with its labor capability based upon the number of hands in the family, with the overall goal of maximizing the household's labor effectiveness and productivity. Other historians suggest that land redistribution was not an innovation of the state or of the landlord but rather a traditional peasant practice aimed at maintaining rough land equality among households based upon each household's size. Whether land redistributions originated from the commune or were imposed by landlords, it is clear that this practice occurred in many parts of Russia and Eastern Europe up until the turn of the twentieth century and even beyond. Land redistribution was common in areas in which agriculture dominated the peasant economy and especially where soil quality was varied (for example, in the black-earth regions of southern Russia and in Ukraine). In areas where agriculture was not important, land redistribution fell into disuse. Peasants of the northern and central provinces rarely practiced land repartition. The periodicity of land redistributions, where they occurred, varied from one to five, ten, or even more years. In addition to its important economic, social, and juridical functions, the commune, indeed village life as a whole, fostered a collective consciousness among the serfs. Through village life, rich in tradition, custom, religious and national holidays, as well as innumerable communal celebrations, serf peasants maintained a sense of solidarity and cohesiveness. Overemphasis on intra-village conflicts has led some observers to question the sense of communality among the peasants.[10] Private conflicts among peasants, however, did not undermine village solidarity. Indeed, one of the chief functions of the commune was to contain and adjudicate conflict; witness to such communal activities and the spirit of unanimity it fostered is too widespread to be doubted. Furthermore, peasants who migrated into cities for employment sustained themselves in the unfamiliar urban environment by forming fraternal associations (in Russia the famous urban *zemliachestvos*) directly based upon the respective peasants' village and district origins.[11] In essence, at the first opportunity peasants who had left the village recreated familiar communal mores, hardly a practice consonant with reflexive mutual hostility.

Solidarity among the serfs expressed itself in numerous cases of collective insubordination, refusal to work, disturbances, and rebellions large in size and duration. Popular protest usually broke out when the quality of justice, as understood by the peasants, deteriorated. The village commune was a crucial element in initiating popular protest. Serfs first presented their disagreements and complaints collectively to their lords or local officials. If the latter failed to resolve the disputes, the serfs usually petitioned legal institutions or state authorities. The last resort was one or another form of popular protest. Naturally, serfs showed the greatest concerns about increase in duties and demands upon them. For example, during 1800–1861, 371 (47 percent) out of 793 disturbances in the central Russian provinces were caused by increases in feudal obligations.[12] In addition to collective forms of protest facilitated by the commune, serfs actively used various forms of individual protest, such as deception, manipulation of legal norms, and fleeing. These latter forms of protest were primarily associated with the serfs' unfree status.[13] Although most Russian cities could not guarantee freedom for fugitive serfs, peasants nonetheless used running away as the primary means to escape serfdom. This practice was particularly widespread during the earliest decades of serfdom. Thus, the strong, collective consciousness noted above among serfs did not undermine their individual motivations, as also witnessed by their individual economic pursuits (trading, temporal migration, and so forth) (Figure 1.2).

Although often organized by local communal institutions, most peasant revolts had no concrete political or generalized economic goals. The persistence of peasant insurrectionism in Russia throughout the centuries of serfdom reflected the structural changes of Russian society, such as the growth of population, state centralization, imposition of new heavy taxes and obligations, the development of a market economy, and the transformation of popular mentality. All of these factors worked together to erode serfdom and bring it to an end.

Figure 1.2 Rebellious peasants.

Suggested readings

Blum, Jerome. "Russian Agriculture in the Last 150 Years of Serfdom," *Agricultural History*, vol. 34, no. 1 (1960).

Dennison, T. K. *The Institutional Framework of Russian Serfdom*. London: Cambridge University Press, 2011.

Emmons, Terence. *The Russian Landed Gentry*. New York, NY: Cambridge University Press, 1968.

Gorshkov, Boris. *A Life under Russian Serfdom*. Budapest, Hungary: Central European University Press, 2005.

Hoch, Steven *Serfdom and Social Control in Russia: Petrovskoe, a Village in Tambov*. Chicago: University of Chicago Press, 1986.

Kimerling Wirtschafter, Elise. *From Serf to Russian Soldier*. Princeton: Princeton University Press, 1990.

Kimerling Wirtschafter, Elise. *Religion and Enlightenment in Catherinian Russia: The Teachings of Metropolitan Platon*. DeKalb: Northern Illinois University Press, 2013.

Kolchin, Peter. *Unfree Labor, American Slavery and Russian Serfdom*. Cambridge, MA: Harvard University Press, 1987.

Smith, R. E. F. *The Enserfment of the Russian Peasantry*. London: Cambridge University Press, 1968.

Peasant Agriculture

Describing Russian peasant agriculture is a daunting task because the country's geography, and therefore its crops, is quite varied. In addition to the East European and the West Siberian Plains, Russia has a series of extensive mountain ranges, gigantic plateaus, and endless lowlands. A further complication arises because agriculture was just one aspect of peasant economic activity. Nevertheless, agriculture in Russia constituted the agrarian question, which stood prominent throughout the imperial and Soviet periods in Russian history.

During the imperial period, most of the population lived in rural areas and the majority worked in agriculture at least part time of the year. Although during the late imperial decades, the urban population grew, agriculture remained the most important sector of the national economy. Only soviet collectivization of agriculture and rapid industrialization changed the balance between the economic sectors and the rural and urban populations. Regardless, agriculture continuously occupied a fundamental position in the economy, society, and in the history of imperial Russia. Agriculture engaged the majority of the population and determined hierarchical social divisions: the social estates. In many respects, agriculture was connected with the origins and development of Russian serfdom, the subject of discussion in the previous chapter. While at various times Russia was the largest exporter of grain, as most scholars argue, its agriculture was developed less efficiently than in Western Europe or in parts of the world with similar climates. Russian agriculture relied on traditional methods and used extensive labor in order to maintain productivity. Productivity concerns in turn generated reforms and regulations, which, it follows, provoked fundamental historical questions and problems. This chapter will offer a general overview of Russian peasant agriculture, focusing on the centuries of serfdom and the late imperial decades.

We begin our account with the end of the Time of Trouble, the early seventeenth century, which had endured a series of external and domestic wars and resulting economic devastation. As a result of this warfare, the land under cultivation diminished and the peasant population decreased.[1] The process of recovery was slow because of the poor soil fertility of the original Muscovite Principality, short growing season, and the lack of labor force. Agricultural productivity was also vulnerable to unpredictable weather conditions. Heavy rains and early frosts, as well as the deficit of moisture in the soil during droughts, caused frequent harvest failures. This was one of the factors of colonization of lands not originally under Moscow's control and the resulting territorial growth of the Muscovite Principality into the Russian tsardom and eventually state; this also influenced the progression of the institution of serfdom.

During the seventeenth century, as colonization began, the Russian state expanded south and east, and eventually included Siberia, the Southern Urals, and eastern Ukraine. The territory stretched from the Dnepr River in the west to the Pacific Ocean in the east and from the White Sea in the north to the South Caucasus and Central Asian steppe. About a half million peasants moved into these new areas from central Russia. By the end of the century, the population of Russia reached over 10 million. Russia became the fourth largest state in Europe after France, the Germanic and Italian lands, and England. The population continued to grow and, by the beginning of the nineteenth century, it reached 40 million, including over 30 million peasants.[2] The populations of Siberia and Northern Caucasus were about 3 and 1 million, respectively. In 1800, the population density was about 8 persons per 1 square kilometer. Further to the south, north, and east of the southwestern and central regions, the population density declined dramatically. In the Volga and Don regions, the population was no more than 1 person per 1 square kilometer. The population density in Siberia was even lower.

In the seventeenth and eighteenth centuries, much of the country's territory still had natural vegetation, much of it forested.[3] According to the tax census of 1678, the majority of Russian peasants still inhabited the forest heartland spreading out in all directions from Moscow. Depending on time and region, lands under cultivation accounted for from one-fifth to one-half of all arable lands. By the end of the nineteenth century, for example, Pskov province in the north and Yaroslavl' province of central Russia cultivated about 30 percent of their arable land. In other provinces, the amount of land under cultivation ranged from 12 to 20 percent. Large amounts of arable and fertile lands were fallows, forests, meadows, and steppes.

Overall, Russian agricultural productivity, including yields from both peasant and noble fields, was low.[4] The net cost of agricultural production was about twice above its market price, even at times of good harvest and ideal weather conditions (a calculation that suggests that peasant labor was simply uncompensated on noble lands, whereas peasants themselves engaged in subsistence farming that did not take into account their labor input). In times of bad harvests, the net cost of crops was three to five times higher than the market price. Thus, Russian agriculture was labor-intensive and grew extensively, involving ever more peasants and lands. This provided the basis for migrations of Russian peasants to the south and southeast of European Russia which had more fertile soil. During the seventeenth and eighteenth centuries, many peasants of the non-black-earth region migrated unlawfully to the newly acquired more fertile regions of the south and Siberia. Since much of the eastern region was forested and meagerly settled, migrations helped populate them, bringing an enormous mass of fertile land into cultivation.

According to the tax and population statistics, in 1678, the male Russian peasant population of the Central Black Earth, Mid-Volga, Lower-Volga, and South Urals regions accounted for about 1 million men, or 29 percent of the male peasant population of Russia. In 1762 the male peasant population of these regions increased to 3.3 million or 41 percent of male peasant population. The male peasant population of Siberia was 49,000 in 1678 (1.3 percent of the total population) and, in 1762 it reached 356,050 men (4.5 percent). Simultaneously, the peasant population of the central non-black earth was proportionally declining in relation to the population of the black earth belt and other regions: from 70 percent in 1678 to 55 percent in 1762. This trend continued throughout the nineteenth century.

Agricultural crops were diverse and depended on the environment, especially climate and soil. With the territorial acquisitions, the Russian State gained more fertile lands. The black-earth region, which included Ukraine, the Central Agricultural Region, Mid-Volga, South-west Urals, Lower-Volga regions, and South-Western Siberia, favored agriculture because of its productive soil. The black-colored soil, known as *chernozem* (literally "black earth"), contains a high percentage of humus, phosphoric acids, phosphorus, and ammonia, all of which make it highly fertile. This region had a great potential for the growth of Russian agriculture. Agricultural productivity in this region was as much as twice higher than elsewhere in Russia. The chief agricultural staples were cereal crops: rye, oat, barley, and wheat. Rye and oats were traditional predominant crops, grown by peasants from times immemorial. Landlords' estates produced wheat for foreign markets, whereas subsistent peasant farming produced entirely for local consumption. Northern Ukraine and the Central Agricultural Region cultivated sugar beets. South-eastern Russia and the southern Ukraine also produced sunflowers (for oil). Potatoes were grown in the northwest parts of the black-earth region and in the Urals.

Aside from predominant crops, Russian peasants commonly cultivated numerous other crops, which had their own characteristics and required great knowledge of agriculture. Even within one geographical region, there could be many kinds of soil that peasants also had to be familiar with and differentiate among in terms of suitable crops. In addition, the weather could produce unexpected conditions that peasants had to tackle. The peasants' choice of cultures was made according to their beliefs and knowledge about what would be suitable for their goals, including techniques, time, and labor input, for their concrete needs, and for the actual environment and soil. In this respect, peasants calculated their time and labor effort and tried to be as efficient as possible. For the sake of time and labor-use efficiency, peasants cultivated a combination of crops in the spring and winter fields. In other words, peasant agriculture was complex rather than simple.

The most widespread culture for most regions of Russia was winter rye. Rye occupied about 50 percent of all winter fields.[5] From an economic ecology perspective, rye better suited the peasants' agricultural methods and capacities and, simply put, was the most productive crop. For a peasant, who followed strictly the agricultural calendar and constantly shifted between outstanding tasks, rye was the most reliable culture. Full-grown rye was stronger and less vulnerable to disease and drought than other crops; furthermore, when spring crops matured, peasants harvested the latter, whereas rye could remain in the fields until late autumn when other crops had already been harvested. Thus, the various cultivations well fit the peasants' work schedule and kept peasants occupied the whole agricultural season without a break. Peasants also cultivated spring rye when they expected a winter crop failure. Peasants considered rye as a crop resistant to weeds and diseases. In their daily diets, Russian peasants preferred rye bread over wheat and considered the former to be better-tasting and healthier. They also believed in certain healing qualities of rye bread. In addition to bread, peasants used rye grain to make various alcoholic and nonalcoholic beverages, including kvass, moonshine (samogon, or "self-fire"), and vodka.

Oats was another preferred crop for Russian peasants and it prevailed on spring fields. Its cultivation required less labor effort and time than many other crops, it was virtually invulnerable to disease and pests, and it was generally easy to grow and maintain. It also needed less area because of the density of seeding. Plowing and harrowing the field was required only once. Oats also did not require fertilization. Although yields were not high, they were steady and reliable. Peasants used oats to supplement their diets and to feed horses and other animals. Russian peasants also cultivated summer barley, whose cultivation fitted well in most areas of Russia. Barley's vegetative (growth) period was the shortest, from eight to nine weeks, compared to from twelve to eighteen weeks for summer rye and wheat. Barley was also second (after oats) as regards consistent productivity. The best yields of barley were gathered from fertilized soil. Barley served peasants as a safety net. When winter crops had not survived, peasants plowed the field again and seeded barley in the spring.[6]

Spring wheat was also widespread throughout Russia, but in smaller quantities than other cultures. Although wheat did not dominate Russian peasant agriculture per se, it predominated on landlords' fields (worked by peasants) for export. Wheat required significant labor effort and either the fertile soil of the black-earth region or newly plowed fields from meadows and cleared woods. The Central Agricultural Region and the black earth regions of Siberia had better conditions for wheat. Over time peasants and agronomists gradually developed skills and knowledge in the selection of appropriate types of wheat. In the eighteenth century they selected a type of wheat suitable for the central non-black soil areas. This type required little fertilizer. They also developed new wheat cultivation techniques, such as autumn plowing and harrowing. In early spring, as soon as the snow had melted and the soil was ready peasants sowed the crop. Nevertheless, in the central non-black-earth region wheat crops' yields and labor requirements could not win out over rye and peasants' wheat crops remained small. In the eighteenth century wheat crops made up from about 10 to 30 percent of summer fields.

Two other cultures, peas and buckwheat, were well adapted for most regions of Russia (northern areas being the main exceptions) and occupied from 8 to 12 percent of summer fields. Neither crops required much labor and both were reliable, with growing periods from nine to twelve weeks. Like oats, buckwheat required plowing only once and, because of certain peculiarities, actually produced better in poor soils than in fertile black earth soils. It also required no manure (the principal fertilizer available to peasants). Peas also grew well on fields without manure. Peas could be harvested at an immature stage, increasing the convenience of the crop. Already in the seventeenth century, peasants began to consume baby peas, for which purpose they harvested it before full maturity. Peasants used both cultures (mature and immature) for food preparation. The pea crop was also used to feed animals. The cultivation of buckwheat stimulated the growth of honey production because the buckwheat flowers, while blossoming, attracted honey bees.

Another important area of peasant agriculture was horticulture. Peasants grew turnips, cabbage, onions, garlic, cucumbers, carrots, beets and melon (which types), apples, plums, cherries, and raspberries among many other vegetables and fruits. Turnips and cabbage were the most widespread vegetables. Among the fruit trees, apple trees predominated. Vegetables and fruits were an important supplement to the peasant diet. In Russia, horticulture was almost exclusively a peasant activity. Orchards were usually situated in areas close to peasant households, although remote areas were also sometimes employed, depending on the availability of appropriate soil and other conditions. In remote areas, peasants often cultivated cabbage because it did not require constant care. Peasants devoted close and careful attention to their orchards; orchards were fenced and fertilized. Peasants from the central provinces also produced orchard seedlings and sold them at local markets.

In the non-black-earth region, which comprised the central Russian provinces with Moscow at the center, where soils were relatively poor, peasants developed many nonagricultural activities, cottage industry, crafts, and trades and commerce, in addition to agriculture. Agriculture in this extensive area was largely limited to industrial crops, such as hemp and flax, in order to sustain cottage industries so vital for their living. For consumption, the central region depended on imports of cereal crops from other areas, whereas it exported the products of cottage industry and industrial crops. Industrial crops, also known as cash crops, were usually sold on national and international markets and enabled peasants to earn some income. Other regions (the north, Siberia, etc.) engaged in animal husbandry, fishing, and vegetable and fruit production, depending on the environment.

Agriculture constituted a substantial part (but not all) of the peasant natural economy. Traditionally peasants engaged in agriculture because they needed to sustain their livelihood—what is known as subsistence agriculture—and pay seigniorial dues or work seigniorial fields. Thus, earlier in Russian history (as elsewhere), peasant agriculture was not oriented to the market but to the peasant household needs. In past times, before the development of broader markets, peasants produced just enough to sustain their living and pay dues. This perhaps helps explain why Russian peasants were initially reluctant to adopt new farming techniques, as so often noted by observers. During the centuries under discussion in this volume, peasant agriculture would become more market oriented, particularly in the central provinces.

By the seventeenth century, peasants were gradually shifting from the traditional two-field crop rotation system to the three-field system. However, the open field system dominated and both two- and three-field crop rotation systems coexisted. In most of the black-earth areas, peasants practiced the open field policy. The open field system of land cultivation developed during medieval centuries and survived in Russia until the Stolypin agrarian reforms. Under this system, each village used two or three fields, which were divided into numerous narrow strips. Peasants grew certain cereal crop, such as rye or wheat, on one field, and on the second other crops. The third field was allowed to lay fallow. The crop fields were fenced temporarily and opened after harvest in order to allow animals to graze on the stubble and provide manure for the soil. During the nongrowing seasons, the peasants would allow their animals to graze on the fields, but the fields were otherwise kept off limits to animals to prevent damage to crops and soil.

In the eighteenth century, the three-field system of crop rotation prevailed in most of European Russia. Recent studies find that the three-field system and strip farming were not as backward as has been previously assumed. In addition, peasants of the non-black-earth region also utilized a long-fallow system alongside the three-field crop rotation, as did their contemporary Western European counterparts. Peasants assigned large areas of previously used and cultivated land to a fallow period of several years in order to regain productivity. They especially preferred the long-fallow system over the short (one-year)-fallow system in cases where there was a lack of adequate cattle to produce sufficient manure.[7] This suggests the practical and rational nature of peasant agriculture—based on experience and knowledge accumulated over lengthy periods of time.

Peasants' rational choices were guided by tradition, which was created by generations of farming experience in Russia. Peasants paid great attention to every detail in the process of cultivation in their choices of cultures and types of harvesting. According to the conditions of other vegetation, such as native grasses, trees, and bushes, peasants could determine the quality of soil. Peasants also knew and distinguished types of soil; for example, in the central provinces alone, there was about a dozen soil categories and peasants were able to recognize each one and determine the processes and time for cultivation. Clay soils, for example, were plowed in the fall, after rains, after allowing them to dry out a little, with the expectation that winter frosts would break off lumps and spring waters would make them soft. Sandy soils were plowed during humid weather, with wide ditches made between lanes. If the field had an inclination, peasants plowed it across a slope so that layers retained water.

Peasants possessed an extensive knowledge of their local environment and agriculture. Based on experience passed down from generation to generation, peasants composed and scrupulously followed an agricultural calendar. Since Russia had a short growing season, strict adherence helped the peasants gain the most from their land. The calendar let peasants know when to plant and sow, as well as suggested the best times to harvest. Plowmen paid especial attention to the timing of spring plowing. They believed that the soil should be ripe for plowing: that is, should be dry enough so that the plow could break it. The timing of plowing, as well as the start of other work, was determined by the most experienced peasants who had acquired a reputation in the local village communities. Their knowledge could hardly be overlooked aside from expert knowledge of village elders; in general peasants knew that if they started plowing the soil when it was wet, a poor harvest would result. Peasants also knew that premature plowing can damage the soil. Years might be required for the soil to fully recover. Wet layers of soil dried by the spring wind became hard as a rock and, naturally, lower fertility resulted. Peasants had to know all the features of the soil in order to cultivate it.

No less important was choosing the correct time for sowing and peasants went to great lengths to determine the right dates. They considered various factors such as the temperature of the soil and air humidity. Since the peasants possessed no instruments to measure, they relied on their own popular lore in order to measure these factors and make the right decision about timing. For example, according to the stages of development of other vegetation, or behavior of animals, reptiles, and insects, they choose when to sow and what crop to sow. When birch trees began to blossom, they knew, it was time to sow oats. The time for sowing barley was when juniper was blooming. The first seasonal croaking of frogs or the first appearance of red bugs in the forest around the rotten stumps suggested the time for sowing the oats. When turtledove began to coo, peasants started to plant hemp. The cuckoo was considered a signal for sowing flax.

The relationship between peasants and their environment was not in one direction. The environment influenced peasant choices of crops and techniques. However, peasants also tended to adapt the environment to fit the needs of their agricultural and other economic activities. Colonization, peasant migration, and settlement eastward and in Siberia had a dramatic impact on the region's steppes and forests. Forests in central Russia thinned out and disappeared. Formerly vegetative areas were turned into agriculturally productive fields. Peasants moved in and settled into areas with familiar climate, where they could perform similar kinds of activities. Peasants were responsible for spreading agriculture into areas which had been previously sparsely populated with indigenous nomadic population or which had been completely unsettled.

In the northern region, which was dominated by vegetation, peasant migrants had to engage in considerable clearing. First, they cleared the forests from plots of land, burned other vegetation and roots, and retained the resulting ashes as a fertilizer. They used this newly cleared field for sowing cereal crops for several years until the soil productivity started to decline. Then, the area shifted to the three-field system, being divided into three parts for winter and spring crops or to lie fallow. Peasants in the north used fertilizers intensively, especially moss, manure, and peat. Peasants in the northern region kept considerable livestock, which produced sufficient manure to fertilize their own land; any excess was sold.

Regional circumstances influenced not only agriculture and livestock breeding, but also determined the character of peasant activities in terms of both methods and tools. For land cultivation, peasants used the wooden plough or the improved plough (the harrow) and for harvesting they utilized scythes, rearing hooks, and flails. In general, peasants employed many variations of ploughs and other agricultural tools depending on differences in soils. Observers noted that, contrary to often-heard opinion, the Russian plough had never been stagnant. It experienced a long evolutionary path, adopting to soil and labor conditions and becoming, over several centuries, simpler and lighter. Over lengthy periods of time and from generation to generation, the Russian peasant had been developing an optimum shape for the plough, in which every detail was carefully considered. For example, in the central industrial provinces peasant used light-weight ploughs, because male peasants of these provinces usually worked outside villages and agriculture was in women's hands. In those areas, women ploughed, harrowed, and sowed. During the first decades of the nineteenth century, peasants adapted winnowers, threshers, rolling breakers, and straw-cutters. The inventors and producers of these devices were often peasants themselves. Thus, agricultural tools reflected peasant ecological mentality and were shaped by their conscious choices.

Throughout several centuries of imperial Russian history, individual farming in Russia remained limited, while communal land cultivation prevailed. Peasants worked their land and the land of their landlords in cooperation with other families of the village commune. Communal institutions, mainly the communal assembly, managed and supervised all agricultural and economic activities of peasants. The assemblies also periodically redistributed communal land among peasant families, in order to maintain a rough equality among them. On average, a peasant household had for its use about 31 acres of land. Nevertheless, in most instances, individual farmers were constantly making decisions themselves. They also consulted with other individuals who were noteworthy in terms of agricultural knowledge, personal experience, and talent. In difficult or controversial cases, in order to determine such matters as soil quality or the extent of hay meadows, peasants commonly resorted to the commune and the communal assembly. In these cases, the communal assembly selected knowledgeable peasants, who were best versed in the given problem. The peasant commune had a flexible body, responsive to the changing sociopolitical conditions. The commune could not disregard public or landlord pressures, but at the same time it acted in the interests of the peasants, distributing labor obligations and dues in a convenient and fair way.

One of the most important and widely debated communal practices was the periodic redistribution of arable land among households. Land redistribution was especially common in the agricultural black earth regions of southern Russia. In other areas, peasants usually did not redistribute lands. In areas where land redistribution prevailed, peasants redistributed lands among the given commune's households every five, ten, or fifteen years, as decided by local peasant custom. According to one old theory, periodic land redistribution had a long tradition, predating serfdom and rooted in rational peasant practices aimed at maintaining land equality among peasant households. Each family received a combination of strips of good and bad land, nearby and distant, and on the hills and in the lowlands. These land strips intermingled. Possessing strips in ecologically various areas, the farmer received an average harvest: in an arid year, strips located in the lowlands could save the harvest and in a rainy year—the elevated strips on hills. Other scholars believe that land redistribution resulted from serfdom. In this view, landlords obligated peasants to redistribute lands among their households, in order to synchronize each household with its labor potential based upon the number of hands in the family and thus to maximize household productivity. It would be a serious mistake, however, to believe that peasant redistributions and communal land tenure was based on the desire to equalize resources according to the family size. Communes never tried to maintain economic equality among their members and did not seek to maintain equity in their primary means of production. Regardless of the origins of the practice, it occurred in certain parts of Russia up until the turn of the twentieth century and even thereafter. Repartitioned lands were always, by definition, lands held in communal ownership.

This aspect of communal land ownership led many interpreters of Russian history to conclude that Russian agriculture failed to modernize in part because the peasants were irrational and inept. Thus, these factors constitute an aspect of alleged Russian backwardness and supposedly contributed to an "agrarian crisis" during the late nineteenth and early twentieth centuries.[8] How ironic, then, that neither peasant communal land ownership nor the continued existence of serfdom (until 1865) prevented dynamic agricultural growth and the general economic development of the Russian countryside. For example, by the turn of the twentieth century, roughly 36 percent of the world's wheat crop came from Russia. Furthermore, it is important to recall that although the commune is typically associated with communal land ownership, it never excluded individual land ownership. In fact, the peasant commune usually involved a combination of collective and individual lands. Whatever their shortcomings, communes hardly undermined individual peasant endeavors and often acted as safety nets for their members. The commune was hardly an obstacle for the enterprising peasant. The peasant could rely on the commune, reckon with it, and act quite independently. This is evidenced by a large number of rich peasants and their concrete histories. Also, the agrarian crisis, to whatever extent it occurred, resulted largely from the transformation (rather than the stagnation) of the countryside, growth of the population and the decline of cottage industries, the subject of discussion of the following chapters (Figure 2.1).

Figure 2.1 Peasants taking a break from work.

Although communal ownership was the predominant type of peasant land tenure in Russia, other types of land tenure coexisted with it. A significant numbers of peasants, serfs as well as state and other categories of peasants bought and owned lands individually. About 66 percent of peasants who owned land came from the central industrial provinces and the rest came from other areas. By the 1850s, serfs, that is, peasants who belonged to landlords, of the central industrial provinces owned 580,392 acres of land. These lands were in almost complete peasant ownership even before 1848. The new 1848 law allowed serfs to buy or acquire real estate in their own names, a matter that had been explored in the previous chapter.[9] Contemporaries noted that the outputs on privately owned lands were significantly higher than on communal redistributed lands. Peasants took greater care in tending these lands. Peasants regarded communal lands as "shaky and temporary," subject to surveys, cuts, and repartition. On their own lands peasants took complete charge. The private lands were exempt from taxation and not subject to repartition or compulsory crop rotation. According to pertinent data, the 1770s and the 1790s were the most active years for land purchases by peasants—about 82 percent of peasant land purchases occurred during those decades.[10]

Peasant purchases of private lands resulted in part from ecological considerations. The evidence suggests that peasants bought much land for noncultivation purposes, either for wood lands or pasture lands. During the second quarter of the nineteenth century, the number of new acquisitions declined, especially in central non-black earth provinces. After all, when nonagricultural activities began to prevail in the central non-black earth provinces, land purchases for farming were not important. In the mid-nineteenth century over a half of Russia's peasants were engaged in nonagricultural activities, a factor that signifies that the peasantry facilitated, rather than hindered, Russia's economic and industrial development. During the first half of the nineteenth century, agriculture was already losing ground to local industry and commerce.[11]

Russian agriculture saw many improvements toward the end of the nineteenth century and especially during and after the 1905 Revolution. An especially significant reform concerned improved crop rotation methods. Peasants learned that to improve and restore the land's fertility, clover could be planted. They also introduced flax into the crop rotation; by the end of the nineteenth century most of Russia was on the three-crop rotation system. Clover offered more food for cattle in the nongrowing season, which led to an increase in the number of cattle and field animals, which in turn increased the amount of manure and, finally, enhanced land fertility. Russia agricultural continued to develop until the eve of the revolution and the country remained one of the world's bread baskets. During the prerevolutionary decades, grain farming was the dominant industry. In 1910–1912, gross production of grain reached an average value of about 4 billion rubles and for all field crops—5 billion rubles. Grain was the main export article of Russia. In 1913 the share of grain production was 47 percent of total exports and 57 percent of agricultural exports. In 1909–1913 grain exports were greatest—11.9 million tons of grain, of which 4.2 million tons of wheat and 3.7 million tons of barley. In the world grain market exports from Russia amounted to 28.1 percent of total world exports. Russian agriculture played an important part in the world economy. Russia's wheat production fed not only its own people but also, because of extensive wheat exports, a significant proportion of the world's population.

In summary, the Russian peasantry possessed significant agricultural knowledge, accumulated from long collective and individual experience. This knowledge allowed Russian peasants to adapt their farming skills to Russia's diverse environment. The peasantry as a group and each peasant individually possessed knowledge about the environment and agriculture. The peasant in the village from an early age steadily acquired this knowledge through gradual involvement in farming and household activities.

Suggested readings

Bartlett, Roger, ed. *Land Commune and Peasant Community in Russia: Communal Forms in Imperial and Early Soviet Society*. Macmillan: Basingstoke and London, 1990.

Blum, Jerome. *Lord and Peasant in Russia from the Ninth to the Nineteenth Century*. Princeton, NJ: Princeton University Press, 1961.

Moon, David. *The Russian Peasantry 1600–1930: The World the Peasants Made*. New York: Addison-Wesley, 1999.

Volin, Lazar. *A Century of Russian Agriculture. From Alexander II to Khrushchev*. Cambridge, MA: Harvard University Press, 1970.

Peasants, Childhood, and Gender Roles

As explored in the previous chapter, peasants possessed wide social and economic experiences, which accumulated over time and were fully reflected in the organization of the economic activities of the family as a small labor community. A clearly worked-out pace of everyday activities of a family was combined with a reasonable distribution of these activities. The same cadence was inherent in each cycle of seasonal work and the agricultural year as a whole. This well-attuned tempo involved specifically designed methods of behavior in adverse weather conditions. And an extremely important role here was played by labor education—the gradual and natural connection of children and adolescents to all the tasks of the family.

This chapter addresses labor education and divisions in the context of gendering and gender roles in the Russian countryside during the imperial period. It specially focuses on the practices of child rearing among peasants and on gendered role divisions. Perhaps not fitting well into the *recently* prevailing portrayals of women, a certain impression of a Russian rural woman—robust and undaunted—often emerges in literature. What did being a man and a woman mean and what did feminine and masculine signify in the Russian countryside? How did peasants define femininity and masculinity? What did gender and sex divisions mean in the rural society of Russia? To aid in answering these questions, gendering here means the practices of rearing, encouraging patterns of behavior, and teaching and dividing responsibilities as ascribed to the stereotypes of biological sex. This chapter seeks to understand the meaning of a gender system in a peasant environment, as well as the role of the institutionalized gender order in child rearing and gender roles.[1]

According to Russian-language ethnographers and scholars of popular culture, rural child rearing occurred alongside and within the productive economic activities of the peasant household. Since familial productive tasks were generally divided between men and women, the process of child rearing was consistent with gendered male and female spheres of economic activity.

Peasants correlated particular labor duties with sex: certain types of work in the fields or performing household tasks were ascribed to a certain biological sex. Two different spheres of productive and household activities for men and woman surfaced in the rural society and children were allocated to these masculine and feminine spheres from an early age, but not at once. Therefore, it may be assumed that, at least at the level of customary law and practice, gender order already took an institutionalized character in the peasant family and rural society before an industrial-capitalist society formalized gender order. It appears that the gender arrangement was influenced by productive activities of the peasant household and the labor arrangement of its members. The latter were important factors that influenced popular stereotypes of gender.

At this moment, let us define the category of children as peasants understood it. Contrary to some scholarly views, peasants actually distinguished infancy and adolescence from the other two stages of life, adulthood and old age, with a complex network of subdivisions, stages, and phases within each stage.[2] These divisions relied upon popular beliefs about human biology and were also entrenched within a broad range of sociocultural assumptions and economic roles. The criteria for transitions from childhood to adulthood and to old age were relative and depended on the individual's physiological condition and readiness to carry out one or another task according to gender and physical condition.[3] Researchers of Russian popular culture have noted that peasants believed that childhood begins with birth and continues until the age of fifteen or seventeen. In reality, depending on locality and the ability to undertake a productive responsibility, the upper limit of childhood ranged from age thirteen to nineteen.[4]

In support of most gender theories which view gender as a socially constructed arrangement, it appears that peasants considered infants and very young children, from the day of birth to age five or six, as neutral or without gender. Collective names for children of this age did not reflect their gender, although personal names were given according to a child's sex. With the exception for given names, children's nicknames did not reveal their biological sex but rather either suggested the child's age (a baby, child, kid, etc.) or behavior associated with that age, such as crying and crawling. Regardless of their sex, both male and female infants were variously called "baby" or "child." Small children were also called *kuviaka* or *kuvatka* (those who cry), *sligoza* (those who drool), *popolza* (those who crawl), and so on, depending on locality.[5] Similarly, the clothing of very young children did not distinguish their biological sex. Peasant children of both sexes usually wore long linen shirts until five or six years of age. Until that age, young boys normally did not wear pants. In most peasant families, children's clothing was produced from old worn-out adult clothes and was passed from elder children to younger ones. Thus, despite their biological sex, children's gender remained neutral until their ability to assume household responsibilities.[6]

Nevertheless, the institutionalized gender order began to influence the practice of child rearing from the day of birth. In some cases Russian orthodox peasants assumed that infants before being baptized were vulnerable to being exposed to evil spirits which could surrogate the baby or change its sex. Besides, on the whole, peasants believed that the child's biological, or as they called it, "natural" sex did not automatically convert into the right behavior normally attributed to the biological sex. Parents used many customs and activities linked to the supernatural and popular religion in order to guard the child's biological sex. In other words, peasants performed certain actions to push the children's upbringing in a way they believed to be fitting for their biological sex. Even with their great variations, in all cases these activities and customs were tied to male and female spheres of household economic activities.

The process of gendering started early, right from the day of birth, and was influenced by local custom. For example, in many northern provinces of Russia parents tied the navel strings (after removal) of new-born baby boys under an object which they associated with the traditional male sphere, such as a hammer or an axe, whereas they tied those of baby girls over objects associated with female occupations, such as spindles and yarn. These objects related not only to male or female activities but also to the occupations that parents desired for their children's future. For example, depending on the parents' desires, the daughter's navel was cut over a spindle or a thread, whereas the son's upon a hammer, axe, or a form for making peasant shoes. Some practices of fastening biological sex involved magical handling of the child's placenta. For example, in Orel province in south-central Russia, a mother would take a piece of her baby's placenta and put it in a place or upon an object she associated with the child's desired future occupation. In Vologda province of northern Russia, the father would hang the placenta of his baby son in the stables while saying "the child grows up with the horse."[7] These different choices for boys and girls clearly indicated that peasants had certain stereotypes about gender, distinguished by beliefs about male and female spheres of productive activity. By magically associating children with one or another sphere, the parents tried to cultivate skills and activities proper to the child's biological sex.

This finding supports the idea of many practitioners of gender studies that gender is a socially and culturally constructed category. Thus, early gendering of infants involved the symbolic association of them with masculinity and femininity spheres of productive activity, even when infants of both sexes were otherwise treated identically. Physical differences between newborn boys and girls suggested sex and gender, yet for peasants, until puberty, gender was not clearly established and required further action on the part of parents.

Furthermore, evidence suggests that Russian peasants distinguished childhood as a unique stage of life. Until a certain age, children had their own sphere of activity, relatively separate from the adult one. The children's sphere was a world where they lived, played, fooled around, and learned to become adults. While being another world, this was also an imitation of the adult one. Many games and recreational activities engaged in by children between the ages of six and fourteen imitated adult occupational and social activities. For example, in some areas peasant children played *konople*, a game that mimicked certain labor tasks in hemp cultivation. With few exceptions, children's games were gendered, following the adult gender order.[8] In the words of an investigator of children's recreational activities, "a game was a particular way of preparing children for adult responsibilities."[9]

Gendering children continued into their adolescence and was reflected in the practice of apprenticing children in productive activities of the household. Apprenticing children served primarily as the means of educating and preparing children for adult life.[10] Boys and girls were gradually assigned "masculine" and "feminine" tasks which they had to learn and be able to do when they become adults. In general, with a few exceptions, initiation of children into agricultural, household, and other productive labor started early, usually from age five or six and involved very simple tasks. As children matured and acquired greater physical strength, parents gradually taught and assigned them more difficult and serious tasks. The process of initiation in some cases was accompanied by additional ritualistic activities and rites. Anthropologists believe that the latter symbolized the transition from childhood to adolescence.[11] For example, in Smolensk province in western Russia, at the age of five or six a young girl for the first time in her life was assigned to spin a single thread. Afterward the thread was burned and the girl was supposed to consume its ashes with water and bread. This ritual was accompanied by a saying: "eat and you will become a good spinner." In other areas of Russia, boys and girls aged five to seven began to wear pants and skirts, modes of dress that also symbolized their transition to a new stage of life.[12] Hence, the transition to adulthood was gendered and began from the age of five or six with the symbolic introduction of children into productive activities and continued for the next several years. During these years, the children were characterized as "undergrown," "under-aged" (*podrostkovye*), or juvenile. This observation questions a modernist hypothesis, namely, that the period from birth to six years of age contained a full transition to adulthood. In this view, from the age of six peasant children started to perform all adult tasks.[13] Findings from the Russian countryside suggest that rather than being completed by the age of six, the transition to adulthood started at the ages of between five and seven and continued for years thereafter.

In general, the institutionalized gender order influenced the types of work children learned to perform. Boys were usually launched into activities associated with masculinity traditionally fulfilled by adult male peasants. Young sons were expected to help their fathers to sow and thresh and to cart manure to the fields. For example, in Narymsk province of Western Siberia, at the age of five or six boys began to assist adult peasants in manuring soil. The most widespread communal function for six- or seven-year-old boys was the herding of animals. Boys who engaged in herding were called *podpasok* or *pastushok* (herd boy, shepherd boy, or cowboy). At about the same age, in many provinces, boys also began to learn how to ride on horseback. In most cases, young boys worked under the supervision of their fathers or older male children.[14]

As boys grew older and gained more physical strength and ability, parents gave them greater responsibilities and assigned them more complicated tasks within the established institutionalized gender order. At the age of seven, eight, or nine, boys began to help adult peasants with land cultivation. In the Shadrinsk district of Western Siberia, boys of this age and occupation were called *pakholki* and *boronovolki* (plow boys and harrow boys). Their work involved leading horses during plowing and harrowing. From age nine or ten, boys began to carry out various other activities: accompanying the cows to water, feeding animals, carting manure, harrowing, helping adults in plowing and harvesting, and carrying provisions for adult males who worked away from the village (in local forests or on nearby rivers, ponds, and so on). From the age of thirteen to fourteen, the male peasant was supposed to work with the scythe, sickle, thresher, and axe, and began to learn how to work with the plough. At the age of fifteen, the son became a "full assistant" (*polnyi pomoshchnik*), as he was called, of his father and could replace him in case of the father's absence or sickness (Figure 3.1).[15]

Girls' activities involved helping mothers to maintain the household, caring for the younger children, and carrying out all agricultural and cottage responsibilities of adult female peasants. These responsibilities included raking, strewing, reaping, binding sheaves, and gleaning. Depending on the province, girls also learned various crafts and cottage industries, which in Russia were

Figure 3.1 A lesson in mowing. Early 1900.

predominantly, although not exclusively, female endeavors. Girls' occupations were usually within the household or the local community, whereas boys' activities were inside as well as outside the village.

Nevertheless, the occupational roles of boys and girls were sometimes interchangeable. In families without male children, girls were taught agricultural tasks normally performed by boys and, vice versa, in families with no female children boys were commonly introduced to female economic and social activities.[16]

Although, regional economic variations determined the character of children's occupations, gender order was still a primary factor. In areas where agriculture predominated—southern, western, and central agricultural areas, the Volga provinces, and Siberia—children performed mostly agricultural tasks. During the nongrowing season in agricultural areas, children engaged in various domestic industries and types of work not associated with farming. While girls usually stayed at home helping women, boys often migrated with fathers and worked away from the village. By the late nineteenth century, with the growth of industry, seasonal migration of rural (mostly male) children to industrial centers increased significantly.[17] This gave boys a somewhat superior position, which would later add to gender inequality when they grew up and become adults.

In addition to farming activity, in areas where hunting and fishing were a significant part of the local economy, boys helped parents in these activities as well. From the age of eight or nine boys learnt how to use the bow and how to set up nets on lakes and ponds for catching wild life. The initiation into fishing and hunting at first started as play, which gradually took more realistic forms. Finally, as they grew older, boys were invited to engage in real hunting and fishing, beginning with simplest and easiest assignments and then going on to the more complicated and difficult ones.[18]

In regions where the local economy was mixed or predominantly nonagricultural, children engaged in cottage industries and crafts. In the central nonagricultural provinces, parents taught children textile making and other crafts that characterized the local economy. Here girls engaged in various cottage industries, whereas boys were initiated into various commercial activities or worked outside the village. Boys sometimes engaged in petty trade. The former serf, Savva Purlevskii, recalled in his memoirs that at the age of eleven (in 1811) he became a petty trader. His mother wove linen cloth and he sold it at local and regional markets. (Serfs in his village traditionally pursued nonagricultural occupations.) In addition to his mother's canvas, Purlevskii also bought flax and locally produced peasant goods and transported them to Moscow or local markets where he sold them. As he grew up, he traveled for longer distances.[19] Thus, productive household activities in the countryside were gendered; female members of family usually stayed at home and males worked outside. In areas with mixed economies, girls usually remained at home and learned various crafts and trades. In Russia peasant cottage industry was virtually a women's sphere. According to a 1787 observer, "women of ... [Moscow province], as is usual everywhere [in central Russia], spin flax and wool and weave canvas and cloth for household use and for sale." This observer recorded similar activities among women in other nonagricultural provinces of central Russia.[20]

Most evidence suggests that Russian peasant children made the transition to adulthood, at least in terms of occupation, at about fifteen years of age. By a certain age, peasant boys and girls were supposed to have learned how to accomplish a certain number of occupational tasks. Those who could not learn how to do work appropriate to their age were subjected to mockery. For instance, a girl who could not learn how to spin by a certain age was called a "no spinner" (*nepriakha*); if by the age of fifteen, a girl could not weave cloth, she was called a "no weaver" (*netkakha*). Boys who had not learned how to make baste shoes were called "shoeless" (*bezlapotnik*). As a contemporary observer noted, in this last case, male peasants who could not make peasant shoes were not respected by fellow villagers and were generally viewed as "losers."[21] This gendered order of productive activities broke down in families with no adult male workers or no male children, where all responsibilities fell upon women and female children.

The upbringing of children as boys and girls started early, initially with the symbolic ascribing of them to male and female spheres of activity, and resulted from the institutionalized gender order for making men and women. Such an institutionalized gender order, so it seems, was a product of popular cultural beliefs and social and economic relational contexts. Gender difference as perceived in popular culture did not ultimately constitute gender inequality or oppression. But institutionalized gender order, that is, the practice of ascribing boys and girls to masculine and feminine spheres of activity, produced gender inequality. As we have seen, boys were introduced into activities which in the future, when they became adults, would give them privileged economic and social position.

Thus, labor duties in peasant families were carefully defined according to the age, gender, and physical abilities of family members. As mentioned in Chapter 1, peasants' full working age usually ranged from about seventeen to sixty-five.[22] In the village small children, under the age of five or six, and people over sixty-five did not work. Children between ages eight and fourteen were considered "half-workers of little strength" (*polurabochie maloi pomoshchi*), whereas juveniles between fourteen and sixteen years of age were "half-workers of greater strength" (*polurabochie bol'shei sily*). Juveniles of fifteen to seventeen years of age were subjected to half labor duty. In impoverished families, or in families in which one of the adults was absent or deceased, children fulfilled all adult responsibilities at an earlier age.[23]

Demographic studies suggest that children under age fifteen constituted about one-third of the peasant population. Children under age five accounted for about 14 percent of the peasant population of northern Russia; children between ages six and ten made up about 11 percent and those aged between eleven and fifteen—about 9 percent.[24] During the nineteenth century, children of age seven and below accounted for about 17.5 percent of the population of European Russia. (In 1858 the population of European Russia was 59.2 million of which about 49 million were peasants.[25]) Infant and child mortality rates were high. During the nineteenth century, only about 50 percent of children survived to age ten.[26] Historians of Russian peasants point out that the high infant mortality resulted from alleged widespread neglect of and indifference toward children in peasant families.[27] Anthropologists maintain that the high death rate among children resulted not from neglect or indifference but from poor living conditions and inadequate medical knowledge. Russian peasant families in fact highly valued their children precisely because of the high mortality rates among them and because of their potential significance as future household and agricultural laborers. One popular peasant saying holds that "Our own harrow-boy (*boronovolok*) is much more valuable than anyone else."

The adult population in village communes provided children with love and care, as well as toleration for some of their mischief. Children were considered to be young and silly and therefore were easily forgiven for pranks. This, however, did not exclude punishment applied within the individual family. When punishment occurred, parents were careful not to cause serious physical harm to their children. A former serf from Yaroslavl' province of central Russia, Savva Purlevskii, recalled that when he was a child in the early nineteenth century, he was beaten by his father "only on rare occasions," because, as he explained, his parents were concerned about his health. His "grandmother would not let anyone beat [him], because [he] was the only child they had."[28] The appreciation of children as future laborers helps explain the low rates of infanticide and child abandonment in Russia (Figure 3.2).[29]

The high mortality rates among infants and young children affected the number of children in peasant families. For example, the 1717 data from the Kubenskii region of Vologda province (northern Russia) suggests that about 47 percent of peasant families had two or three children, whereas 22.4 percent had one child. It is worth to note that about 14 percent of peasant families had no children at all. It is not clear, however, whether these families ever had any children or had none at the time of census. Nevertheless, an average family had two or three children. In Russia extended two generational families with two adult male and two adult female members predominated.[30]

Figure 3.2 Haymaking with mowing machine. *c.* 1900.

Eventually, children grew up into adult men and women. As adults they were expected to do what they had been taught as children. Women generally performed work associated with the female sphere. In the absence of male members of the family, women performed men's tasks. In cottage industries, women usually engaged in the process of making goods, whereas men were responsible for the sale of what had been produced. This certainly gave men an advantage. With the rise of peasant migration during the nineteenth century, women mostly stayed at home in the villages, where they assumed male tasks and responsibilities. Even so, women had some property rights. Women's dowries and their earnings from handicrafts were considered as their property. Widows with children had some rights of inheritance as well. In addition to property rights, women also had some authority within the household. The wife of the head of the household (*bol'shak*) had authority over her younger female and male family members. Women also became heads of households if their husbands died without leaving an adult male heir, although in most cases their rights to vote in the communal assemblies, a traditional male role, were limited. In general, women had modest power outside their households. Peasant institutions and local courts offered women some protection. Township courts and communes offered a degree of protection to women who were victimized excessively by their husbands. Although these inadequate rewards, power, and security were not equal with women's labor input, they were enough to prevent women as a group from protesting against their inequality. After all, women were both actors and victims, able to accommodate themselves to the existing gendered order.

Suggested readings

Gorshkov, Boris B. *Russia's Factory Children: State, Society and Law, 1800–1917.* Pittsburg: University of Pittsburg Press, 2009.

Kelly, Catriona. *Children's World: Growing up in Russia, 1890–1991.* New Haven, CT; London: Yale University Press, 2007.

The Field and the Loom: Peasant Economy

When in 1826, an observer visited the village of Ivanovo of Vladimir province in the central non-black-earth region, he wrote that "agriculture here is in a poor condition because the residents find the weaving of calico more profitable and easier than field work...."[1] Vladimir province was well known as a nonagricultural land and a center of textile making but the survival of the peasant family depended on both agricultural and nonagricultural pursuits everywhere. Even in southern agrarian areas rural life could not be sustained by agriculture alone and demanded of the peasantry various nonagricultural occupations, such as carpentry, blacksmithing, tailoring, shoemaking, boat making, weaving, and many others. A great number of peasants throughout imperial Russia performed multiple economic activities, from day laborers to entrepreneurs. The local and imperial markets largely depended on the peasantry and the latter dominated the Russian marketplace. The local economy and occupations of peasants depended on the environment. In the northern and central non-black earth regions, where soils were poor, agriculture combined work on land or with livestock with various cottage industries, handicraft, work outside the village, and commerce. During the nineteenth century, in certain provinces and regions agriculture became a seasonal occupation and the nonagricultural activities of peasants prevailed. The prominent Russian economic and social historian M. I. Tugan-Baranovsky commented in 1898 about the eighteenth-century Russian economy that "nothing could be more mistaken than the idea that Muscovite Russia was an exclusively agricultural country."[2] This chapter will examine peasant economy. Peasant nonagricultural activities and the tradition of textile making, especially, were important factors of Russia's industrial development.[3]

As we have explored in the previous chapters, the legal definition of peasants hardly fully reflected their actual social and economic activities—peasantry, whether state, landlord's, or royal, was not an occupation. The peasant could be a serf or a peasant of any other category and simultaneously engage in a cottage industry, run a small workshop, be involved in a trade, or even possess a manufacturing enterprise and hire labor of other people, including sometimes people of "higher" social estates. It was particularly true for the central non-black earth region, where peasants were multi-occupational and performed various social and economic roles (Figure 4.1).

The central non-black-earth region, which later became known as the Central Industrial Region, where the Russian centralized state first arose, was the area where industry first took shape. The region included the provinces of Yaroslavl', Kaluga, Kostroma, Moscow, Nizhniy Novgorod, Tier' Vladimir, and usually Ryazan' and Tula, all of which were known in nineteenth-century Russia as the "industrial provinces" (*promyshlennye gubernii*). During the eighteenth century these provinces witnessed the earliest and the most significant development of a market economy. In many provinces of this region agriculture became peasant's lesser occupation. In Moscow province, for example, peasants devoted to agriculture only 3.5 months a year and the rest of the year they worked in domestic industries, crafts, and trade.[4]

According to the data on state peasants, the majority of them in the central non-black-earth and northern regions engaged in nonagricultural activities. For example, Vladimir province's 92.44 percent of the peasants engaged at least

Figure 4.1 Making wooden spoons.

part-time in one or another nonagricultural activity. In Moscow province, 89 percent of state peasants performed nonagricultural activities, in Kostroma province—86.5 percent, in Novgorod province—80.5 percent, in Pskov province—80 percent, in Yaroslavl' province—75.8 percent, and in Nizhnii Novgorod—65.7 percent.[5] The same was true for serfs of these areas, where life could not be sustained by agriculture alone. The dependence on agriculture in these provinces was low and during the first half of the nineteenth century was declining. Peasants there *utilized* grain and other agricultural commodities imported from the southern agrarian provinces and Ukraine.

The environment, as well as various economic factors, obligations to the state, and certain personal inducements motivated peasants to seek extra earnings outside agriculture. They had to maintain their own households and pay feudal and manorial dues, as well as the state taxes. Peasant involvement in nonagricultural activities was particularly extensive in those provinces of the region where rent (*obrok*) dominated over corveé (*barschina*). In the 1760s, 70–75 percent of the peasants of the central non-black-earth region paid rent. By the mid-nineteenth century, as the market economy accelerated, this figure approached 80–85 percent.[6]

In fact, it was the ecological circumstances that ultimately led to the predominance of rent. In non-black earth regions, geography and climate stimulated the development of various cottage industries, manufacturing, and crafts. Vladimir province, where soil fertility was low, provides a significant example of this. A famous textile entrepreneur and historian of Ivanovo, Iakov Garelin, described the impact of geography and climate on the development of the local economy:

> The low productivity of [Vladimir's] land did not allow the peasant to support his family.... [Serf-peasants] abandoned their land and went to the factories. All the Ivanovo residents turned themselves from agriculturalists into factory workers; almost every home presented itself as a small weaving shop because most women wove calico at home and teen-age girls made bobbins; adult men worked all day at the factory printing calico and twelve-fifteen years old boys prepared colors.[7]

Besides these geographical and climatic factors and the need to meet manorial dues, there were many other personal motivations for nonagricultural activities, as we will see, which unlike traditional, agricultural occupations, offered the peasantry greater opportunities for territorial, economic, and social mobility (Table 4.1).

Table 4.1 Occupations of the state peasants involved in nonagricultural activities in the mid-nineteenth century (in percentages)

Province	Employed as workers	Small entrepreneurs, small traders, and craftsmen	Entrepreneurs and merchants
Central industrial region:			
Iaroslavl	44	40	16
Kostroma	50	40	10
Moscow	54	35	11
Riazan'	25	65	10
Tver'	46	44	10
Vladimir	50	42	8
Northern region:			
Novgorod	46	42	12
Pskov	25	65	10
Mid-Volga:			
Samara	12	78	10

Source: Isaev, *Rol' tekstil'noi promyshlennosti*, 49.

According to statistics, presented in Table 4.1, 44–54 percent of the state peasants engaged in nonagricultural occupations were hired workers, 35–65 percent were small entrepreneurs, craftsmen, or self-employed in services, and about 12 percent were merchants and entrepreneurs. Serf peasants, who constituted the majority of peasant-migrants, pursued similar kinds of economic activities. Like state peasants, serfs were involved in entrepreneurial ventures and marketing activities, possessed manufacturing units and workshops, traded, worked in services, and labored in factories.

It was a long-standing tradition that peasants of non-black earth provinces actively pursued nonagricultural activities, providing the local market with necessary manufactured goods, and paying their dues to the landlords and to the state. In this respect the peasants' contribution to the local and national economies was crucial. The mid-nineteenth-century historian and economist A. K. Korsak, in a discussion of peasant cottage industry and widespread peasant involvement in commerce, even argued that peasants played the most vital role of all social elements in the economic development of pre-reform Russia.[8]

Textile production was the traditional occupation of peasants in the central industrial region. During the long winters of central Russia, peasants spun, knit, and wove domestic linen, wool, and imported cotton, and silk bought from petty traders and merchants, and sold their products at local markets. These crafts existed in the form of cottage industry, known in Russia as *kustarnaia promyshlennost'*. During the previous centuries peasants produced textiles for household use and for local and sometimes for distant markets. Also, in many provinces, peasants used their craft production for payment in kind to the landlord. For example, in 1593–1594 the church peasants who populated the lands of Troitsa-Sergiev Monastery paid rent in linen canvas. In 1745 the peasants of the village of Borisoglebskoe (of Kostroma province) paid the landlord 497 meters of linen canvas and 443 meters of unbleached linen.[9]

Linen making was the most widespread textile occupation because of the natural availability of the needed raw materials, their relative cheapness, good demand, and technological simplicity. In the 1760s cottage industry consumed about 65 percent out of 16.38 million kg of linen and hemp utilized by Russia's textile industry as a whole and produced about 140 million arshin (1 arshin = 0.71 m) of canvas.[10] A revealing picture of the entire process of linen making comes from a description by an observer who wrote in the late 1820s:

peasants themselves grow the linen plant and harvest it, water, dry, and prepare the fiber; then [they] themselves spin it on distaff and weave it on their looms in their izbas (village homes) and finally bleach and press it…. The peasant family performs all operations up to finishing [the linen]. Linen canvas production is established in all villages; there is almost no peasant home in which peasants do not spin or weave. Peasant work, all their working equipment and the production itself, all fits into the peasant household. Tools for braking and scutching linen are simple hand-made drakes and scutcher; [tools] for carding there are wooden hatchets or bristle brushes; for spinning simple distaffs; for weaving, when needed, [peasants] locate a loom in a corner of the izba and take it away when the work is done… Having prepared the yarn [peasant women and girls]… weave; the loom is almost never out of action; either the female head of the household, the daughter-in-law, or the daughters and nieces, or sometimes the males, whoever has time, sits at the loom and the reeds hum a noise without stopping. Having done the weaving, [they] bleach…,wash…, dry… [and] press… [canvas].[11]

Thus, as this passage illustrates, the working equipment was quite simple, easy to operate, and usually constructed by peasants themselves from widely available local material: wood, bristle, and so on. A narrow loom which produced fabric up to 0.45 meter in width was the most widespread type of weaving equipment. The same observer explained that in Russia the large weaving loom was not popular among peasants because operating on it required "a strong individual."[12] In the village, weaving was usually the work of women and young girls.

Peasant cottage industry was predominantly run by women. Male peasants of the region usually sought work outside the village while leaving the household and cottage industry to women. "Women [of Nikitskii district of Moscow province]," wrote a contemporary in 1787, "as [is] usual everywhere, spin linen and wool and weave canvas and wool cloth for the household use and for sale."[13] Similar accounts come from other districts of the province, as well as from other provinces where female peasants produced various textile goods for household use, for sale on the local markets and fairs, and for traveling merchants.[14] In the 1780s in Tver' province, about 280 thousand female peasants wove canvas during the nongrowing season. Each woman produced annually about 57 meters of the fabric of the province's 16.33 million annual total.

The making of wool and silk goods was also a significantly widespread occupation in the countryside. Despite the fact that these two materials were expensive, there was a significant demand for them among the population of the Russian Northern provinces. In the mid-nineteenth century, the entire Russian wool cottage industry, which involved 1.6 millions peasants, utilized about 29.5 millions kg of wool and produced 38.34 millions meters of cloth.[15]

Most peasants usually did not perform printing and dyeing themselves since these kinds of work required special knowledge and experience. "Traveling" printers and dyers (known in Russia as *naboishchiki* and *krasheninniki*), who knew how to prepare dye of various colors on the basis of plant and mineral components and who had mastered other secrets of the craft, traveled throughout the countryside printing and dyeing canvas, wool cloth, threads, and other textile products of the peasants' industry. These traveling craftsmen were usually peasant-migrants. During the late eighteenth and the early nineteenth centuries, the migrants founded small workshops in district centers where they dyed and printed fabrics produced by the local population. For example, the printers and dyers of the village of Pistsovo (Kostroma province), the serfs of the princes Dolgorukii, were well known from Penza and Belozersk to Arkhangelsk and even in Siberia. This fact signifies the geographic mobility of the peasants of the Central Industrial Region.

During the eighteenth century, peasant cottage industry of the central non-black-earth region was largely a seasonal business for an entire family, which usually did not employ outside workers and did not function during periods of agricultural work. Peasants counted neither the time nor the labor they spent to produce a certain item. This, however, did not mean that peasants viewed the industry merely as a means of producing exclusively for the household or that they were not interested in profit. In the course of the late eighteenth and the first decades of the nineteenth century, cottage industry was increasingly becoming market oriented. For example, in 1773 about 40 percent of the peasants of Moscow province worked partly for the local market and even for traveling merchants who traded nationwide.[16] Many of these traders sold textile goods in the southern agricultural provinces. In rare cases, peasants conducted their cottage industry independently. Mostly, they depend on middlemen, entrepreneurs of various kinds, big and petty, who gained a good part of their profit at the peasants' expense. These middlemen were also usually of the peasant estate. During the first half of the nineteenth century, proto-industrial and new industrial forms of production already began to compete with peasant cottage industry. Already by the end of the eighteenth century, many peasants engaged in putting out work or worked for local manufacturers.

Trading peasants

Most of these "traveling" merchants were the famous trading peasants or *torguiushchie krest'iane*, as they were known in the bureaucratic language, who would later undertake entrepreneurial risk and start factories. Although some historians have mentioned the existence of trading peasants as a social category during the pre-reform decades, the role of this important social group in the Russia's economic development still remains largely unexplored.

As mentioned above, depending upon province, 35–65 percent of peasants involved in nonagricultural economy were trading peasants. Most trading peasants conducted their business outside their permanent place of residence and therefore were peasant-migrants, but this category also applied to peasants who stayed in the village and were involved in trade (Figure 4.2).

Trading peasants dominated Russia's local and national markets and fairs. Markets usually functioned throughout the year and fairs were conducted during specified periods, commonly seasonal holidays. Both existed in almost every provincial or district town and represented the major part of Russia's domestic trade. In 1780 there were 450 urban and 1,100 rural fairs in Russia. By the mid-nineteenth century the number of fairs had grown to 4,000. This statistic did not include numerous small bazaars and open markets which webbed Russia's countryside. Trading peasants traveled throughout the country to sell the products of peasant cottage industry at these markets and fairs. Peasant trade,

Figure 4.2 Trading peasants.

markets and fairs played a prominent role in the marketing of goods produced by cottage industry. Peasant petty traders bought goods at small village markets and sold them wholesale at large fairs to merchants.

Mid-nineteenth-century Russian literature reflects peasant trader activities. In Gogol's novel *Dead Souls*, for example, one of the landlord Sobakevich's deceased serfs had successfully traded in Moscow and paid the landlord 500 banknote rubles (about 170 silver rubles) a year in *obrok* (rent). In popular parlance peasant petty traders were known variously as *ofeni* or *afeni* (untranslatable), *korobeiniki* (box-carriers), *khodebshchiki* (traveling peddlers). *Ofeni* established themselves as the most prominent actors of the market. In order to meet competition from other traders, *ofeni* developed their own subculture and used a corporate language, known as ofeni language, consisting of specific words, terms, expressions, and slang, the meaning of which was unknown to outsiders. As a Vladimir newspaper observed, in 1847 there were about 5,000 ofeni in Vladimir province alone. Trading peasants traveled great distances. For example, "thousands" of *khodebshchiki* from the Central industrial region were well known at Ukrainian fairs.

Trading peasants played an important role in Russia's urban economy. In 1844 the revenue office of St. Petersburg collected from trading peasants taxes of 53,659 silver rubles (compared to 71,871 silver rubles paid by merchants). The sum paid by trading peasants, however, did not include taxes paid to the city's budget by peasants who "temporarily" entered guilds or worked in various services. Thus, the trading peasants were a highly significant economic category of the peasant estate; this category eventually produced many able entrepreneurs for the textile industry. As contemporaries observed, most prominent entrepreneurs of the mid-nineteenth century had at one time been trading peasants.

Peasant migration

The most active element of the economy of pre-reform Russia was the peasant-migrant. Peasant migrants were a segment of the peasant estate, both men and women, adults and children, who temporarily conducted various kinds of work, usually nonagricultural, away from their permanent living place. They were known as *otkhodniki* or migrants. In the nineteenth century about a quarter of the peasants of the Russian central provinces migrated annually to perform their economic or social activities outside the village. Migrations and seasonal work outside the village manifested peasants' initiative and the ability to conduct their own business. The resettlement and migrations were voluntary. Such movements as these—over long distances to new environmental, economic, and sometimes social conditions—demanded prior exploration and careful planning. They also helped spread a wide range of information, involved participation in the business community, and promoted courage, endurance, and adaptive skills. Also, migrations to distant cities and counties demanded flexibility as regards the social and professional behavior of peasant-migrants.

Travelers in late eighteenth- and early nineteenth-century Russia witnessed peasants moving from their villages into the urban or other rural areas in order to pursue various economic or social activities. In 1804 agents of the Free Economic Society reported that "in the summer as well as in the winter," peasants "joining together into *arteli* (work associations), travel to various provinces in order to get employment." Peasant migration was also widespread in the summer. After the spring cultivation work was completed, peasants looked for activities outside the village during the summer months and then returned home in late August for harvesting. Foreign visitors described how "in the summer, peasants stream into the towns from all over in order to work as petty traders, carpenters, masons, etc." Available data from certain provinces shows that even by the end of the eighteenth century, depending on the province, the number of male migrants of the region already ranged from 5 to 30 percent of the entire adult male population. For example, in the 1770s in Kostroma province about one-third of the adult male population migrated in order to obtain nonagricultural employment or engage in trade. In 1798, 73,500 Yaroslavl' province male peasants (about 20 percent of the province's adult male population) temporarily left their home villages; in 1799, about 49,000 peasants out of 434,000 (about 11 percent of the entire male population) of Moscow province left for temporary work.

Besides the economic factors motivating peasant-migration, the obvious willingness of some peasants to escape from the control of the landlord or local officials and the strong desire for independent activities and personal liberty through possible future emancipation—always a lively issue among the peasants—clearly contributed to peasant mobility. In addition, as some historians have pointed out, serf peasants were inattentive to their agricultural pursuits and therefore did not seek to improve agricultural technology. Since landlords could easily supervise agriculture and appropriate peasants' profits, peasants were more interested in nonagricultural work outside the village, income from which they could easily conceal from the landlord. One serf (who later became a merchant of the Second Guild) wrote in his memoirs that "serf peasants did not care about their domestic economy 'because [the landlord] would find out about it and take away' [their profits]".[17]

In the first decades of the nineteenth century, Russia witnessed significant demographic change. The population of the Central Industrial Region experienced more dramatic growth than during the previous centuries. The urban population of the region increased by 30–60 percent, partly due to the seasonal migration. Obviously, the role of peasant-migration in the urban economy continually increased. The figures of Table 4.2 illustrate the number and percent of internal passports and tickets issued during the 1850s to male peasant-migrants in Yaroslavl', Kostroma, Moscow, Tver', and Vladimir provinces of the Central Industrial Region.

Throughout the first half of the nineteenth century approximately a quarter of peasants of the Central Industrial Region seasonally migrated each year. Table 4.3 shows the dynamics of peasant migration during the 1840s–1850s according to the number of passports issued annually and grain production in Yaroslavl' and Moscow provinces.

As Table 4.3 shows, in Moscow province annual crop production decreased during the 1840s and 1850s, while the number of passports issued to peasants for seasonal work increased significantly. In Vladimir province, crop production

Table 4.2 Peasant-migration in several central non-black earth provinces in 1854–1857

Province (Year)	Total number of adult male peasants	Passports and tickets issued to the peasants	
		Number	Percent
Yaroslavl' province (1826)		45,503	
Yaroslavl' province (1842)		48,639	
Yaroslavl' province (1856)	391,200	85,784	22
Kostroma province (1856)	394,500	97,791	25
Moscow province (1857)	499,600	116,889	23
Tver' province (1856)	602,400	174,494	29
Vladimir province (1854)	401,500	87,769	22

Table 4.3 Dynamics of peasant migration and grain production in Moscow and Yaroslavl' provinces

Number of passports issued			Grain sowing and harvesting (kg per person)				
Year	Yaroslavl' province	Moscow province	Year	Yaroslavl' province		Moscow province	
				Sown	Harvested	Sown	Harvested
1843	54,713		1843	183	252.0	148.5	274.5
1844	55,077	85,378	1844	183	252.0	148.5	274.5
1845	56,997	88,383	1845	183	252.0	148.5	274.5
1846	56,045	90,596	1846	207	388.5	136.5	231.0
1847	55,720	89,012	1847	207	388.5	136.5	231.0
1848	53,581	87,296	1848	207	388.5	136.5	231.0
1850	53,831	91,172	1850	207	388.5	136.5	231.0
1852		98,614	1852			126.0	148.5
1853		100,816	1853			126.0	148.5
1855		97,770	1855			126.0	148.5
1856		100,265	1856			135.0	199.5
1857		125,763	1857			135.0	199.5

increased and the number of peasant-migrants also grew during 1842–1846. This suggests that there was no significant relationship between migration and the harvest. As mentioned above, during the entire period the central industrial provinces imported most of their grain.

As noted above in Table 4.2, from 22 to 29 percent of the peasants temporarily migrated into the cities. Impressive as these statistics are, they cannot be taken entirely at face value, because they included only those peasants who received documents for leave in a given year and did not cover those who had emigrated in the previous years and remained on leave. Additionally these figures did not account for thousands of peasants who traveled without passports or tickets within thirty miles of their home villages, as permitted by tsarist legislation. Peasants also sometimes violated the law and migrated without legal permission. Therefore, the actual number of peasant-migrants in any year was considerably higher. More importantly, the accumulated proportion of the population involved in temporary migration at one time or another during the decades of the 1830s to the 1850s exceeded the number in any given briefer period. Table 4.2 illustrates, by the way, that the absolute number of serf peasant-migrants was higher than the number of state peasant-migrants. This was also true for other provinces of the region. In the 1850s about 64 percent of all passports were issued to landlord's peasants. This suggests that the serfs' overall participation in seasonal migration and the urban economy was greater than that of state peasants, a reversal of usual expectations. Thus, large numbers of peasants of the central non-black earth provinces, most of whom were landlords' serfs, exercised significant geographic mobility, creating an invisible but tight linkage between the village commune and the outside world.

Peasant mobility and activities outside agriculture were regulated by the law. Early imperial legislation regulating peasant migration dates back to the seventeenth and eighteenth centuries. Having in fact completed peasant enserfment, the law of 1649, known as the *Ulozhenie* of 1649, created the possibility for temporary leave from the permanent living place. Articles 32 (Chapter XI), 67, and 68 (Chapter XX) of the *Ulozhenie* granted peasants, with the agreement of the local authority, the right to migrate for the purpose of achieving temporary employment. The law stated that "no matter whose, peasants... who wish to hire themselves out... to people of any rank are permitted [to do so]."[18] This grant resulted, of course, not from the goodwill of the autocracy but rather from the need to meet the economic necessities of the state and of the peasantry. As peasant migration accelerated during the eighteenth and the first half of the nineteenth centuries, further legislation regulated this activity by introducing various letters of leave and internal passports, as well as specifying procedures for obtaining and extending them. In order to leave the village, the peasants had to have special permission (passport, ticket or written permission, depending on the leave term and distance) from their local authority. (In fact, no individual from any social estate, including nobility, could move from his/her permanent place of residence without legal permission.) State peasants acquired their documents from the local state bureaucracy whereas serf peasants—either from noble landlords or from bailiffs and elders, who often were serfs themselves. After the period of stay expired, the *otkhodnik* was supposed to come back to the village.

Additionally, the law on social estates provided peasants with virtually complete freedom for economic activities. The corresponding laws minutely regulated migrants' standings, depending on the activities they pursued. Factory legislation regulated the status of peasant-migrants who worked as factory laborers, as well as those who possessed factories; the trade and banking laws regulated the activities of trading peasants; and so on ad infinitum.

In sum, the expansion of cottage industry and market activities during the last decades of the eighteenth and the early nineteenth century brought significant energy to the village, providing a basis for economic and social advancement that hardly existed in the "purely" agricultural society. The multiple economic activities of peasants served as an important foundation for the further development undergone by the textile manufacturing during the first half of the nineteenth century.

Suggested readings

Blackwell, William. *The Beginnings of Russian Industrialization, 1800–1860*. Princeton, NJ, Princeton University Press, 1968.

Blackwell, William. *Russian Economic Development from Peter the Great to Stalin*. New York: New Viewpoints, 1974.

Fitzpatrick, Anne L. *The Great Russian Fair: Nizhnii Novgorod, 1840–90*. New York: St. Martin's Press, 1990.

Kahan, Arcadius. *Russian Economic History: The Nineteenth Century*. Chicago: University of Chicago Press, 1989.

Kingston-Mann, E. and Mixer, T., eds. *Peasant Economy, Culture, and Politics of European Russia, 1800–1921*. Princeton: Princeton University Press, 1990.

Morrison, Daniel. *"Trading Peasants" and Urbanization in Eighteenth-Century Russia: The Central Industrial Region*. New York: Garland Pub., 1987.

Peasants and Russia's Early Industrialization

Circa 1740, Kondratii, a serf of the nobleman Bibikov in Grebnevo village of Moscow province, engaged part-time in cottage industry as a weaver. Later, he temporarily migrated to Moscow and worked as a weaver in Lazarev's silk mill. In 1758 he returned to his village and with his three sons, Fedor, Kirill, and Egor, opened a silk manufacturing workshop. Around 1760, the sons adapted the surname Kondrashev, after their father's name. The Kondrashev business seems to have gone so well that by 1783 they became prominent manufacturers and were prosperous enough to donate several tens of thousands of rubles for the construction of a new church in the village.[1] Later, the Kondrashev brothers split and each organized his own workshop. In 1796, Kondrashev workshops produced silk ribbons, taffeta, kerchiefs, and satin valued at 108,200 paper rubles that year.[2] In 1800 Kirill Kondrashev passed his business to his son Mikhail who expanded the father's enterprise. In 1815, his workshop had 73 looms; in 1820–1823 it employed 147 people and had 133 looms in one stone building (5 by 9 square meters) and seven additional wooden buildings. The mill produced various expensive silk goods and inexpensive fabrics from silk combined with cotton.[3] Later, in 1828, Mikhail expanded his enterprise and installed jacquard looms, said to be constructed according to a foreign original by one of the mill's workers.[4]

The Kondrashevs became a famous family in the entrepreneurial world of Russia. In 1820 Mikhail Kondrashev became a merchant of the third guild. In 1831, his son, Ivan M. Kondrashev, who took over the father's business, was awarded the honorary title of Entrepreneurial Advisor (*Manufaktur-Sovetnik*) by the Imperial Russian Senate for his successful entrepreneurial activity.[5] In the late 1830s Ivan further expanded his enterprise: in 1835 the factory had 300 looms; in 1843 it used 731 looms (including 300 jacquard machines) and thirteen silk twisting machines and employed 1,579 workers. The annual production in 1843 was valued at 283,800 silver rubles.[6] In the 1850 London exposition, the silk wares of Kondrashev's mill were "noted and approved."[7] The history of the

Kondrashevs' entrepreneurial activities is not exceptional. An examination of late eighteenth- and early nineteenth-century Russia will find numerous examples of entrepreneurial-minded peasants such as the Prokhorovs, Mosolovs, Ermakovs, and many like them.

Most economic historians of imperial Russia agree that during the first decades of the nineteenth century the Russian economy witnessed significant changes. Unlike the economic development of the eighteenth century, which resulted mainly from the support and demands of the state, the economic growth of the first half of the nineteenth century was primarily fostered by consumer demand and largely depended on private, individual initiative.[8] The role of the peasant entrepreneur in this development was both remarkable and largely unnoticed in existing histories. If the industrial enterprises of the nobility were focused primarily on the demands of the state and the nobility itself, peasant units of production, as we shall see, were market-oriented and worked for the needs of the majority of the population. Although some histories have addressed some aspects of peasant-entrepreneurship, this category has not yet been a topic of thorough academic research. Historians have not yet fully emphasized the role of the peasantry and especially of peasant-entrepreneurs in Russian industrialization.[9] This chapter examines peasant-entrepreneurs and their role in the development of textile manufacturing and the mechanization of textile production during Russia's early industrialization, it mostly utilizes primary sources.

Peasants like the Kondrashevs played an important role in the development of textile manufacturing in Russia during the first half of the nineteenth century. Although in the mid-nineteenth century the largest number of textile mills in the central non-black earth provinces belonged to individuals of the *kupechestvo* estate (the merchant or middle class) and of the *meshchanstvo* (townspeople), most of these individuals themselves were of recent peasant origins.[10] The founders of the most important textile factories initially came from serf and state peasants, having worked their way up as small entrepreneurs, merchants, traders, *kustari* (craftsmen), or weavers. The Moscow manufacturing council observed in 1863 that "the most stable [and] important mills and plants" had grown from the peasant trade.[11]

The experiences of various entrepreneurial peasants were similar but not identical. It would be possible, however, to suggest that most peasant entrepreneurs were formerly prosperous weavers, like the above-mentioned Kondratii. Weaving enabled some individual peasants to accumulate the money necessary to start their own businesses. In several years of working as a weaver, the peasant could make money enough to open a workshop with hired weavers or to organize a commercial house (*torgovyi dom* as it was called). In their workshops and commercial houses, peasants usually functioned as managers or intermediaries and most no longer engaged in actual weaving.

Another notable example of a successful commercial house of peasant origins comes from the history of the Prokhorovs, a famous entrepreneurial family. In 1795, having made sufficient money by weaving silk, Vasilii Ivanovich Prokhorov, who descended from monastery serfs, organized a commercial house. In this enterprise, Prokhorov was an intermediary among local peasant-textile makers. Prokhorov and his sons bought cotton yarn imported from England and distributed it among peasant-weavers. The Prokhorovs then sent the woven cloth to bleachers, dyers and printers and finally sold the finished fabric to merchants and traders wholesale. Later, the Prokhorovs founded the *Trekhgornaia maniufaktura* (Three Mountains Factory), the largest cotton enterprise in Moscow and Russia and several other textile factories in the region. By mid-century, the Three Mountains Factory was located in four large three-story brick buildings and twelve wooden buildings.[12] Like the Kondrashevs and Prokhorovs many peasants started as weavers, small shopkeepers or petty traders and eventually turned their modest textile businesses into larger enterprises equipped with modern machines (Figure 5.1).

Perhaps the single most striking example of peasant industrialist activity arises from the history of Ivanovo-Vosnesensk. During the first quarter of the nineteenth century, prominent serf peasant-traders established several textile mills in the small village of Ivanovo, on the estate of the Sheremet'evs, a powerful noble family. Within a decade the village was transformed into the textile city later known as the "Russian Manchester." Similar serf activities occurred in other provinces of the central industrial region.[13] In his insightful account of the origins of the industrial revolution in Russia, William Blackwell wrote about the early nineteenth century that "the serf industrialist established himself as a fixed and prominent part of the Russian social scenery, [and] as a modern type of capitalist" (Figure 5.2).[14]

Entrepreneurial activities were not limited to serf peasants, as represented by the Kondrashevs and Prokhorovs. State peasants were also widely involved in Russia's entrepreneurial life, a fact less known in historiography. For example, Peter Yemel'anov, a state peasant, possessed a cotton-finishing mill in the Rogozhskii district of Moscow in 1853. The factory used ten steam caldrons and one steam engine, employed ninety workers, and produced velveteen and calico valued at 28,200 silver rubles a year. Other enterprises owned by state peasants

Figure 5.1 Vasilii Prokhorov.

employed an even higher number of people. A textile mill belonging to the state peasant Rodion Mosolov in the Kolomenskii district in 1853 employed 245 laborers and produced goods valued annually at 86,000 silver rubles. Compared to other businesses of this kind, these manufactories were rather small; they

Figure 5.2 Ivanvo-Voznesensk.

were, however, some of the biggest enterprises owned by state peasants. Most peasants, state and serf, owned smaller businesses, which on average employed ten to twenty workers.[15]

In the countryside peasant-entrepreneurs often dominated and even monopolized business activities. In some districts of Moscow province, certain types of industry were owned and run almost exclusively by peasants. In the Klinskii district, for example, twenty-five out of a total of twenty-six cotton weaving mills belonged to individuals of the peasant estate. The digest of industry in Moscow province classified some of these enterprises as "factories," whereas most were workshops with five to ten workers. Several were real "factories" that used steam engines and employed fifty to ninety people. Peasants also possessed all nine leather manufactories of this district. In the Volokolamskii district of the province, peasants owned fifteen out of seventeen cotton weaving enterprises.[16]

On a smaller scale, female peasant-entrepreneurs, like their male counterparts, also played a notable role in the industrial development. Historians have as yet to reflect on this small, yet remarkable group of early Russian industrialists. Most of these women had been or were peasant-migrants or had been engaged in cottage industry. In comparison to enterprises possessed by male peasant entrepreneurs, female businesses were smaller in size, the number of people employed, and the annual volume of production. The Moscow province digest of industry lists several enterprises owned by peasant-women. For example, Maria Terekhova possessed a small cotton weaving and finishing mill in the Bogorodskii district of Moscow province. In 1853 the factory employed 63 workers and produced various clothing products with annual production valued at 14,000 silver rubles. A female peasant-entrepreneur ran a porcelain factory in the Bronnitskii district of the province that employed thirty three people in 1853 and produced porcelain goods valued at 6,500 silver rubles. Although, compared to some other cotton and porcelain mills of the district, these were small-sized enterprises, they were still thriving businesses.[17]

Female entrepreneurs in the textile industry usually belonged to the estates of merchants or townspeople or were identified as honored citizens or *tsekhovye* (guild members). Most of the two last categories of women were of a peasant background and had recently attained the title of honorary citizen or entered the guild. In 1853 women of all these categories (and including a few from the nobility) owned about 11 percent (107) of the total number of Moscow and Moscow district enterprises. The very existence of the category of female and female-peasant entrepreneurs within a patriarchal society is significant in and of itself. As regards the peasant component, it suggests that female peasants also desired individual economic activity, personal freedom and were willing to undertake entrepreneurial risk. Most notably, female engagement in business represented for their male peers a unique example of women's managerial ability and, arguably, served as an important historical background to the late nineteenth- and early-twentieth-century feminist movement in Russia.[18]

The category of peasant-entrepreneur was fluid and dynamic. As we shall see in Chapter 7, most well-off peasant manufacturers eventually entered social estates more appropriate to their achieved status—merchant's, townsman's or honored citizen's—the categories to which owners of large businesses usually belonged, after which they were no longer categorized as peasants. Their upward mobility should not obscure their peasant origin.

As the histories of the Kondrashev and Prokhorov families described above show, peasant textile making underwent a whole process of industrial development, a transformation from small workshops with a few simple instruments to large mills with modern machinery and technology. Table 5.1 shows the dynamics of change of peasant textile workshops during the first half of the nineteenth century.

Table 5.1 Peasant textile workshops of the central non-black-earth region during the first half of the nineteenth century

| | Manufacturing | | | | | | | | | Total number | | |
| | Silk number | | | Linen number | | | Cotton number | | | | | |
	Workshops	Workers	Workers per shop	Workshops	Workers	Workers per shop	Workshops	Workers	Workers per shop	Workshops	Workers	Workers per shop
1797	135	1,378	10	69	1,970	29	17	708	41	221	4,056	18
1803	135	1,378	10	69	1,970	29	17	708	41	221	4,056	18
1813	72	1,240	17	33	668	20	174	7,790	45	279	9,698	35
1823	63	1,142	18	50	937	19	255	6,454	25	368	8,533	23
1853	17	228	13	3	235	78	164	6,297	38	184	6,760	37
1856	12	274	23	3	94	31	106	7,360	69	121	7,728	63

TsGADA (Central State Archive of Ancient Acts), *fond 277, opis' 16, dela 5, 7, 8, 9*; RGIA, *fond 17, opis' 1, delo 45*; ibid., *fond 18, opis' 2, dela 61–65, 83–89, 221–223, 287–293, 393, 1515–1533; opis' 4, delo 225*. See also Tarasov and Isaev, 91, 92, 97.

The archival records contain only fragmentary evidence about peasant textile workshops; therefore the figures of Table 5.1 reflect only these workshops which reported about their production, number of workers, and equipment. Some peasant enterprises remained uncovered by any statistics. In general, the available evidence represented in Table 5.1 illustrates the growth of peasant textile workshops in terms of their size and the number of people employed. The most dramatic growth occurred just after the Napoleonic War, known in Russia as the Patriotic War of 1812, and throughout the early 1820s. After 1823 the number of peasant workshops decreased in all branches of the industry (including the cotton) as a result of the actual decline of some enterprises and the transition of other enterprises into larger units. This transition is also reflected in the increased average number of workers per workshop. In 1797, the average workshop employed eighteen workers, and by 1857, this number had increased to sixty-three.

The decline in the number of peasant workshops in part represents the success of certain peasant-entrepreneurs. Peasant-entrepreneurs like the Kondrashevs and Prokhorovs enlarged their enterprises by building new modernized mills, introducing machinery and technology, and employing more workers. These enlarged manufacturing units were registered as "factories" and, of course, were no longer counted as "peasant workshops" in statistics.

The development of peasant textile workshops contributed to the general growth of the textile industry during the first half of the nineteenth century. Table 5.2 shows the dynamics of development of the four major branches of the industry of Russia.

According to the statistics of Table 5.2, the volume of production and the average productivity per worker and per unit of production increased heavily. The number of workers in the industry increased from 84,000 in 1803–1805 to 291,000 in the late 1850s. At the same time, the volume of production grew from 16.8 million meters to 217.1 a year. Overall, the average productivity per worker increased from 200 meters of fabric to 746 (almost fourfold). Additionally, the average number of workers per factory grew from 89 to 168, and the average volume of production per factory increased from 17,872 meters to 125,130 annually.

These units of production, called in statistics "factories," usually combined putting out with centralized systems. The figures of Table 5.2, however, do not count putting out work. Table 5.3 illustrates the number of machines used and workers employed in both the putting out and centralized systems in the four major branches of the textile industry; this creates a more accurate picture of the development of textile industry.

Table 5.2 The dynamics of development of the Russian textile industry during the first half of the nineteenth century

Years	Number of "factories"	Number of looms	Number of workers			Volume of production, meters	Average worker's productivity, meters
			Free	Possessional	Total		
Linen manufacturing							
1805	199	17,660	21,875	9,950	31,825	11,336,923	356.2
1823	195	12,933	14,197	8,489	22,686	9,534,050	420.3
1825	196	14,654	18,720	8,112	26,832	11,479,336	427.8
1857–1861	101	15,000	17,490	2,604	20,094	13,295,329	611.7
Wool manufacturing							
1803	170	3,276	7,087	32,788	39,875	2,384,714	59.8
1825	324	11,705	51,898	63,603		5,284,090	83.1
1857	641	117,025				19,900,043	170.0
1858–1861	638	32,737	62,393	60,976	123,369	24,333,645	197.2

Years	Number of "factories"	Number of looms	Number of workers			Volume of production, meters	Average worker's productivity, meters
			Free	Possessional	Total		
Silk manufacturing							
1803	351	5,305	6,276	2,790	9,066	1,242,620	137.1
1823	149	4,670	6,227	1,669	7,896	1,954,800	247.6
1852	572	14,500	17,753	0	17,753	6,007,015	338.4
1857	256	14,000	15,744	0	15,744	8,039,033	510.6
Cotton manufacturing							
1803	220	2,522	3,079	141	3,220	1,915,186	594.8
1823	420	22,020	N/A	N/A	35,559	21,355,515	600.6
1825	550	31,990	N/A	N/A	46,969	32,537,960	692.8
1857	740	100,000	N/A	N/A	131,606	171,539,200	1,303.4

The table was drawn from the following sources: TsGADA, *fond* 276, *opis'* 1, *delo* 1726, *listy* 3–71; ibid., *fond* 277, *opis'* 14, *delo* 586, *listy* 59–60; and RGIA, *fond* 18, *opis'* 2, *dela* 393, 1517, 1518, 1693, 1719.

Table 5.3 Dynamics of "putting out" and centralized systems in the textile industry of Russia during the first half of the nineteenth century

Year	Number of looms			Number of workers			Total
				Possessional	Free employed		
	In factories	"In villages"	Total	In factories[a]	In factories	"In villages"	
Linen industry:							
1790s	16,101	8,000	24,101	9,000	19,095	112,414	140,509
1850s	15,000	15,000	30,000	2,250	17,490	127,500	147,240
Wool industry:							
1800s	3,276	500	3,776	21,222	7,087	8,912	39,921
1850s	32,737	10,000	42,737	45,309	62,390	19,532	127,231
Silk industry:							
1800s	4,505	10,500	15,500	2,750	6,276	4,000	49,026
1850	14,000	26,000	40,000	0	17,753	85,000	102,753
Cotton industry:							
1790s	2,522	7,500	10,022	141	3,079	11,250	14,470
1850s	100,000	370,000	470,000	3,642	157,645	544,000	705,296

Isaev, 130–131, 144, 152, 164–165.

[a]For discussion of "possessional" workers, see Chapter 6.

Table 5.3 shows that the number of workers who worked at home increased even more rapidly and was greater than the number of workers who worked in factories. According to contemporaries many peasants for whom weaving was a familiar cottage industry occupation were willing to engage in this putting out work. An observer wrote in 1783 that "many rural residents" wove and "earned wages" by weaving for manufacturers.[19] The commercial journal, *Zhurnal manufaktyr i torgovli*, reported in 1830 that putting out work was widespread in all provinces of the Central Industrial Region, and, in particular, in Yaroslavl', Kaluga, Kostroma, Moscow and Vladimir.[20] In the 1840s the cotton mills of the village of Ivanovo (Vladimir province) "alone absorbed [the production of] more than 50,000 neighboring inhabitants" who engaged in putting out work.[21] Throughout the province more than 150,000 peasants performed putting out work in the cotton industry.[22] Available reports from the 1850s showed that 58 (out of 200 cotton mills overall) of Vladimir province mills had 918 looms and employed 5,821 workers working inside the walls of these mills and 65,644 workers laboring at homes as a part of the putting out system.[23]

Not all putting-out work was conducted in peasant homes. Statistics on putting-out work often counted work performed in villages in buildings called *svetlitsy* (large usually wood cabins), built as branches of a mill, situated to bring the factory closer to the work force. Both putting out work and work in such village establishments were called "work in a village." Therefore it is hard to define whether the work was done at home or in a factory's establishment located in a village. For example, the entrepreneurs of Kostroma province supplied the local rural population with looms, reeds, warps and other materials. The rural residents worked either at home or in such *svetlitsy* establishments built by the manufacturers. There were 190 village *svetlitsy* with 1,382 looms in Kostroma province in 1792. Similar manufacturing establishments functioned in villages in other provinces of the central industrial region.[24]

The figures presented in Tables 5.1 and 5.2 also reveal that the growth of the cotton industry was the most profound of all the branches of the industry. The statistics illustrate that the annual growth of the production of linen, silk and wool was smaller than the annual growth of cotton production. In 1797 (see Table 5.1), there were 135 registered peasant silk workshops with 1,378 workers (roughly ten workers per shop) and only seventeen cotton workshops with 708 workers. These cotton units were already larger than their silk and linen counterparts, on average employing forty-one workers each. By 1823 the number of silk workshops decreased to sixty-three and the number of cotton mills increased to 255.

The growth of the cotton industry during the first half of the nineteenth century is well reflected in the statistics on the imports of cotton fiber and yarn to Russia during the period illustrated in Table 5.4.

Table 5.4 indicates that from 1822 to 1858 the import of cotton fiber tripled. At the same time, from 1842 the import of cotton yarn began to decline and, in 1861, accounted for only about 10 percent of the yarn consumed by Russian textile mills which suggests a significant late development of the Russian spinning industry.

The success of the cotton industry impressed contemporaries as enormous. The description of the first exhibition of Russia's manufactured goods in 1829 explained that the rapid development of the cotton industry resulted from the natural qualities of the cotton fiber which, as the author believed, did not require preparatory operations such as wetting, drying, and so on as in a linen and wool manufacturing. Unlike other fibers, cotton was highly adaptable for mechanization, as well as easy to spin, weave, bleach, dye, or print.[25]

Table 5.4 Dynamics of imports of cotton fiber and yarn into Russia during the 1820s–1850s

Years	Import of cotton	Import of yarn
	In *pud*	In *pud*
1822–1826	69,757	278,149
1827–1831	103,080	457,712
1832–1836	179,925	560,100
1837–1841	330,155	580,092
1842–1846	610,402	593,420
1847–1851	1,247,954	279,510
1852–1858	1,834,642	106,668

P. Nebol'sin, *Statisticheskoe obozrenie vneshnei torgovli Rossii* 2 parts (St. Petersburg, 1850), 2:83–84; *Kommercheskaia gazeta* 89 (Moscow, 1839); ibid., 142 (1842); 129 (1844); 134 (1846); 143 (1850); 1 (1852); 20, 149 (1854); 1, 143 (1856); 1 (1858). Also see Tugan-Baranovsky, *Russkaia fabrika*, 50.

Nineteenth-century engineers, economists, and industrialists emphasized the high profitability of the cotton industry. The journal *Zhurnal manufaktur i torgovli* (Journal of Manufacturing and Commerce) pointed out in 1844 that the price of wool fiber usually accounted for about one third of the average price for wool cloth made from it, while the average price for cotton was only one eighth of the price of the finished fabric.[26] One *pud* (16 kg) of cotton turned out 256 m of cotton fabric while one *pud* of card linen produced 81.6 m of canvas. Producing 81.6 m of bleached canvas cost 13 rubles while making 256 m of bleached calico cost only 10 rubles.[27] Thus, the economic advantage of cotton over other materials became obvious to many entrepreneurs.

The cotton industry and its production were the most adaptable to the needs of the vast majority of the population. Peasant-entrepreneurs, who usually oriented their production toward lower social levels, were the most interested in the production of inexpensive cotton goods. Most peasant-entrepreneurs, who started as linen, silk or wool producers, actually switched their production to cotton making, or more often, started to produce silk or woolen cloth combined with cotton, as in the case of Kondrashevs' mill.

Contemporary observers noticed cotton's great potential as a popular product. They commented that broad elements of the population had begun to utilize cotton goods, which encouraged production as well. "No one of all the industries in Russia spread so quickly and to such an extent as the cotton industry," wrote an observer. "Consumption of these goods was encouraged by the beauty and cheapness of cotton." In Russia "common people began to wear cotton shirts instead of linen ones. Therefore the cotton industry will develop according to the demands of the common people."[28]

During the first half of the nineteenth century, Moscow and Vladimir provinces became the major centers of cotton production. Both provinces were early leading centers of the textile industry of the Central Industrial Region and Russia as a whole and experienced the most dramatic and continuous economic development. The city of Moscow and its province, for example, boasted the largest number of cotton workers and the greatest volume of cotton production in the country. In 1858 about eighteen out of the fifty four spinning factories in Russia that used modern technology were in Moscow province.[29] They made about a quarter of all cotton yarn produced in Russia. In 1859, 410 out of 659 cotton weaving factories and about one-third of cotton finishing factories of Russia were located in the province.[30] Table 5.5 presents the dynamics of the growth of cotton production in Moscow.

As Table 5.5 illustrates, during the mid-nineteenth century Moscow's cotton industry underwent a whole processes of intensification and concentration of production and labor. Despite the decreased number of factories and workers respectively by 8.5 percent and 11.5 percent, the volume of production grew by 17 percent and the average worker productivity increased by 32 percent. Although the prices for cotton products dropped by 15–20 percent during this period and the prices for raw cotton were increasing (in the late 1850s), both of which depressed the industry somewhat, the volume of production was nevertheless growing.[31]

During the period of the 1840s and 1850s, throughout the Central Industrial Region many small textile mills were incorporated into large factories with the goal of concentrating capital in order to mechanize and increase production. For

Table 5.5 Cotton industry of the city of Moscow in 1843–1860

Year	Number of factories[a]	Number of workers	Average number of workers per factory	Production (rubles)	
				Total	Per worker
1843	141	18,143	128.7	6,686,000.00	368.52
1853	129	16,049	124.4	7,816,000.00	487.01

Compiled from *Istoria Moskvy*, 3:199.

[a]This number includes spinning, weaving and finishing factories. In 1843 there were only three spinning factories; in 1854 their number reached four.

example, in 1848, the owners of several medium- and small-size enterprises founded a large stock corporation, known as Lukin, Skuratov and Co. This stock company consisted of eighteen coowners headed by Lukin and Skuratov. The total amount of investments into this enterprise, 570,000 silver rubles, was divided into fifty seven shares.[32] The incorporation of small enterprises facilitated the further expansion of the industry, its mechanization and the growth of production and, together, provided a way to meet the challenges of the developing market in textile goods.

The growth of production and average worker productivity, particularly notable by the end of the 1840s, was achieved by mechanization. The mechanization of textile factories was an important moment in the development of the industry. Although the peasants' role in mechanization was by no means exclusive, their involvement in and contribution to the process was meaningful. This aspect is almost completely ignored by western historiography of Russian industrialization. Peasant-entrepreneurs were often initiators in introducing new advanced equipment in their workshops. Many mechanics, drawers, and other professionals involved in mechanization were also peasants.

The cotton industry experienced mechanization earlier than other segments of the textile industry. An observer noticed in 1857 that "during the last 50 years Russia made significant strides in the development of the cotton industry. These strides defined a whole epoch in the modernization of this industry." [33] Until the beginning of the nineteenth century, there was no cotton spinning industry in Russia. Cotton spinning had also been unknown among the rural population.

Most cotton yarn utilized in cotton weaving workshops and mills was imported from England. According to contemporaries, English cotton yarn was of relatively low quality and sufficiently expensive that it did not satisfy Russian manufacturers. Consequently, they sought to establish the spinning and production of cotton in Russia.[34] During the first decade of the nineteenth century spinning machines were introduced chiefly in Moscow, the center of the textile industry, as well as in St. Petersburg in the Aleksandrovskaia mill. According to an 1811 report, by 1810 the first imported spinning machines were installed in Moscow "in many calico factories."[35]

The first machines for the cotton industry, imported from France and Belgium during the first quarter of the nineteenth century, were relatively simple in their construction and therefore could be easily reproduced by manufacturers. There is a good evidence from a number of manufacturing enterprises that most of their machinery was copied from foreign originals and constructed by their own mechanics and workers most of whom were state and serf peasants. For example, by 1810, the equipment of the cotton weaving mill of the Moscow merchants Pantelleev and Aleksandrov (45 water frames, 45 mules, 108 spindles and carding machines) was produced and installed by the mill workers' "own effort." In 1810, about forty-five people were engaged in machine making in this mill including one master-mechanic, one mechanic-assistant, and forty-three other metal workers.[36] Similar evidence comes from the Grachev and Bykovskii mills in Moscow. Grachev's enterprise was equipped with twenty-two spinning machines with 108 spindles, 15 mules and 15 carding machines. All this machinery was produced in the mill by its workers. The Bykovskii mill had twenty spinning machines and ten carding machines, most of which were also constructed in the mill.[37] According to a 1812 report, in Moscow there were eleven private mills with 780 spinning machines at the beginning of this year.[38] In 1812, however, all these mills disappeared because of the war and the fire.

Most mechanics involved in the construction of machinery for the industry had acquired their experience while working in the more advanced mills that had the highest level of technology in comparison to other mills. One such mill was *Aleksndrovskaia manufakrura* in St. Petersburg, the earliest mechanized mill in Russia. For example, in the Grachev mill the construction of machinery was organized by the peasant mechanic Gladkii who had worked in the Aleksandrovskaia mill. This establishment was the earliest mechanized mill in Russia. In 1812, after the fire of 1812 destroyed Moscow's spinning industry, the Aleksandrovskaia mill was granted a ten-year monopoly to produce machines for the cotton industry. The mill, however, could not produce sufficient machines and was able to satisfy only its own needs.

The Moscow cotton spinning industry that was destroyed in 1812 revived in the early 1820s with the help of the introduction of a tariff on the import of cotton yarn. In 1824 Russian-made spinning machines were installed in the Pokhvisnev cotton mill. These machines were modified copies of foreign originals constructed by a serf mechanic, Stepan Petrov. The owner of the mill romanticized about the mechanic: "he improved and developed the work of the machines due to his genius, which characterizes Russian peasant."[39] Most spinning mills of the 1820s were relatively small in size and did not differ much from the first spinning factories that existed before 1812. By the end of the 1830s there were sixteen spinning mills in Russia with 200,000 spindles and 30,000 *pud* (180,000 kg) annual production; most of these factories were located in Moscow, St. Petersburg and Vladimir provinces. In 1858 their number approached fifty four with 1,535,000 spindles and 1,799,423 *pud* annual production. Table 5.6 illustrates the number of mechanized spinning factories in Russia and the volume of their production in 1858.

Table 5.6 Mechanized cotton spinning factories in Russia in 1858

| Province | Number of | | Production, |
	Spinning mills	Spindles	Silver rubles
St. Petersburg	13	605,000	9,600,000
Moscow	18	370,000	5,920,000
Vladimir	9	210,000	3,350,000
Other	14	350,000	5,600,000
Total	54	1,536,000	24,470,000

Obzor razlichnykh otraslei manufakturnoi promyshlennosti v Rossii 2 vols.
(St. Petersburg, 1863), 2:462–464.

According to Table 5.6, in 1858 Moscow and Vladimir provinces produced cotton yarn valued at 9,270,000 silver rubles. This accounted for 37.9 percent of the cotton industry in Russia. During 1810–1858 the average productivity of one spinning machine increased as much as eightfold. In 1861, about 90 percent of the yarn utilized in Russian mills was produced in Russia and about 10 percent was imported from abroad.

The development of weaving equipment was much slower than that of spinning equipment. Until 1800, the major machine used in weaving was the hand-operated loom. The flying jenny began to spread from the second decade of the nineteenth century. Just as in the cotton industry, the peasants' contribution to the mechanization of the weaving process was significant. According to a mechanic of Vladimir province, I. Nesytov, after the war of 1812 French war prisoners "taught Russian peasants all they knew about how to improve the hand-operated loom; the peasants learned from them about the flying jenny."[40] As a contemporary commented, the peasants of Vladimir province "were entrepreneurial [and]… quick to understand the usefulness of all technical improvements."[41] In the 1830s the peasant brother Chudov opened a workshop and started to make flying jenny looms. Similarly, in villages of Yaroslavl' and Kostroma provinces "the loom with the flying jenny spread immediately once the peasant learned how to make it."[42]

In 1824, in Moscow a serf, Trifon Egorov, constructed jacquard machines according to the drawings of a foreign original. He was actually a self-taught mechanic and had worked at several other factories as a drawer. His machines were installed in some mills of the city. Contemporaries often noted that the introduction of the jacquard machines was initiated by peasant-entrepreneurs. A Moscow newspaper wrote in 1827: "thanks to the peasant, the use of jacquard machines grew year by year."[43] The machines were constructed by "common mechanics," most of whom were peasants and serfs.[44]

According to Garelin, mechanical looms were first introduced Russia in 1808 in the Aleksandrovskaia mill in St. Petersburg. In Moscow province they appeared in the 1830s in a few mills. In the central black-earth region, mechanical weaving spread widely only in the 1850s. According to the available statistics, in 1860 of thirty-two cotton textile mills equipped with 10,109 mechanical looms, 82 percent (8,089 looms) were in St. Petersburg, Moscow, and Vladimir provinces. St. Petersburg's mills had 3,584 (35 percent) mechanic looms, Moscow province mills 2,773 (27.4 percent) looms, and Vladimir province mills 1,732 looms. The proportion of mechanical weaving production in the cotton industry in 1850 was about 20–24 percent of the total.[45]

The transformation process of textile manufacturing into a modern industry was closely connected to the use of steam engines. The widespread use of the engines started during the late 1830s. In 1839 Moscow and Vladimir province mills had twenty-eight steam engines at an average of sixteen horsepowers each; in 1859 there were eighty-five engines with thirty-five horsepowers. At the same time, the use of water and horsepower was reduced. Table 5.7 illustrates the dynamics of the growth of steam-powered machinery in the cotton industry of Moscow and Moscow province.

By the 1840s, steam power began to squeeze out the traditional sources of power: water, horse, and even man which still were the basic sources of power in Moscow cotton factories of the 1820s–1830s. Table 5.7 demonstrates that from the beginning of the 1840s to the end of the 1850s the number of steam engines had almost doubled. Also, their total power increased by as much as 2.5 times.[46] Besides that, the number of weaving machines had expanded 30 percent by 1853 and continued to grow afterward.

Table 5.7 Growth of basic equipment in the cotton industry of Moscow and Moscow province

Equipment	1843	1853	1858
Steam engines	80	95	152
Water power	70	38	
Horsepower	163	106	
Weaving machines	49,000	63,676	
Jacquard machines	4,865	4,824	

Kazantsev, *Rabochie Moskvy*, 16.

Most Russian industrialists adopted a favorable attitude toward mechanization. A letter written in the late 1850 by a group of Moscow entrepreneurs (the Prokhorovs were among them) to the finance minister indicates that the price of a foreign-made steam engine of 40 horsepowers for a spinning factory of 15,000 spindles was 14,000 silver rubles. Besides that, the entrepreneurs complained, the transportation of such heavy machines to Moscow increased their price by an additional 30 percent.[47] Despite these serious difficulties, the modernization of the industry continued. If at the beginning of the 1850s, only seven to ten steam engines were mounted each year, by 1860 this number increased to thirty-one per year.[48]

The use of steam engines in the textile industry stimulated the development of mechanical workshops and plants. In 1825 there were three socialized mechanical factories that produced engines and machines for the industry. In 1859 there were 55 such works with an annual production valued at 7,970,000 silver rubles.[49] Also, Russia continued to import machinery from abroad. Table 5.8 shows the dynamics of import of machinery to Russia. As noted, until 1842 machines were imported to Russia mainly from Belgium and France. Usually foreign companies had their sales representatives in Russia. After 1842, England lifted all obstacles on the export of its machinery. Imported English machines as the most advanced prevailed among textile manufacturers. For example an entire shop floor of the Lepeshkin mill was equipped with English spinning machines with 16,000 spindles and an English steam engine of 100 horsepower. Another shop-floor of the mill had French and Belgium machines.

In 1847, in order to reduce the dependence on imports, the Moscow section of the Manufacturing Council organized the construction of a new machine-building plant. That same year, the plant began to produce its first machines. The plant used British technology and produced steam engines, spinning and weaving machines, and other equipment for the textile industry.[50] Its output contributed heavily to the mechanization process of textile mills, but the plant

Table 5.8 Value of various machines imported to Russia, 1824–1860

Years	Imported, in silver rubles	Years	Imported, in silver rubles
1824–1828	42,529	1844–1846	1,164,402
1829–1833	73,763	1851–1853	2,735,000
1834–1838	409,455	1856–1860	3,103,510

L. B. Koshman, "Iz istoriii promyshlennogo perevorota v Rossii" *Vestnik Moskovskogo universiteta. Istoriia* 5 (Moscow, 1969):35–44, 42.

could not fulfill the growing need and the industry continued its dependence on imported machinery which during 1856–1860 valued in average over three million silver rubles, as illustrated by the figure of Table 5.8.

In summary, as this chapter suggests, Russian early industrialization resulted from the activities of the peasantry, in other words, was "from below." Peasants' involvement in this economic transition was significant. As we have seen many industrialists were peasants, while many other entrepreneurs had recent peasant social backgrounds. The findings of this chapter also provide a clearer understanding of the peasants' role in the mechanization of the industry. Most of the mechanics and machine builders were peasants. This mechanization and enlargement of production were performed on the initiative of the peasant industrialists and without significant intervention from the state. The story about the development of the textile industry and the peasants' role in it does not end with the mechanization and enlargement of workshops. Because of peasant involvement, the industry's labor force experienced a significant transformation as well.

Suggested readings

Blackwell, William L. *The Beginnings of Russian Industrialization, 1800–1860*. Princeton, NJ: Princeton University Press, 1968.

Morrison, Daniel. *"Trading Peasants" and Urbanization in Eighteenth-Century Russia: The Central Industrial Region*. New York: Garland Pub., 1987.

Rieber, Alfred J. *Merchants and Entrepreneurs in Imperial Russia*. Chapel Hill: University of North Carolina Press, 1982.

The Peasant and the Formation of Industrial Labor Forces

In the course of the first half of the nineteenth century pre-reform Russia's industrial labor force experienced a significant transformation. Serf labor (labor of individuals, whether landlords' serfs or state peasants, juridically attached to an enterprise), widely practiced in the manorial and possessional factories during the previous centuries, declined partly because of its low productivity and partly due to the development of factories owned by individuals of the non-gentry estates. Peasant-migrants were increasingly becoming the major source for the industrial workforce. This chapter will examine this change, and explore categories of workers, and their gender-age structure, as well as workers' relations with entrepreneurs and early workers associations.

Manorial and "possessional" peasants

In eighteenth-century Russia, state- and gentry-owned factories, known respectively as "possessional" and "manorial" factories, depended heavily on the labor of so-called possessional and manorial peasants. These peasants were legally tied to an enterprise and consequently to its owner and therefore were not supposed to leave the enterprise without specific permission, a restriction introduced during the reign of Peter I. Both categories of these "tied" laborers were paid; the payment, however, was at a much lower rate (as low as one third) than the labor of "free" contracted workers. "Possessional" and "manorial" peasant resided in villages near their enterprises and maintained their own households. They were permitted to marry and have families. Owners of possessional and manorial enterprises, whether state or noble, were supposed to support their workers and provide them with appropriate living conditions.[1]

These two types of workers were the major labor force of state- and gentry-owned factories in Russia throughout the eighteenth century. During the first half of the nineteenth century, with the growth of the commercial activities of the peasantry, the number of enterprises owned by the non-noble estates greatly increased. Non-gentry individuals, according to the imperial legislation, could not possess serfs and therefore could not use "possessional" labor. Their factories relied on free hired labor. Simultaneously, possessional and manorial manufacturing was declining and these operations were not able to provide their workers with employment.

During the first half of the nineteenth century, manorial and possessional factories faced large-scale worker unrest.[2] This unrest resulted not from labor conditions but from the fact that, as noted, these factories were not able to assign the workers with work and consequently were not paying wages. The workers demanded either to work or to be set free to find other means of earning a livelihood. From the end of the eighteenth century the total number of manorial and possessional workers began to decline, as well as the number of manorial and possessional factories. The law of 1835 allowed owners or managers of manorial and possessional factories to set their "serf" workers free. These workers, as the law specified, could enter into either the merchant or townsman estate.

As a result of these two factors, in the 1840s–1850s possessional labor had almost disappeared from Moscow's cotton mills. In 1846 there were still 973 possessional peasants working in the city and by the end of the 1850s almost none.[3] Nationwide, in 1825, in the cotton and silk industries, free laborers composed, respectively, 83.1 and 94.8 percent and, in 1857, approached 100 and 97 percent, respectively. The wool industry, which relied heavily on serfs (in 1825, they accounted for 82.6 percent) still used their labor extensively but at a lower rate. In 1857, 50.6 percent of the wool industry labor force was free laborers. Of course, this lagged behind the average national level. In all industries of Russia, the free labor force accounted for 54.3 percent in 1825 and for 77.5 percent in 1858,[4] a very rapid growth in terms of percentages at a time when the labor force overall was growing rapidly.

Peasant-migrants as the major workforce

Free laborers were usually recruited from peasant-migrants. From the 1800s peasant-*otkhodniki*, male and female, adults and children, began to dominate the factory labor force. In Moscow, for example, in 1848, they constituted about

80–90 percent of the city's total industrial labor force. In 1853 Moscow had 436 large enterprises with the total of 45,359 workers. About 645 (1.4 percent) laborers of these enterprises were possessional workers and about 10–20 percent were workers of urban estates.[5] Migrants composed the major part of cotton workers, the largest Moscow industry. A contemporary report showed that most peasant-*otkhodniki* of Serpukhovskii, Ruzskii, Volokolamskii, Dmitrovskii, and other districts of Moscow province took jobs in Moscow cotton mills.[6] As a whole, the city's industry, whose technology required numerous laborers, greatly depended on the *otkhodniki*. An observer wrote in 1845 that Moscow entrepreneurs "employ landlords and state peasants who come from distant regions.... Up to 40,000 of such people have stayed in Moscow [every year]."[7]

The predominance of peasant-migrants' labor was therefore absolute and heavily influenced economic development. Having migrated to a city, the peasant-migrant was still officially considered "a rural inhabitant" (sel'skii obyvatel') along with his or her "temporary urban" status and bound to his or her permanent place of residence. Furthermore, the serf peasant-migrant was still legally subject to the landowner. Therefore, the *otkhodniki*, whether state peasant or serf, had to return to the home village after the period stated in his/her passport had ended (extensions required approval from local authorities). Additionally, peasant-migrants' ties to the countryside went far beyond the legal aspects. Most peasants-*otkhodniki* possessed a certain amount of land in the village commune and, during the months of fieldwork in the spring and summer, many of them returned to the countryside for fieldwork even within the allowed period of work in the city. (Even after the 1861 emancipation of the serfs, this practice continued because of special fiscal arrangements that legally tied peasants to their ascribed place of living.) In certain cases, peasants considered their migration to the strange urban area as temporary and under duress and had no intention of abandoning their beloved rural residences. Repelled by harsh working and living conditions, some migrants abandoned their unexpired contracts and returned to the village.[8] Thus, the majority of industrial workers maintained close ties with the countryside whether they wished to or not. An individual with an allotment of land, rather than a proletarian cut off from land, was the typical industrial worker through 1917 and beyond.[9] In the 1840s and 1850s this was universal.

Peasant-migration was an insufficient source for the formation of a fully modernized industrial labor market. The close connections of peasant-*otkhodniki* to the countryside caused a high incidence of fluctuation in the labor

Table 6.1 Dynamics of labor fluidity in two cotton mills of Moscow

Cotton weaving factories	Bavykin's	Guchkov F.A.
Number of workers on January 1, 1846	243	874
Changes in the number (January 1, 1846– January 1, 1847):		
Hired new workers	331	212
Workers who left	264	74
Number of workers on January 1, 1847	310	1,012
Changes in the number (January 1, 1847– January 1, 1948):		
Hired new workers	340	1,885
Workers who left	310	1,758
Number of workers on January 1, 1848	340	1,139

Kazantsev, *Rabochie Moskvy*, 82

force in Russian industries. Table 6.1 presents the dynamics of labor fluidity in two cotton mills of the Lefortovo District of Moscow.

As Table 6.1 illustrates, peasant-migrants were not and could not be a permanent and stable labor force. The lack of an alternative, and the constant need for skilled workers, motivated factory owners and managers to try to keep the most experienced workers. They used various methods to obtain the extension of passports for their workers, thus expanding the period these valued individuals could be away from their villages. Even so, only in some exceptional cases did certain peasants work in the city for as long as 15 years;[10] in most cases, they remained only for a briefer period—from six months to two years. According to a contemporary account, at Moscow factories, the working year usually lasted for up to nine months; from June through September factories significantly reduced their production because most workers left for the countryside.[11]

Structure and gender-age composition of peasant factory workers

The temporary nature of peasant-migration and the migrants' close ties with the countryside also had significant implications for the social structure, gender-age composition, and work habits of factory workers. Adult males predominated within the factory labor force. In 1846, in Moscow city, for example, 40,181 out of 41,874 workers were men and only 1,693, women.[12] This predominance resulted from the demand for male workers based upon the need of most semi-mechanized industries for male strength to perform laborious operations. It also highlights the role of the female peasants in rural economy and society. They had enormous duties in maintaining the household: this included care for children, gardening, and taking care of domestic animals. The household, however, was not the only area of a woman's responsibility. Peasant women were actively involved in cottage industries, such as spinning, weaving, or porcelain making that provided invaluable income for the family. During the 1850s, however, with the growth of industries in and around the cities, more and more women gradually became involved in factory labor.[13]

As in the case of male migrants, the number of landowners' female peasant-migrants (that is, female serfs) also exceeded that of state women-*otkhodniki*. Table 6.2 shows the social composition of female workers in two districts of Moscow province in 1851.

As Table 6.2 illustrates, in 1851 approximately 70 percent of female workers were peasant women-migrants; about 40 percent of them were female serfs and about 20 percent—state peasant women. This difference suggests that the economy of landlords' estates had less demand for female labor than the economy of state villages. Traditionally, state villages had well developed cottage industries that relied heavily on female labor. It is worthwhile noting that in addition to those of peasant origin, about 20 percent of female workers were women from the lower middle class and about 7 percent were from other segments of the lower orders.

The Russian industrial labor force also involved children, who usually came to urban areas with one of their parents or were recruited in the countryside and

Table 6.2 Social composition of female workers in 1851

District:	Bogorodskii	Moskovskii
Social estate:		
Serf peasants	3,181 (46.4 percent)	1,080 (38.5 percent)
State peasants	1,796 (25.9 percent)	507 (18.1 percent)
Royal peasants		378 (13.4 percent)
Soldiers' wives (or soldiers' widows)	469 (6.8 percent)	314 (11.2 percent)
Meshchane (townspeople)	1,430 (20.9 percent)	312 (11.1 percent)
Other (including possessional workers)		216 (7.7 percent)

TsGIAM, *fond* 17, *opis'* 24, *delo* 330, *listy* 19-57.

brought by employers. Deprived of their childhood, these children learned early on all the responsibilities and grievances of adult life. They shared with their parents the burden of duties and obligations to the state or to the landlord and became an important element in the survival strategies of the family. Industries used not only the labor of children who came as migrants; they employed children of the cities' poor, as well as inmates of foundling homes. Throughout the central industrial region, children were exploited as unskilled laborers for certain auxiliary operations, especially in the textile industry. In the cotton weaving industry, for example, children very often assisted their fathers by carrying bobbins, cleaning the loom, and so on. The labor of children was paid at the lowest rate (usually one third of that of the adult male worker).

Despite the efforts of the state to put some restrictions on the use of children as factory workers (see discussion below), the problem still persisted. In 1844 there were about 3,000 children working in industries of Moscow province, two-thirds of whom worked in the cotton industry. By the end of the 1850s, as peasant migration accelerated, the number of children employed in the industries of the province increased to 10,184 and accounted for 15.2 percent of industrial workers, a remarkable statistic. As unfortunate as these children were, a certain percentage of them received the elementary and technical education provided at some factories. For serf children, migration and factory labor often offered the only possibility to get an education.[14]

Factory workers were also identified according to their level of skill. There were three major identities of workers-master-foremen (*mastera*), workmen (*masterovye*), and common laborers (*chernorabochie*). The latter group usually consisted of unskilled peasant-migrants who had little or no experience in industrial work. They worked in various auxiliary functions, particularly in the textile industry, and made up the largest part of the industrial labor force. *Masterovye* were more experienced workers; they had certain specialties and were responsible for carrying out specific operations. Mastera were known as the most experienced workers; in large factories they usually were responsible for complicated technological processes and supervised the work of others. Naturally, the level of skill directly determined workers' wages. In 1856, for example, at N. Garelin's Cotton Printery a master working as mechanic could make as much as 83.3 silver rubles a month, while a *masterovoi* (apprentice) working as a printer earned 10.83 silver rubles and a common laborer received 5.42.[15]

Wages of female workers, whose labor was considered to require "less" physical strength and skill (such as yarn winding, yarn unwinding, planing, throwsting, bleaching, sorting, and cleaning machines), were lower than those of their male colleagues. For example, in the 1840s women weavers at the Great Yaroslavl' Manufactory earned 0.60–0.80 banknote rubles (about 0.20–0.27 silver rubles) a day, while the male workers made 1.30–2.00 banknote rubles. At the same time, average monthly wages of working children were about 1.50–1.80 silver rubles.[16] Nevertheless, in the opinion of Haxthausen, in the mid-nineteenth century, Russian female factory workers on average earned up to twice as much as their German peers. The German observer generalized that "in no country are wages (of factory workers) so high as in Russia…. As for real wages, the advantage of the Russian worker over his foreign counterpart is still greater."[17] Whatever the accuracy of these estimates, it would seem that at that time, confronted by the general instability of the labor force, Russian factories kept wages at a reasonably high level.

The early factory legislation

In order to provide a stable labor force for developing industries, during the second quarter of the century Russian entrepreneurs helped bring about significant changes in the laws that regulated peasant mobility. During the 1830s–1850s, under pressure from the Moscow Section of the Manufacturing Council, the imperial government approved a series of decrees that simplified the procedures for issuing and extending passports for peasant-migrants.[18] On May 24, 1835, the government issued a new law which denied the right of landowners and local authorities to recall employed peasants-migrants from factories until the expiration date of the passport or permission for temporary leave.[19] The law initially was limited to Moscow and St. Petersburg and their districts, but in the late 1830s–early 1840s it was extended to most industrial provinces.[20] This law, which was intended to regulate the relations between the worker and the entrepreneur, in fact challenged the basis of serfdom by limiting landlords' rights over their subjects. Further legislation of 1848–1849 entirely abolished written permits for temporary migration within 30 miles.[21] This legislation would have applied to thousands of peasants of every district of every province who sought nonagricultural employment, of whatever length, in areas near their native villages, but were uncounted in any statistics because, by law, they had no written permits.

In August 1845 the government attempted to regulate child labor at factories by prohibiting night work for children under twelve years of age. The introduction of this legislation was probably provoked by the workers' disturbances at

Voskresensk cotton mill (Dmitrov district of Moscow province) in 1844. The mill employed a large number of peasant children. The concerned government officials soon found out that child labor was a common practice in most Russian industries. The law of 1845, however, completely lacked any provision for its enforcement and obviously was violated by the employers.[22] As mentioned above, the number of children employed in industries continued to grow.

Doubtlessly, these developments alone could not bring about a sufficient increase in labor sources. The existence of serfdom simply did not allow for the development of a modern, extensive labor market. Nevertheless, the legislation of the second quarter of the century regarding peasant-migration was of enormous historical importance, providing an important foundation for the final abolition of serfdom during 1861–1864 by significantly weakening the legal bonds that tied millions of serfs and state peasants to their landlords or home villages.

Peasant-migrants' close connections to the village exerted a tremendous impact on the relationship between the employer and the employee. High labor fluidity hindered the organization of effective labor supervision. Legislation attempted to determine the relationship between the employer and the employee. The law of 1835 stipulated that the employment of all workers was based upon the conclusion of a personal contract between employer and employee which specified the responsibilities of both sides. Since most workers were peasant-migrants, whose period of stay in the city was determined by their passports, the period of the contract's validity was usually limited by the term of the passport. Workers were not supposed to leave their places of work until the expiration of the contracted employment period.[23] This regulation however was difficult to enforce. Many entrepreneurs and managers complained that workers left their enterprises before the contracted time for the countryside or for better employment opportunities.[24] In a labor-short market, there was little that the entrepreneurs could do except improve conditions and pay.

Early workers associations

The industrial environment was novel to the experiences of most peasant-migrants. Facing the uncertainty and strangeness of an urban area and guided by a feeling of regional identity, peasant-migrants from the same area, whether village, hamlet, township, county, or province, grouped themselves into informal, extra-legal fraternal associations, *zemliachestva* and *arteli*. According to one commentary *zemliachestva* and *arteli* had existed "from time immemorial."[25] These associations functioned as important social agencies, providing crucial social, economic, and cultural services for members employed away from the native village.[26] *Zemliachestva* and *arteli* provided financial and mutual assistance, helped to obtain employment, and served as the means of communication between the city and the countryside and thus mitigated the harshness of peasants' the new life. Through the informal regional ties of *zemliachestva* and *arteli*, peasant-migrants from the same area could maintain certain customs, traditions, practices, and cultural values of their native land.

The maintenance of close ties with fellow villagers through active involvement in *zemliachestva* and *arteli* should not be interpreted merely as a desire of peasant-migrants to maintain rural traditions and customs.[27] These ties were especially vital to them since migration involved high risk taking. Migrants acted within the conditions of the free-market economy—any venture could fail at any time—in which case the *zemliachestva* could act as safety net. Also being in a *zemliachestvo* or *artel'* did not automatically segregate their members from the rest of society.[28] Besides regional identities peasant-migrants might also have other identities and ties and might be involved in other social groups and subcultures as well. For example, one may note that some migrants practiced religion and others made contacts at taverns and clubs, or even educational establishments, all of which broadened their ties beyond the *zemliachestva* and *arteli*.

These ties also promoted and facilitated collective action. Perhaps the earliest incident of collective labor protest among free hired workers in Russia occurred at a large Moscow province enterprise where workers-*zemliaki* (fellow-villagers) dominated.[29] In the summer of 1844, 300 workers (*fabrichnye liudi*, as they were identified in an official report) of the Lepieshkin cotton-spinning mill in Dmitrovskii district protested against unsatisfactory wages and labor conditions went on strike. All these workers (*fabrichnie liudi*) were at the same time serf peasant-migrants from the same estate of Kaluga province.[30] During the first half of the nineteenth century, however, serious collective protest (such as strikes) among free laborers seldom occurred because workers usually preferred to leave an undesirable place of work and look for better job opportunities.

In the process of adaptation and adjustment to the new industrial environment, during the late nineteenth and early twentieth centuries peasant-migrants gradually turned their *zemliachestva* and *arteli* into worker's unions, cooperatives, and other modern organizations of laborers. Thus, besides their socializing nature, *zemliachestva* and *arteli* served as a transitional mode, bridging preindustrial and industrial practices. These associations were voluntary, informal and extra-legal until 1905. The legislation of 1905 provided a legal basis for the establishment of formal associations. Even then, however, peasant-migrants preferred to seek informal contacts with one another and preserved their informal and extra-legal *arteli* and *zemliachestva*, alongside their formal organizations (Figure 6.1).[31]

Figure 6.1 Peasants visiting St. Petersburg, 1850.

The active involvement of the peasantry in industrial development signified the formation of the free-hired industrial labor force. Unable to use the labor of "possessional" workers, peasant- and middle class-owned factories employed free contracted workers. These free laborers particularly dominated in the cotton industry, which was owned mostly by non-gentry individuals. The peasant-migrants constituted the major part of free laborers. Far from being "proletarians," migrant workers possessed land and kept close connections with the home villages. These ties and the temporary nature of the factory work had important implications for the patterns of the formation of workers' associations which provided their members with mutual assistance and support. In many cases peasant-migrants viewed their industrial work as temporary and expected to return to the village. As the free labor force became dominant, the state introduced legislation in order to regulate labor relations and provide the growing industry with labor force.

In summary, during the first part of the nineteenth century, the industrial labor force witnessed a profound transformation discussed in this chapter. Yet, entry into the factory labor force provided many workers with the opportunity for economic and social advancement. The most experienced and qualified workers became masters or often started their own businesses. Many were able to enter higher social estates. The next chapter will examine education and the social mobility of peasants involved in commercial and industrial activities.

Suggested readings

Gorshkov, Boris B. *Russia's Factory Children: State, Society and Law, 1800-1917*. Pittsburg: University of Pittsburg Press, 2009.

Johnson, Robert E. *Peasant and Proletarian: The Working Class of Moscow in the Late Nineteenth Century*. New Brunswick, NJ: Rutgers University Press, 1979.

Zelnik, Reginald E. *Labor and Society in Tsarist Russia: The Factory Workers of St. Petersburg, 1850-1870*. Stanford: Stanford University Press, 1971.

Social Mobility of the Peasantry

Economic developments of the first half of the nineteenth century in Russia had a significant impact on upward social mobility. Through nonagricultural activity, economic advancement, and education, many individuals from the peasantry, a "lower" social segment, entered "upper" social positions. Although the social achievement of some was remarkable, the economic development during the pre-reform decades, *c.* 1800–1861, was uneven, leaving many citizens untouched. Some areas remained agricultural, particularly these of the black-earth regions, whereas other parts witnessed remarkable economic and social changes. This chapter will discuss pre-reform imperial legislation, which provided a solid juridical basis for the economic and social betterment of the peasantry, as well as education and social mobility.

Pre-reform legislation

The growth of the economy and the development of the textile industry, in particular, provoked remarkable changes in the imperial laws regulating peasants' economic activities and their status during the first half of the nineteenth century. An extraordinary but little known aspect of pre-reform imperial legislation is that it provided peasants of "all categories" with virtually complete freedom to engage in economic activities "such as those given to merchants" and "townspeople," and, in the case of trading serfs, even allowed a certain immunity from interference by the landlord. Legally, just like all other social estates, serf and state peasants could buy, inherit, possess, and run almost any kind of business and real estate (except for real estate populated with people).[1] According to the law, economic activities were divided into "licensed" and "free." Four categories of peasant trade licenses existed. The first category granted peasants "the right to conduct all kinds of trade allowed to merchants of the first guild" (this included wholesaling, possessing ships and ship faring, possessing and managing stores, shops, various manufacturing units, factories and mills). The only exceptions were the owning and managing of banking and insurance businesses. The second and third categories pertained respectively to all the trading rights and activities of the second and third merchants' guilds. The license of the fourth type enabled peasants to conduct all economic activities "given to *meshchane* (townsmen)." Peasants licensed in the first three categories even had the right to trade at the St. Petersburg goods exchange.[2] The category of (non-licensed) free trading activities enabled peasants to enter guilds (*tsekha*) temporarily, keep artisans' workshops (with a limited number of workers) and small stores in and outside the home village, and conduct petty trade, cab driving, and numerous other activities "peculiar to the peasant mode."[3]

In order to provide serfs with more freedom to conduct their business, the laws of 1827 and 1828 "limited the power of the landlord" over serf-peasants who engaged in "commercial business." As the law stated, the landlord could not "extract" the serf from his activity "once he received a trade license."[4] The legislation of March 3, 1848, granted serfs the right to buy and possess in their own name enterprises and real estate such as land and buildings.[5]

All disputes and conflicts that arose from peasants' economic activity were to be resolved in the appropriate state institution, such as public chamber (*kazionnaia palata*); city *duma*, council, or hall (*ratusha*); local police office; or district, commercial, and arbitration courts in the localities where they conducted their business.[6] The records of the office of the Moscow governor-general reveal that the peasants seized this legal opportunity on the widest scale. The peasants complained, requested, appealed, and made other legal interactions with the office.[7] Thus, peasants involved in commercial and industrial activities lived in a non-isolated legal world and acted within and according to the normal network of state laws and institutions. This fact alone serves as an important corrective to the persisting historiographical notion of peasant legal "isolation." The integration of the peasant estate into the pre-reform Russia legal network provided an important legal background for social activity and advancement of individual peasants.

Development of professional education

Peasant activities in the textile industry exerted an important impact on the development of professional and technical education and learning. Peasants became acquainted with the economy and industry and learned crafts and trades. Involvement in various textile occupations required peasants to make certain calculations and keep records. For example, peasants involved in weaving had to keep count of their work and of the necessary materials. They had to estimate an accurate quantity of warp and weft to make a fabric of a particular weight, width, and size. Often lacking formal education and literacy, peasant-migrants had to keep many numbers and numerous calculations in their heads. A mid-nineteenth-century observer wrote about the peasants of the central Russian provinces in which the population largely engaged in textile making: "[peasants] of Kostroma, Vladimir, Moscow, and other [industrial] provinces, although they have never studied, are able to calculate and make relatively difficult calculations in their heads alone. Naturally, for them, education is an acute necessity."[8]

Apparently, peasants' nonagricultural activities not only stimulated peasants' ability to learn but their willingness to pursue an education as well. The importance and necessity of formal education became evident to many peasants as demonstrated by their tendency to send their children to schools and often to attend themselves. Deeply concerned about qualified cadres for industry, which was both growing and mechanizing at a time when the government restricted education for lower social estates to elementary schooling, Moscow entrepreneurs, on their own private initiative, established technical schools, Sunday schools, and schools for teenage workers. Newly introduced industrial techniques required educated workers able to operate the new machines.

The history of trade and technical schools founded by the brothers Timofei and Konstantin Prokhorov, the co-owners of the Three Mountains (*Trekhgornaia*) Factory, is a notable example. The first such school opened in 1816 for 200 children of the factory's workers (most of whom were peasant-migrants) and of the Moscow poor. To maintain the school, the Prokhorovs spent annually about 20,000 banknote rubles, a remarkable sum by contemporary standards. In 1833, Timofei Prokhorov opened another school for both children and adults. This was a two grade school; the students received instruction in accounting, linear and pattern drawing, management, calculus, Russian, and theology. Education in both of Prokhorov's schools was free.[9] In the 1840s–1850s there were no less than thirty-four factory schools in Moscow province. Teenage girls were among the students at some of these schools—eighty female students attended Prokhorov's, Guchkov's, and Roshfor's factory schools.[10] The curriculum for the female students in Prokhorov's school was "somewhat narrower" than that for their male peers and focused on theology and reading.[11]

In addition, in 1843 ten Sunday factory schools were opened in Moscow province with 1,050 students. A modest number of factory schools existed in other provinces of the central industrial region. Although all these schools were private, the government attempted to regulate and make uniform their general curriculum. Students of these schools received an education in industrial technology, industrial chemistry, factory management, mechanical drawing, machine construction, accounting, and other technical and financial disciplines as well as in general subjects such as theology and calculus.[12] According to a report for 1844, "the major part of students of private factory schools belongs to the peasant estate [including serfs] and less that one seventh are from meshchane (townspeople)." Additionally, children of serf peasants also attended certain state schools. The Finance Ministry's technical drawing schools represent an interesting example. Among 882 students of the schools, 109 (12.5 percent) were serfs' children; 131 (15 percent)—children of peasants of other categories; 31 (3.5 percent)—nobles'; 56 (6 percent)—families of high military officials; 18 (2 percent)—clergy; 2 (0.2 percent)—state bureaucracy; 14 (1.6 percent)—orphans; 2 (0.2 percent)—honored citizens; 52 (6 percent)—"people of various ranks" (*raznochintsy*); and 467 (53 percent) belonged to other social estates, mostly townspeople.[13] In the classroom, children of serf and state peasants were not segregated from those of other social estates. The significance of these educational establishments was that they provided peasants and people of other "low" estates with one of the necessary bases for upward social and economic advancement and many availed themselves of it.

Social mobility

As mentioned, a significant number of late imperial Russian entrepreneurs, merchants, and honored citizens had peasant social backgrounds and had become petty traders, intermediaries, or artisans on the way up the socioeconomic ladder. The phenomenon of significant peasant social mobility, as illustrated by the wealthy merchant of serf origin buying a noble estate, was reflected in many literary works of the nineteenth and early twentieth centuries. One may recall Chekhov's hero Yermolai Lopakhin from *The Cherry Orchard*. Entrepreneur Lopakhin, having bought the estate of his father's former master Ranevskaia, proclaimed, "I bought it..., I bought it..., I bought the estate where my grandfather and father were slaves."[14] A similar example comes from A. N. Ostrovsky's play *Les* (Forest). In this and other plays, the author illustrates the emergence and maturing of a new social force, the middle class with all its energy and brashness.

Although Lopakhin and Vosmibratov (in *Les*) were literary personages, thousands of people like them existed in real life. The Prokhorovs, one of the biggest industrialist families of Moscow, were a classic example. There were many other real-life protagonists of the famous literary personages. Savelii Vasil'ev Morozov, a serf of the nobleman N. G. Riumin, engaged actively in trade in the early-nineteenth-century Moscow markets. His small workshop produced silk point lace which he sold in Moscow. In 1820 he bought himself and his four sons out of serfdom for 17,000 banknote rubles and entered the first guild merchant estate. In 1825 he founded a cotton weaving factory in Moscow and several factories in the province. By the mid-1850s, Morozov's enterprises had an estimated value of 6 million silver rubles with annual production of 2 million silver rubles. By the 1860s, the famous Savva Morozov had become one of the biggest entrepreneurs and landowners of Russia.[15] Following similar paths, during 1828–1835 about thirty-two Ivanovo serf-entrepreneurs bought themselves out of serfdom. The Garelins, peasant-entrepreneurs and owners of the third largest cotton mill in the city (employing 1,407 workers in 1817), were among the thirty-two.[16]

Peasant-entrepreneurs also sought to enter "higher" social estates, mainly merchant and *meshchanstvo*, a process that accelerated throughout the first half of the nineteenth century.[17] Contemporaries commented that the merchant estate, *kupechestvo*, was in constant flux. The most prominent "old" merchants' families replenished the upper stratum, the nobility, while peasants were enlarging the merchant estate. Mid-nineteenth-century observers wrote that the merchant estate "mainly consists of new individuals who came from the lowest social estates"; "the self-made peasant [is] becoming the head of the merchant community" and a prominent figure in "public affairs."[18] According to Isaev, during the late eighteenth and the first half of the nineteenth century the middle-class population grew as much as tenfold largely at the expense of the peasant estate.[19] In sum, the changes in pre-reform legislation, the development of professional education, and upward social mobility created a necessary basis for the formation of the middle class in post-reform Russia.

Suggested readings

Gorshkov, Boris B., "Serfs on the Move: Peasant Seasonal Migration in Pre-Reform Russia, 1800–1861," *Kritika*, vol. 1, no. 4 (Fall 2000): 627–656.

Gorshkov, Boris B., "Democratizing Habermas: Peasant Public Sphere in Pre-Reform Russia," *Russian History/Histoire Russe* 31 (Winter 2004): 373–385.

Gorshkov, Boris B., *A Life under Russian Serfdom: The Memoirs of Savva Dmitrievich Purlevskii, 1800–1868*. Budapest and New York: Central European University Press, 2005.

Peasants and the Public Sphere

Until recently, scholars of Russian history conventionally agreed that civil society and public opinion were typical only of certain Western nations. In this view, neither civil society nor public opinion existed in autocratic imperial Russia. In contrast, today scholars display a notable interest in imperial Russia's civil society and public opinion. Several recent books and articles explore aspects of late imperial Russian civil society.[1] Some historians focus on civil society composed of educated elites, whereas others, including myself, concentrate on civil society constituted by broad social strata. This chapter will turn its attention to civil society and public opinion among the peasantry.

What is civil society? The ancient Greek understanding defined it as a political society where supposedly "free" and "equal" citizens joined together and directly engaged in formulating state politics. The Enlightenment notion of civil society emphasized the boundary between the state and civil society. It stressed associative social relationships and the rights and freedoms of the individual. More recent perceptions accentuate the direct participation of civil society in state politics. Some recent scholars still emphasize the relative autonomy of civil society and suggest influence and persuasion rather than power and money as a basis of the functioning of civil society. The concept of civil society has depended on the ideological and political priorities of scholars, especially when the relationship between civil society and capitalism is concerned.[2] Thus, there is no definitive understanding of civil society and its concept has been elastic.

Nevertheless, certain basic conceptions of civil society exist and can be fruitfully utilized for analysis of the relationship between the state and society. For instance, most social thinkers have argued that civil society is a site of interaction between the state and society. The rudiment of civil society is the self-organization of individuals into free associations aimed at pursuing common interests. Scholars emphasized primarily male middle-class discursive publicness. Emerging from capitalist development, the public sphere replenished and finally replaced the previous, ancient forms of public communication.

The discursive bourgeois public space which involved critical and reasonable discussion of a well-informed and educated public produced the new social and ideological category of public opinion which became a powerful instrument of the middle class for the guidance of state decision making.

While the general concept of the public sphere as an imagined site where critical and reasoned discussion takes place and produces public opinion is productive, it has been utilized in a quite limited spectrum. First, this delimited category of the public sphere does not account for the complexity, ambiguity, change, and internal dynamics in society. Second, the public sphere is narrowed to include only the male middle class and excludes other important social groups and subcultures, in particular the subaltern social strata, for instance, women, workers, and peasants.[3]

The association of civil society exclusively with the middle class often leads scholars to an assertion that in societies where the middle class is small, absent, or atypical, civil society does not exist. This is especially true for scholars of Russian history. They ignore the possibility that other social groups, such as the peasantry and workers, might also constitute a civil society. Yet, these social groups engaged in public discourse, influenced public opinion, and, consequently, were able to influence the process of state decision making. In this chapter I want to focus on peasant publicness.

As explored in previous chapters, the peasantry, some 85 percent of the empire's population, was everywhere multi-occupational and their input into the local and national economies went far beyond producing agricultural commodities and paying taxes. In the Russian economy, the peasants' commercial activities not only supplemented but virtually supplanted the activities of the relatively small, legally defined middle class. According to various studies, a significant portion of peasants—from 40 to 70 percent, depending upon the region—engaged at least part-time in trade and commerce. These peasants traded, possessed manufacturing establishments and workshops, and were involved in various entrepreneurial and commercial ventures. They pursued these activities both in the countryside and in urban areas. Imperial Russian cities collected about one-third of their annual tax revenues from registered trading peasants. Nationwide, in 1851, the floating capital of peasant entrepreneurs reached 25 million silver rubles, an enormous sum.[4]

It is also worthwhile remembering that peasants always exercised territorial mobility. Numerous peasants conducted business or worked outside their native villages, especially at certain times of the year. This so-called seasonal migration involved, at any given time, about a quarter of the peasants, including serfs. These peasants constantly moved back and forth between urban or industrial areas and the countryside or between various rural areas. They created an invisible but tight linkage between the village commune and the rest of the country.[5] Thus, a significant bulk of peasants, by virtue of their commercial activities and mobility, performed middle-class functions and, to that extent, were in fact middle class, at least while engaged in those activities. Economic historians illustrate the dramatic expansion of peasant economic activities during the late eighteenth and the nineteenth centuries.[6] Peasant economic activity provided peasants with a degree of institutional, social, and cultural independence (or autonomy) from the existing state structures and, at the same time, insured that they were not isolated from the rest of society. This nuanced approach to the peasantry opens the way for a broader application of the public sphere.

The expanding economic activities of the peasantry had broad social and cultural implications. The recent works of historians and earlier studies by anthropologists and folklorists have leveled devastating criticisms against traditional theories of peasant darkness. They suggest instead that peasants had a deep general awareness of the world outside the village. Their territorial mobility and economic activities stimulated their knowledge of local and national politics and acquainted them directly with imperial laws. Peasants knew about the local and national economy, the market, and the decrees that regulated their economic activities. They also aptly utilized this knowledge for their economic and social pursuits.[7] They derived their knowledge of these matters from official and nonofficial sources and spread it to other peasants by the traditional means of oral communication—conversation, rumor, gossip, stories, anecdotes, and so forth.

Themes of peasant discourse varied. Peasants revealed a lively interest not only in sensational events, curiosities, and local communal life, topics that scholars tend to emphasize. They also discussed contemporary events and the latest political issues, recent wars, governmental affairs, imperial decrees, the emperor's personality and political legitimacy, and so forth. For example, the peasant war of 1773–1775, the 1812 war, the military conflicts with the Ottoman Empire, not to mention the potential abolition of feudal obligations and the emancipation from serfdom, all served as lively topics of peasant interest and conversation during the late eighteenth and the first half of the nineteenth century. The topics of abolition and emancipation received particular attention among peasants after the 1812 war and on the eve of the 1861 reforms.[8]

The spread of news occurred in association with peasant-migrants and traveling peasant-traders who moved back and forth between villages and cities, soldiers returning from military service or the front, or the so-called village intelligentsia (*derevenskaia intelligentsiia*)—local priests, communal teachers, postmasters, field nurses, and clerks (many of whom were also of recent peasant origins). A few literate and prosperous peasants had libraries and subscribed to literary and political journals. For example, Savva Dmitrievich Purlevskii, a former serf from Yaroslavl' province recollected in his memoirs that in the early nineteenth century his father had a sizable library that included works by Nikolai Karamzin and Denis Fonvisin. He also subscribed to the liberal literary and political journal *Vestnik Evropy*. Another former serf recalled that he inherited from his father a library of about 2,000 volumes.[9]

Although literate peasants during the nineteenth and earlier centuries were exceptions, their function in the countryside was meaningful. Literate peasants read various publications—newspapers, journals, and books—and broadcast the news and ideas among their fellow countrymen. Literate peasant-migrants who worked in cities sent letters to the countryside that informed fellow-villagers about the latest political, economic, social, and cultural developments. In addition to these methods, local and national fairs and marketplaces, as well as numerous country inns, taverns, and drinking establishments, which webbed Russia's countryside, served as institutions of peasant sociability. These localities were public spaces where peasants could learn about and discuss news or exchange opinion about public issues among themselves and with people of other social estates.

In view of rural peasants' limited literacy and narrow access to the printed word, these forms of communication served as a sort of popular journalism, accessible to most peasants and virtually free from state censorship and the control of dominant social strata. Scholars find that the news and rumors that circulated among peasants were sometimes reliable and accurate, sometimes permeated with invented or confused details, and sometimes entirely fantastical. Of course, inaccuracies and falsehood permeate the printed word as well. Peasant awareness of political and other major issues was not significantly inferior to that of persons of other social categories. Peasants often proved themselves quite well informed, especially about issues that directly related to their interests.[10]

Their grasp of social issues, the economy, and the laws facilitated peasants' economic and social activities, as well as their interactions with the state. Many scholarly studies show that both serfs and state peasants often used regular state institutions to seek adjudication of conflict, legal protection of their interests, or, in the case of serfs, even emancipation from serfdom. In their appeals to state institutions, peasants frequently displayed their juridical knowledge by referring to concrete state decrees. The sources of this knowledge varied. Some decrees were printed in separate leaflets and thereby made accessible to peasants, while others were copied by hand from various legislative publications and circulated among peasants. Ultimately, much of this knowledge was handed down by means of oral communication. Literate peasants often served as informal solicitors (*chelobitchiki*) for their uneducated fellow-countrymen.[11]

Peasants revealed a surprising degree of awareness of the 1861 reform during its preparation in 1855–1856. They discussed the conditions of emancipation and formed their own opinions of the entire reform project. The act of 1847, which allowed peasants of indebted estates to redeem themselves, and the 1856 decree, which allowed serfs who resided on their own lands to enter the estate of state peasants, were subjects of particularly lively interest and discussion among peasants. One peasant-migrant from Smolensk province wrote back to his home village that "one hears about the transfer of landlords' peasants into [the category of] state peasantry. According to newspapers, many serfs are freed from their landlords and reside on their own lands."[12] Their awareness of the 1847 and 1856 laws encouraged serfs, even those who did not come under the laws' terms, to claim freedom from bondage.

Peasant discourse and the exchange of opinions about various topics facilitated forms of critical thinking that inherently questioned the established laws and rules and, it follows, helped form new popular perceptions. Peasants often displayed skepticism toward the activities of government officials and even toward certain state policies. They did not, however, restrict themselves to negative or belittling remarks. Peasants also expressed their own attitudes toward the social, economic, and political issues in question. For example, peasants increasingly challenged taxation, dues, various laws and decrees, the institution of serfdom, and the very principle of aristocratic rule. Thus, peasants engaged in critical and reasoned discussion about common issues. They formulated conceptions of the common good, which in turn resulted in what can be defined as public opinion.

The tendency for peasants to criticize the government and existing social relations finds a reflection in peasant writings of the era. In a brief unpublished essay written in 1858, a serf, Mikhail Mikhailov, questioned both serfdom and the landlords' authority and insisted that "all people were equal before God." Referring to the Holy Scriptures, Mikhailov stated that "persons cannot hold sway over other persons." Peasants, it followed, must gain their freedom.[13] Mikhailov did not restrict his attacks on serfdom to written tracts. He also utilized St. Petersburg's taverns and drinking establishments, always crowded with people of all social strata, to spread his ideas, to which lower-class individuals were especially sympathetic. Peasants also expressed a belief that everyone should have the right to "utilize fully the fruits of his own labor," an obvious attack on the underlying principle of exploited serf labor. These and other critical popular perceptions were quite widespread and became even more so during the entire half-century before the 1861 legislation.[14] Clearly, the dominant language of the period's peasant discourse stressed the idea of freedom. It denounced serfdom's oppressions, both minor and major. This language suggests that peasants could no longer come to terms with serfdom. As a group, peasants had begun to perceive serfdom as an unacceptable, unjust, and definitely not inevitable condition. Of interest is that by the 1800s peasant opposition to serfdom, whatever it had been earlier, was not mute, inarticulate, or passive.

The peasant public sphere also helped peasants form new perceptions about themselves and their place in society. Peasants, and especially serfs, directly challenged the landlord's authority and indeed increasingly perceived themselves as free persons. This perception is well reflected in the peasants' increasing tendency to refuse to obey the landlords' orders, perform labor duties, or pay dues.[15] Studies of popular protest illustrate that many instances of peasant disobedience accompanied, indeed were based upon, a questioning of the lord's authority over them. As one nobleman put the matter, "the spirit of freedom (*dukh svobody*) has captured the peasants' minds."[16] In 1844 over 200 peasants on the estate of the nobleman Svechin of Yaroslavl' province suddenly refused to obey him because they had come to "believe in the possibility of gaining freedom."[17] During the 1840s and 1850s, numerous refusals to conduct corveé and other labor duties took place in estates of Prince Golitsin because, as a report stated, the peasants "perceived themselves as free."[18]

During the nineteenth century, many peasants utilized existing legal channels to file petitions with the state authorities (at so-called *prisutstvennye mesta*) for emancipation from serfdom. Such petitions, noted tsarist bureaucrats with concern, if not alarm, grew practically by the day. For example, in a 1827 report, Yaroslavl' provincial official stated that the provincial institutions are filled with "a great multiplicity" of peasant petitions for "freedom from the landlords' possession."[19] A contributory factor in the growth of emancipation petitions was the fact that the pertinent statutes automatically granted all peasants who submitted such petitions the status of temporary freedom from the landlord until the official decision of the case, which, in tsarist Russia, could occupy quite a stretch of time. The temporary free status included temporary exemption from all fiscal and labor obligations to their landlords. Naturally, the failure of our peasant historiography to note the existence of the statutes in question, not to mention the peasants' utilization of them, constitutes a great weakness in our historical understanding of the pre-emancipation era.

What is defined here as the peasant public sphere was also a site of conflict. Social awareness and perceptions of freedom helped facilitate and organize peasant popular protest. According to studies of popular protest from 1801 to 1861 there were about 1,467 significant outbreaks of peasant resistance.[20] Historians note that most of these outbreaks were well organized. In part, this was because the peasant commune took an active part in their organization. In this regard, the peasant commune served as a voluntary public sphere where peasants joined together to address the particular issue they faced. Of special note is that the peasant commune existed throughout Russia. Peasants normally attempted to resolve disputes by resorting to strictly legal methods, that is, by first presenting their complaints to the appropriate local authorities. If this approach failed to achieve what they perceived as "justice," peasants then resorted to protest. Some historians argue that not only economic exploitation— the increase of feudal obligations—caused popular protest, but the peasants' increasing will to freedom from feudal dependence.[21]

Thus, the peasant public sphere provided peasants with important knowledge about economic, legal, and political matters, all of which simultaneously facilitated their interactions with a broader public sphere of imperial Russia. Peasant social and economic activism was noted by contemporary intellectuals, public activists, and government officials. Journal and newspaper publications during the pre-reform decades disclose the fascination that many educated contemporaries and government bureaucrats had in regards to the peasants' social and economic abilities. Many publications were devoted to peasants' economic and social pursuits.[22] In association with this view of the peasants, most contemporaries, including high state officials, increasingly viewed serfdom as a social evil.

The imperial Russian state also showed a certain interest in peasant public opinion.[23] State institutions revealed an interest in people's attitudes about such matters as the personalities of contemporary emperors, ongoing recruitment, and state fiscal policies. Prominent public figures recognized the importance of broad public opinion, by which they meant the opinion of all social groups, for formulating and carrying out state politics. For example, in a message to Aleksandr II, S. Bezobrazov argued that no decree should be enacted without broad public discussion. "The emperor," he claimed, "approves only those laws that public opinion supports." The term "the institution of public opinion" stands prominently in many writings and government publications of the mid-nineteenth century.[24] The reader should be aware that "public opinion" routinely included peasant opinion, an aspect that numerous historians are, even today, unaware of.

Various offices of the Ministry of Internal Affairs and the notorious Third Department of the Imperial Chancellery monitored and studied public opinion. Historians usually view the Third Department as a political police and emphasize its police and censoring functions. Nonetheless, activities of the Third Department were broader and went far beyond policing and tracking society. In a broader sense, the Third Department was a site of interaction between the state and society. The reports and numerous records of public opinion, particularly for the late eighteenth and nineteenth centuries and data it gathered provided the state with important guiding principles in decision making. Various state institutions revealed a particular interest in the peasants' public attitudes on the eve of the 1861 reform.[25] Most reports emphasize the persistence of the idea of freedom in peasant discourse. For example, one report of the Third Department noted that "the idea about freedom is burning among the peasants and becomes ever stronger and stronger."[26]

The peasant interaction with the state helped bring about important pre-emancipation laws that restricted the landlords' authority over serfs, provided peasants with greater freedom for their economic and social activities, and granted peasants immunities from landlords.[27] For example, the law of 1812 granted serfs the right to engage in entrepreneurial activities in their own names and officially introduced the well-known legal category of "trading peasants." The law gave peasants of all categories virtually complete freedom for economic activities "such as those given to merchants and townspeople." Serfs were granted some immunity from interference by the lord. To be sure, before 1812, serfs actively pursued economic activities but acted legally on behalf (in the power) of their lords, a fact that often caused discord. In order to facilitate peasant involvement in business without the lords' interference, the Imperial Senate issued the new law. In 1811, before the law's introduction, the finance minister, D. A. Gur'ev, advised the Senate about the necessity of such a law and wrote that "peasants run various sorts of businesses in the names of merchants or on the lords' behalf." The abnormality, he felt, had to be corrected.

Furthermore, the law of 1827 restricted the lords' authority over peasants who engaged in commercial endeavors. The law forbade landlords to "divert" peasants who obtained trading licenses from their business activities. Of special interest is the law of 1835. This law prohibited lords and other "local authorities" from recalling peasant-migrants temporarily employed outside the estate. The law of 1848 granted serfs the right to possess in their own names private enterprises. As noted above, the law of 1856 set free serfs who settled on their own lands (that is, which they had purchased). The laws that regulated seasonal migration provided peasants, including serfs, the right to travel for employment or conduct their own business and to prolong their stay without undue interference from their landlords. These laws were of tremendous significance. They challenged the foundation of serfdom by reducing the power of the lord over peasants. When one examines these series of laws in their historical context, it becomes obvious that they were direct state responses to peasant economic and social activities and to publicly expressed peasants attitudes, as well as to those of society in general.

The reality is that peasant public life and civil society in imperial Russia influenced imperial policy making. Peasant publicity influenced the peasant-oriented legislation of the first half on the nineteenth century. It also exerted an effect on the 1861 law, which became the decisive word in a lengthy process of abolition that started long before the final decision and that was reflected in the earlier laws. The roots of this process lay in long-term developments in the civil society of pre-reform Russia. Recent studies of serfdom suggest the institution's flexibility, social viability, and its capacity to accommodate peasants' material needs and economic development. But what brought the institution to its end? Perhaps the answer can be best found in the new perceptions and values that emphasized freedom and that, in the eyes of many contemporaries, made serfdom a culturally outmoded institution. As much as anyone, Russia's peasants themselves were responsible for these crucial changes in attitude.

Suggested readings

Bradley, Joseph. "Subjects into Citizens: Societies, Civil Society, and Autocracy in Tsarist Russia," *The American Historical Review*, vol. 107, no. 4 (Oct. 2002): 1094–1123.

Burbank, Jane. *Russian Peasants Go to Court: Legal Culture in the Countryside, 1905–1917*. Bloomington: Indiana University Press, 2004.

Gorshkov, Boris B. *A Life under Russian Serfdom: Memoirs of Savva Dmitrievich Purlevskii*. Budapest, New York: Central European University Press, 2005.

Gorshkov, Boris B. "Democratizing Hebermas: Peasant Public Sphere in Pre-Reform Russia," *Russian History/Histoire Russe* 31 (Winter 2004): 373–385.

Peasants and the End of Serfdom

At long last, the legendary 1861 "All-Merciful Manifesto" of Alexander II, the emperor of Russia (*c.* 1855–1881), liberated over twenty million serfs from legal bondage to Russia's landlords. A subsequent law gave freedom to state peasants. Within the context of Europe, Russia was among the last monarchies to grant liberation from servitude. This process started with the French Revolution, which abolished feudalism in France, and ended in 1864 with the emancipation of Hungarian serfs. As regards imperial Russia, the manifesto opened up an epoch of changes that became known as the Great Reforms. This chapter will explore the end of serfdom in Russia, focusing on the decades which preceded it, its legal aspects and results, and, perhaps unexpectedly for most readers, peasant agency.

Why in fact did the system of peasant servitude and legal bondage in Russia end, and why and how did serfs receive their legal freedom? These questions have produced many scholarly studies, as well as some controversies. Generally, historians underscore economic and political causes allegedly responsible for the legendary manifesto. Economic accounts suggest that the 1861 act was a result of the so-called crisis of feudalism. In this interpretation, the newly emerging capitalist forms of production conflicted with the old feudal economy that produced peasant disturbances and resistance. As a consequence, this conflict led to what some historians call a "revolutionary situation," a lethal condition that eventually brought serfdom to an end.[1] This interpretation is associated with the Marxist school of thought. Political explanations usually stress the defeat of Russia in the Crimean War (1853–1856).[2] This defeat, according to this interpretation, was the apogee of Russia's alleged backwardness and weakness. Political explanations also accentuate the role of the state bureaucracy in instigating the reform of 1861. From this viewpoint, the defeat forced the Russian conservative autocracy to recognize the necessity of reforms. In order to carry out vital military and indusial reforms, the government allegedly finally decided to free the peasant population (Figure 9.1).

Figure 9.1 Reading the manifesto to the peasants.

Regardless, in contrast to these approaches which focus on mid-nineteenth-century crises, long-term economic, social, and cultural developments in Russia since the late eighteenth century can also be seen as necessitating the end of serfdom. As explored in previous chapters, Russian serfdom was, to a surprising degree, flexible, socially viable, and capable of accommodating peasants' material needs and economic development. The decay of serfdom in Russia began long before the manifesto of 1861 abolished it and perhaps for somewhat different reasons than most historians have recognized. To some degree, its decay was reflected in long-term peasant and popular attitudes and in imperial decrees, which, long before 1861, progressively loosened peasant bondage. This chapter will not reject any of the approaches but rather will try to reconcile them. Perhaps they all had a vital influence on the course and outcome of the reform.

As mentioned in previous chapters, peasants were the largest segment of Russia's population, constituting about 85 percent of the total. Approximately half of these were landlords' serfs. According to the Tenth Imperial Census (1857), the 10,694,445 male serfs accounted for about 49 percent of all male peasants and 34 percent of the empire's male population. Along with being the predominant majority of the population, peasants were in several respects the most vital social group in Russia, especially as regards their economic activities. With the absence of a large traditional middle class (urban dwellers engaged in commerce, trade, production, and so forth) in Russia, the peasants' activities occupied the middle-class economic sphere. Furthermore, their economic, cultural, and social significance enabled peasants, and specifically serfs, to establish and maintain a balance between the diverse and habitually conflicting interests of the state, the landlord, and themselves. The economic significance of the serfs at the same time induced the state to regulate lord–peasant relations and allowed peasants to establish limits on the landlords' and local officials' prerogatives. Apparently, the Russian national economy could not survive without peasant and serf activities. Serfs' economic significance explains certain juridical ambiguities of Russian serfdom. As noted in a previous chapter, the 1649 legislation that established serfdom concurrently allowed peasants to sustain their everyday life needs. For example, imperial laws enabled peasants to seek temporary employment or engage in work activities outside the village and allowed serfs to engage in various trading, commercial, and entrepreneurial ventures, in effect granting serfs the right to leave the village. Regarding their feudal duties, serfs were supposed to perform work for landlords—corveé (*barshchina*) part of the time or pay money rent (*obrok*)—depending on the local economy and arrangements. A 1797 decree banned landlords from requiring their serfs to work more than three days a week, as well as to work on Sundays and holidays. Those peasants on money rent paid landlords between 30 and 50 percent of their annual income. As the market economy accelerated during the first half of the nineteenth century, many landlords shifted their serfs to money rent. In general, serfs who paid rent in money enjoyed greater freedom from the landlords for their independent pursuits.

It is important to remind the reader that neither the state nor the landlord had an interest in completely containing the peasant. In order to sustain the national economy and the economic needs of the landlord, the state needed to provide the peasantry, as a demographically and economically predominant social group, with certain legal protections and freedoms for territorial mobility, as well as for economic and social pursuits. Obviously, this legal aspect distinguished serfdom from American slavery and brought it closer to European feudalism. Contrasting Russian serfdom with American slavery, some contemporary Americans noted that in Russia "a serf could not be beaten to death or separated from his family and sold like any other piece of merchandise," practices endured by many American slaves.

Supplementary to the legal limits on the landlord's authority provided by the state, Russian serfs themselves deployed a broad range of means to curtail the lord's influence. Living on their land for centuries, serfs created and maintained traditions, customs, cultural values, and institutions. These provided for the survival of peasants by keeping a balance between external forces and their own individual and communal interests and needs. Hallowed tradition and indigenous institutions enabled peasants to set limits on the landlords' or state power and authority.

All these legal, institutional, social, and economic factors underlay the important internal dynamics and changes within serfdom during the centuries of its existence. New economic, social, and cultural realities that emerged during the first half of the nineteenth century, in turn, challenged serfdom's foundations. The expansion of the peasantry's economic and social activities had widespread consequences and became important precursors for the 1861 reform. It had an impact on education and on the territorial and social mobility of the serfs. Peasant engagement in various crafts and trades acquainted them with the national and local economies and with pertinent state and local laws and regulations. Through economic advancement and education, some serfs even entered the upper social strata. Although the number of such fortunate individuals was small when compared to the total serf population, the phenomenon impressed contemporary observers. One mid-nineteenth-century commentator pointed out that self-made peasants were forging to the head of merchant communities and emerging as leaders in public affairs. Some mid-nineteenth-century scholars even began to describe peasants as the most economically important social estate.[3] All these factors suggest the development of new favorable attitudes toward the peasant estate and the wide recognition of peasants as an important economic and social force. In association with this view of the peasants, most contemporaries, including high state officials, increasingly viewed serfdom as a social evil. This opinion was epitomized in the numerous publications and literary works of mid-nineteenth-century authors that attacked serfdom.

Russian public discourse of the first half of the nineteenth century stressed the ideas of freedom and equality. Serf-oriented research illustrates that these ideas were not limited to only a few enlightened individuals, but penetrated the minds and discourses of common people. Moreover, over the first half of the century, the perceptions of serfs about themselves and their serf status also dramatically changed. Serfs increasingly viewed themselves as "free persons." Studies suggest that the number of peasant refusals to perform feudal duties increased during the first half of the nineteenth century. Peasants refused to work or pay rent because they perceived themselves as free persons.[4]

It is crucial to emphasize that the process of emancipation of serfs started long before the final 1861 decision. When one examines the series of laws that regulated relations between landlords and their peasants in their historical context, it becomes obvious that these laws were direct state responses to peasant economic and social activities. Peasant publicness also influenced the peasant-oriented legislation of the first half of the nineteenth century. The roots of the process of emancipation of serfs lay in long-term developments in the society and culture of pre-reform Russia. Beginning in the early nineteenth century, new laws eased peasant entry into nonagricultural activities, in part by restricting the lord's authority over serfs. New decrees enabled serfs to engage in virtually all kinds of economic activities and regulated those activities. A series of laws progressively limited the power of the lords over peasants engaged in licensed commercial and business enterprises and introduced private property rights for serfs. These laws ultimately applied to many tens of thousands of serfs. The laws gave peasants of all categories virtually complete freedom for economic activities "such as those given to merchants and townspeople." Serfs were granted significant immunities from interference by the lord. Although rarely mentioned, these laws were of a tremendous historical significance. They challenged the foundation of serfdom by reducing the power of the lord over peasants.[5]

During the first half of the nineteenth century, the state took harsh measures against lords who violated the provisions that regulated their relations with serfs. Over a hundred noble estates were under state guardianship because of the landlords' mistreatment of serfs. In such cases serfs' feudal obligations and payments went directly to the state, not the landlord. In all these and other cases, the law limited the authority of landlords over the estates and serfs. By the mid-nineteenth century, these processes had gradually undermined the position of the nobility and led to serfdom's decline, even before it was abolished. In this light, the emancipation of 1861 was a culmination of a long process that began in the early nineteenth century.

The ideas of the enlightenment and liberalism penetrated into Russia prior to and especially during the reign of Nicholas I (1825–1855), usually portrayed as a time of stagnation. During his reign, the government appointed numerous commissions with the goal of abolishing serfdom. Support for emancipation came from educated elites and reform-minded statesmen. The reformist members of the government prepared various projects. But the resistance of the landowning nobility prevented a positive outcome. The landowning gentry initially agreed with the idea of setting the serfs free but wished to do so without giving them land. Nevertheless, during the early nineteenth century, serfdom had experienced some fundamental transformations, in addition to which the proportion of serfs in the general population had declined. By 1859, more than two-thirds of estates and two-thirds of serfs were mortgaged for the loans taken from the state. Thus, liberation of serfs could occur even without the emancipation manifesto. One of the ministers of Nicholas I, P. D. Kiselev, suggested that, if the state had reinforced the collection of loan payments, most landlords would have failed to pay off their debt to the state and, therefore, would have to lose their peasants to the state. Serfs, thus, would be transformed to the status of state peasants. These factors, rarely considered in historical discussions of serfdom, would facilitate the decision of 1861.

In Russia by the mid-nineteenth century only a few radically minded conservatives, usually members of the landed gentry, still supported the institution of serfdom and staunchly opposed its abolition. The defeat in the Crimean War, however, made the position of these advocates of serfdom untenable and simultaneously solidified the position of those who desired liberal reforms. The defeat served as the final impetus to end the outmoded institution. In November 1857, Alexander II formulated a memorandum with his own vision of emancipation. The memorandum promulgated the elimination of personal dependence of serfs and preservation of the right of landlords to keep land while granting to peasants a certain amount of land for which they would be obligated to pay a rent or to work for the landlord. Legal dependence was to be ended within a transition period of ten years. The government appointed a "secret committee" to work out an act on abolition of serfdom. The committee, however, consisted of conservative state bureaucrats who opposed emancipation. It worked out a plan for emancipation according to which peasants were to gain their freedom but receive no arable land. The procedures for freeing serfs outlined in this project were extremely complicated. The project was not accepted and in 1858 the government established the Main Committee, consisting of more forward-thinking individuals, to carry out a new project of serf emancipation. The government also established provincial gentry committees to discuss emancipation at the local level.

In general, most nobles agreed with the government's emancipation effort. It is clear, however, that they wanted to carve out for themselves as many privileges as possible. For instance, lords from provinces where agriculture dominated the economy and was the major source of wealth wanted to retain land and free their serfs without land or with very small allotments, all suggestions similar to those outlined in the 1857 commission proposal. Nevertheless, as an active social force, serfs also exercised some influence on this process of lawmaking. They publicly expressed their attitudes on the emancipation project. The state institutions studied peasant opinion about the reform. Most state reports emphasized the peasants' desire both to gain legal freedom and retain their land.

During 1859–1860 the materials on public opinion about emancipation, as well as the official opinions of the local gentry committees, went to the Editing Commission and finally to the Main Committee. After brief consideration by the State Council, Alexander II signed the 1861 act of emancipation. The act granted the status of "free rural inhabitants" to over twenty million serfs. According to the act, serfs had the right, under certain rather complex conditions to be described later, to purchase or, in some cases, receive free, much of the land they had utilized before 1861. This became one of the most important legal acts in the history of imperial Russia.

The manifesto, entitled "The General provisions on the peasants who have left serfdom," stated that "peasants have ceased to be considered serfs and have begun to be considered temporarily dependent." The document gave these peasants the rights of free citizens and granted the rights to marry without landlord's agreement. Houses, buildings, and all other possessions of peasants were recognized as their personal property. Peasants also received elective self-management. The lowest economic unit of self-management was a rural society (commune, the already existing *obschina* or as the peasants called it, *mir*), the maximum (administrative) unit—the county (in Russian *uezd*). Landowners were permitted to keep all property on all their remaining lands, but were obliged to allow peasants to use their land, pasture, wood, and other estate facilities as appropriate. The land was given to peasant communes, not to individual peasants. The Manifesto also allowed peasants to purchase land from the landlords in private or collective possession. The peasant commune received the status of a rural society. The commune, at the same time, retained its all traditional functions, as an economic union and the lowest administrative unit of the state. Communes continued to redistribute the land among their members, and established the right to use pastures and forests. At the same time, the Manifesto gave the commune all responsibilities for distributing taxes and maintaining order within its territory.

The foregoing description of serfdom during its last decades suggests that the 1861 abolition of serfdom had perhaps brought serfs somewhat less new freedom than some contemporaries and many serfs had expected. Clearly, before the 1861 decree serfs exercised some freedoms regarding their economic and social activities and decisions, as well as territorial mobility. After the law's introduction, however, former serfs still remained subjects of their village communes. For instance, in order to leave the village they had to obtain permission from the communes or other local authorities rather than from the landlords. The law also retained most of above-described functions and authorities of the commune. Simultaneously, the law extended some feudal obligations of serfs for certain periods of time, an arrangement that tended to keep peasants in their home villages. Some evidence suggests that the number of peasants who seasonally migrated actually decreased somewhat during the first decade after the emancipation, a phenomenon caused by the terms of the emancipation law.

On the one hand, these provisions clearly aimed at retaining for the landlords at least some of the economic powers they formerly enjoyed over serfs, as well as to protect as much as possible their former privileges. Regardless, the whole project of serf emancipation can be credited to the efforts of members of the liberal-minded intelligentsia and statesmen. Individuals, such as Nicholas Miliutin, Georges Samarin, Grand Duke Konstantine, and Grant Duchess Elena Pavlovna, who identified themselves as "liberals," participated in the project and exercised an influence on its preparation. Thus, the law was a compromise between the conservatives who completely opposed emancipation and the liberals who were moved to action by their belief in freedom. The liberals influenced the emperor to speed up the passage and implementation of the new law, whatever its shortcomings.

It must be noted that the 1861 law emancipated serfs with land, although the methodology by which they were to receive land was complicated and protracted (decades later some peasants were still working on the landlords' plots while awaiting to receive their own land). After peasant and landlord's fields were separated (under conditions to be explained below), the state would compensate landlords for the land they lost, whereas former serfs had to pay the state so-called redemption payments over a period of forty-nine years for land they received. (In this procedure, the peasantry would gradually recompensate the state for funds given to nobles when peasant and noble land was separated.) In reality, the state withheld about a half of the nobles' compensation, in order to pay off landlord's past-due debts owed to the Imperial Bank for existing mortgages on serfs and land. The rest of the compensation was paid by specially issued state bonds.

This compensation began, however, only after a division of land between nobles, on the one hand, and former serf-peasants, on the other. And this division process began, according to the emancipation laws, only when any given noble agreed to it. Until then, peasants continued to labor on noble estates under the same economic conditions and burdens as under serfdom. The only difference for the time being was that peasants were personally free and not subject to the landlords other than during work time. Under those conditions, one might think that nobles would have little motivation to initiate a division of land between themselves and their former serfs. Yet only when nobles agreed to the land division would they receive financial compensation (up front, one might say) for the land ceded to peasants (their former serfs). For nobles who were often heavily in debt, this certainly offered a motivation for land separation. Some nobles began the separation at once, while others lagged: many simply were not willing to change at all, while others felt that the existing arrangements profited them. Even two decades later, when new laws finally enforced land separation, 15 percent of noble estates had still not carried out land separation.

According to various studies, serfs overall received from 10 to 18 percent less and, in the southern provinces, from 25 to 40 percent less land than they had utilized before 1861 (agricultural lands given to nobles were meant to provide them with future income and prevent their impoverishment). Landlords, who accounted for 1 percent of the population, retained about 265.5 million acres of land, whereas former serfs (34 percent of the population) retained 313.2 million acres. It should be noted that some of the land retained by nobles consisted of forest land and other uncultivated and in some cases uncultivable land. Most scholars suggest that serfs received an inadequate amount of land and in allotments hardly sufficient to sustain their households. Other historians, however, point out that land had provided peasants with only a part of their incomes, the rest of which came from economic activities not associated with land. In many cases, particularly in the areas where nonagricultural economic activities prevailed, peasants preferred to take a "dar (gift)" free allotment of land, misleadingly sometimes called a "beggar" allotment so as to pay no redemptions. Peasants who received these "gift" allotments were called *darstvennye*. "Beggar" allotments or "gifts" from landlords were provided by article 123 of the emancipation provisions which allowed peasants to accept free of payment one-fourth of the normal allotment they would have otherwise received. In such cases, they renounced the rest of the land they would have received at separation. In some provinces, peasants preferred to accept the beggar allotment and significant majorities did so. Overall about 33 percent of former serfs took so-called beggar allotments, although the percentages varied greatly according to local conditions. In some provincial districts, as many as 97 percent of peasants opted to take these free land donations. It bears repeating: in cases when former serfs took beggar allotments, they were exempt from all redemption payments. In order to estimate a redemption payment for every specific case, the government carried out land surveys (which had never been carried out before in much of Russia) and prepared inventories of landholdings and feudal obligations of former serfs. Peasants and landlords had to sign the inventory and thus agree on a final settlement. This process was often quite stormy and proceeded with the help of "peace mediators" to be discussed below. In many cases, the land price was estimated at up to twice as much as its market value before 1861, a practice that benefited the lords and burdened the peasants. (Officially, the tsarist regime stated that it would not compensate nobles for their loss of serfs, whereas many observers felt that the inflated prices nobles received for the land they ceded to peasants at the time of separation constituted a hidden payment for their loss of serf labor.) In any case, inflated land prices help explain why in many cases former serfs had no desire to receive large land parcels and preferred the smaller but free "beggar" allotments. Another calculation contributed to beggar allotments: in many provinces, peasants could rent land for less than they would pay in redemptions to possess the same amount of land: many post-emancipation nobles were quite willing to rent land to peasants which tended to lower rental prices. As noted in a previous chapter, most Russian nobles did not view themselves as "agriculturalists" but rather as state bureaucrats, officers, or persons of leisure. Decades later, population growth, especially notable among peasants, led to land shortages that drastically increased land rent, genuinely reducing these peasants to the status of "beggars." Regardless, at the time of noble-peasant land separation, a beggar allotment was a rational choice in many parts of Russia.

Overall, former serfs had paid off almost 1.6 billion rubles of land indebtedness (redemption payments), by 1905, when revolutionary developments led the government to abolish the redemption payments once and for all. The estimated actual value of that land was 897 million rubles, which signifies that peasants had overpaid roughly 40 percent for the land they received.[6] Meanwhile, state peasants (those living on state-owned lands, mostly former church land confiscated during the eighteenth century) paid almost 1.6 billion rubles of redemption payments by 1905, whereas the value of land they had received was estimated at about 650 million rubles. According to these accounts, land allotted to state peasants was priced much higher than the land that went to former serfs within the same region.[7] The motivation for this imbalance is not clear but the end result was that former state peasants, who in general were more prosperous than former serfs, helped repay the government for payments it provided the nobles for the land they lost to their former serf peasants during emancipation. The land arrangements of the 1861 law, along with the rapid growth of the population and resulting unemployment and land shortages in the countryside, contributed to agrarian problems during the late nineteenth and early twentieth centuries.

Even so, upon close examination much of the process was marked by ecological/environmental outlooks on the part of peasants and, surprisingly, involved government figures. Despite first appearances, peasants in the ring of provinces around Moscow and some other areas who overwhelmingly chose the relatively small "free allotments" (one fourth of the full allotment in the area) did so on the basis of a clear understanding of their current and future needs. These peasants already earned most of their income from cottage industry, merchantry, factory work in cities and towns, and other pursuits. An arrangement that gave them several acres of land free of charge sufficed to allow them to raise fruits, vegetables, livestock, fowls, and so forth for their use and to sell at local markets. Plus they were freed from all noble control and indebtedness. Even when some peasants (smaller percentages) in heavy grain regions to the west and south chose the free allotments, this was done by a fine calculation between overpriced land and their knowledge that local landlords would have to hire them at a market price for labor to raise grain,(no other labor being available). Why overpay for land when you could work it for a decent salary with no other obligation? The government's decision to allow for this arrangement did not have the goal of impoverishing peasants but to allow them to choose for themselves, according to region and their own inclinations and their considerable knowledge of local conditions. Unforeseen economic developments decades later changed the equation, impoverishing some, enriching others, and leaving many unaffected.

The emancipation's land settlement caused dismay among former serfs, who had expected to receive, without redemption payments, all the land they had worked as serfs. The emancipation set off a series of revolts and disturbances that swept throughout the Russian countryside. Scholars estimate that about 1,889 disorders occurred in 1861.[8] The complicated nature of the emancipation and lack of confidence in the local nobles and authorities provoked peasant riots. Peasants believed that the local gentry deceived them by manipulating the terms of the emancipation legislation. Some peasants believed that the price on land was highly overestimated and refused to sign or otherwise confirm landholding inventories, which would have signified their acceptance of the terms of emancipation. Contributing to peasant unrest was the phenomenon of "Golden Charters." Certain unscrupulous individuals travelled through rural districts offering, for a fee, to read what they called the real emancipation decree (the Golden Charter), which was much more favorable for the peasants: they were freed with all the land without payment. Rumors spread that gained some credence among peasants to the effect that unscrupulous nobles suppressed the actual decree that *Batiushka tsar'* ("Little Father Tsar") had intended. Peasant riots often ensued. In addition to peasant disturbances, during the early 1860s student uprisings broke out in cities, a development that reflects the fact that liberal-minded students had expected political reforms, along with peasant and land reform. In Tver (Central Russia) the provincial noble assembly called in vain for convocation of a constitutional assembly in order to create a national constitutional government in Russia. Although the government of Alexander II had to take harsh measures to quell these and other disturbances and to restore order, it continued the reform efforts. Simultaneously, the dissatisfaction of many educated Russians with the emancipation terms spurred the development of the revolutionary movement in Russia, a matter of vast significance for Russia's future.

In order to moderate the process of emancipation and, most importantly, to arbitrate the land settlement between peasants and landlords, the state introduced the institution of peace arbitrators.[9] Among the peace arbitrators were progressive minded individuals, such as Leo Tolstoy, who was well known for his sympathy for the peasantry. Others had different outlooks, not so favorable for the peasants. The first two years of the reforms' implementation proved to be the most difficult. All statutory certificates and inventories were to be drafted and put in place. At the same time, the arbitrators mediated all disputes, explained the provisions, observed the formation and activities of peasants' self-government, oversaw the execution of peasants duties and conclusions of repurchase transactions, and so on. The imperial government in general stayed away from the institution's activities and intervened only to prevent abuses of power by some reactionary, anti-peasant arbitrators. In many cases, the state was worried less about the control over the quality of their work (in any case, because of the vast size of the country and numbers of such arbitrators, such control would have been almost impossible), than about protests of the lords and peasants that the arbitrators' activities of the might cause.

The institution of peace arbitrator was relatively short-lived (it ended roughly twenty years later). Nevertheless, it had an enormous social implication in a long-term perspective. It paved the path for the further development of a civil society. The institution furthered the process of integration of various social groups within Russian society. Activities of the arbitrators brought together peasants, lords, and authorities, creating important horizontal lines of interaction and to some degree replacing or weakening vertical ones. Although the emancipation did not meet the expectations of peasants and the liberal intelligentsia, it ended human bondage for over twenty-three million Russian serfs, a signal event in Russian history. It contributed to the decline of the noble class in Russia and the simultaneous rise of the middle and laboring classes during the late imperial period. The emancipation and other accompanying reforms stimulated rapid capitalist development during the late nineteenth century. The law of 1861 set in motion a transformation of the Russian Empire.

Suggested readings

Blum, Jerome. *The End of the Old Order in Rural Europe*. Princeton, NJ: University of Princeton Press, 1978.

Easly, Roxanne. *The Emancipation of the Serfs in Russia: Peace Arbitrators and the Development of Civil Society*. Routledge Series on Russian and East European Studies. Routledge: London and New York, 2009.

Emmons, Terrence, ed. *Emancipation of the Russian Serfs*. New York: Holt, Rinehart and Winston, 1970.

Field, Daniel. *The End of Serfdom: Nobility and Bureaucracy in Russia, 1855–1861*. Cambridge, MA: Harvard University Press, 1976.

Moon, David. *The Abolition of Serfdom in Russia, 1762–1907*. London: Longman, 2001.

Smith, Alison K. "Freed Serfs without Free People: Manumission in Imperial Russia," *AHR*, vol. 118, no. 4 (2013): 1029–1052.

Post-Emancipation Peasant Economy and Society

The final decisive point in the process of emancipation of the peasants in 1861 marked the beginning of a reform movement during the 1860s. In 1864 laws created local self-government, called *zemstvos*, and introduced juridical reforms, which simultaneously established principles of equality before the law and provided peasants the opportunity to engage in the process of law making at the local level. The post-emancipation decades marked a new era of railroads, banks and industries, rational law and public representation, new forms of scientific knowledge and social control, new management methods and standards, new language and style of public debates, and new political ideas. All of these came to Russia. In this sense, 1860s–1870s marked a turning point which sharply impacted the state's policies toward the village and the peasantry. The old approaches necessitated rethinking, while at the same time the new reality posed unforeseen challenges, which in turn required new answers and solutions. This chapter will assess the results of the reforms and will focus as much as possible on micro-level case studies and on peasant agency.

The end of serfdom opened the way for the development of capitalism in agriculture. By 1870, Russia reached the fifth place in the world in terms of industrial output and continued thereafter to develop its industries. If in 1870, the share of Russia in the global industry was 4 percent, after France (10 percent), Germany (13 percent), the United States (23 percent), and England (32 percent), by 1900, Russia produced more than 6 percent of the world industrial goods, France—8 percent, Germany—14 percent, England—22 percent, and the United States—31 percent. Russian industrial production developed eight times faster than agriculture. Agriculture also, though more slowly than industry, became more commercialized and entrepreneurial than it had been. This was manifested by the increase of production of grain for sale, for both domestic and foreign markets. From 1861 to 1896, the volume of grain shipments by Russian

Railways increased by two times, and grain export grew by five times. By 1881 Russia's grain export reached 3.2 billion kg. Russia was the world's leading exporter of grain.

The reform of 1861 undermined the foundations of the feudal economy and ended the legal attachment of the peasant to the land and the landlord. The peasant economy was now detached from that of the landlord. The landlord lost direct authority over peasants and had to rebuild his economy on a capitalist basis. But the transition from *barshchina* to the capitalist system was not instantaneous. On the one hand, the nobles' economy lacked the necessary means for capitalist production, that is, people who were accustomed to free contracted labor, ownership of agricultural tools (they *usually* belonged to peasants), and, in general, the capitalist organization of agriculture. On the other hand, the *barshchina* system, although it had been eroded, still retained some relevance. For example, under the terms of the emancipation the landlords still utilized the so-called temporary dependent economic status of the peasantry. Peasants still worked landlords' fields with their own tools, paid rent in money or in kind (usually grain), or paid various fees and fines (for damage done by cattle, felling of trees, etc.). In a direct way, these forms of lord–peasant relations were relics of serfdom, temporarily preserved under the terms of the emancipation. Labor productivity remained low and farming methods outmoded. For example, peasants in this status were paid much less than free hired workers.

As narrated in the previous chapter, the redemption of peasant lands depended on agreement between the landowners and peasants and occurred under no particular time limit. According to the law, landlords could require former *barshchina* serfs to redeem their allotments beginning two years after the emancipation decree. In such cases, lords would receive 80 percent of the land's value paid in redeemable government bonds. Ironically, the *barshchina* peasants had little interest in hurrying the redemption process. They were quick to realize that, under the new conditions, the landlords could not easily control *barshchina* labor, because the landlords' authority over peasants was now virtually nonexistent. Thus, since their former serfs often did not desire immediate redemption, during the early 1860s many *barshchina* landlords, especially in the black-earth region, demanded that the government revise the 1861 law and introduce immediate mandatory redemption, a request that the government, however, refused. Nevertheless, the government understood that in many regions where *barshchina* dominated the nobles' estates had become vulnerable and were, in fact, declining. When the redemption process began in 1863, at the will of the landlord, the *barshchina* peasants often refused to buy land at the government's price and abandoned their allotments. In these cases, being aware that the lord had no right to refuse them to do so, former serfs preferred to take the so-called beggar allotments (one fourth of the normal allotment), which, the reader may recall, were essentially free of charge. This, plus the fact that leased land was quite cheap (less than redemption payments), explains why in many black-earth provinces the small free allotments were widespread: this pertained mainly to the southeast parts of Russia and some eastern provinces: Perm, the southern part of the Voronezh, Tambov, Samara, and Saratov. As a consequence, this later resulted in land hunger among the peasantry of the black-earth region (land shortages later in the century eventually drastically increased prices for leasing land).

Nonetheless, for the moment, the general economic situation for the black-earth zone was promising and, on the whole, beneficial. Meanwhile, in the 1860s, grain prices in foreign markets increased considerably, doubling in some cases. Since the end of the 1840s, after the abolition of the restrictive Corn Laws in England and facilitated by the growth of Western Europe's urban population, the demand for Russian grain increased sharply. At the same time, workers' wages in the Russian Empire grew by 80–100 percent and most workers spent these wages buying bread and other necessities. Hence, farmers of the black-earth provinces had the opportunity to bring new lands under cultivation; the extent and intensity of cultivation grew rapidly. If in the 1860s, in European Russia alone, about 240 million acres of land were under cultivation, in 1887 this figure increased to about 316 million acres (almost 25 percent).[1]

However, throughout Russia the tillage area was tremendously irregular. In non-black-earth regions, landlords often abandoned their farming activities entirely. In these provinces, the area under cultivation diminished radically. In the north-west region, the area under cultivation remained constant, although nonetheless agricultural productivity increased because of the introduction of crop rotation and other modes of agricultural intensification and new forms of management. In the central black-earth region, the area under cultivation increased by only 5 percent, because most arable lands in this region had already been plowed before the reform. In the Middle Volga provinces, the area under cultivation grew by fully 35 percent between 1861 and 1881; in Ukrainian provinces, it increased by 13 percent; in Novorossia (the deep south of Russia)— by 98 percent; and in Southern Volga provinces—by 36 percent. Nevertheless, regardless of this general extensive growth of cultivation, the nobles' agricultural business did not increase. For the most part, the former serf-owners failed to use the opportunity offered by high prices on grain, despite the large amounts of capital in the form of government loans and redemption payments they received. The nobility rarely made new investments in agriculture and instead preferred to rent out their land to peasants. Consequently, much of this notable agricultural intensification can be laid to the peasantry.[2]

During the post-reform decades, peasant renting of lands increased. In the northern provinces, where animal husbandry was highly developed, peasants rented mainly meadows and pastures; in the southern provinces, peasants usually rented arable land for farming. In general, in the 1880s in European Russia, there were about 184 million acres of land under cultivation, of which over 128 million acres were on peasant communal lands, about 32.4 million acres were on rented lands (mostly by peasants), and 23.5 million acres of land were on private farms, mostly owned by nobles. Thus, about 87 percent of all lands under cultivation belonged to peasant communes and about 13 percent belonged to private owners. In 1882, in 48 provinces of European Russia peasant communes owned about 12.13 million workhorses and individual owners had 1.5 million workhorses. Evidently, the noble landlords could handle only about 38 percent of their land, whereas the rest they rented out to peasants.[3]

The latest studies suggest that although twenty years after the emancipation former serf owners retained ownership of much of their land, their participation in the agricultural economy declined while their debts grew relentlessly. As mentioned in the previous chapter, on the eve of emancipation, most landlords' estates (about 70 percent) had been mortgaged, while at the same time the majority of lords had outstanding unpaid debts. When post-emancipation nobles initiated the separation of their land from that of the peasants (the so-called redemption process), the state withheld the landlords' debts from the compensation payments. Consequently, during the very early post-emancipation years the lords' indebtedness declined somewhat. However, by the mid-1860s, the outstanding debt of the nobility started to grow again and, by the end of the 1860s it reached 230 million rubles. By the beginning of the 1880s, it approached 400 million rubles and by the end of that decade—600 million. Despite these enormous loans from the newly founded post-emancipation banks, in the black-earth region the agricultural economy of the noble estates grew only very modestly. The main agricultural expansion in this region occurred only because of peasant farming and the expansion of land rented from the landlords. By the 1880s, the nobility rented out to peasants about 135 million acres of land in the provinces of European Russia. During the 1890s, with the help of the newly established Peasant and Noble Banks, many noble estates were liquidated. In general, the process of sale of landlords' estates accelerated after the 1861 reforms. Between 1859 and 1875, an average of 1.4 million acres of nobles' land was sold every year and between 1875 and 1879, the sales increased to 2 million acres per year and during the early 1890s—to 2.1 million acres. Annual sales of nobles' lands increased thereafter and by the beginning of this twentieth century reached 2.7 million acres a year.[4] In 1906, as a result of the 1905 revolution and Stolypin agrarian reform, over 20 million acres of nobles' land were put up for sale. Statistics indelibly reveal that in Russia by the early twentieth century noble landowning was yielding to that of the peasantry and, to a much lesser extent, the middle classes.

Meanwhile, by the end of the nineteenth century, there were two poles of land ownership: at one pole stood 10.5 million peasant communal households (roughly 50 million people) with approximately 189 million acres of land (keeping in mind that peasant family holdings varied vastly), and at the other, 30,000 large farms and estates, mostly of noble landlords, with about 150,000 people with the same amount (189 million acres) of land as the entire peasantry. An average peasant household had about 19 acres of land, insufficient to maintain economic well-being, especially as regards households at the lower end of acreage holdings. (Of course, peasants resorted to renting land when they could afford the price.)

Existing scholarship has reached no consensus on the conditions of the peasantry after the reforms. Approaching the question from a macro-level perspective and examining state-generated data and statistics on grain production, rural wages, land prices and rents, taxes, and government relief measures, some historians see the existence of a series of crises in the countryside during the post-reform decades.[5] These crises, in this macro-level analytical trend, affected peasant agriculture and living standards, as well as the entire sociopolitical system. These scholars adhere to the idea of peasant impoverishment during the late tsarist decades. Although such scholars do not reject that reality that there was improvement in agriculture and per capita grain production, they emphasize a significant ongoing crisis in the important central black-earth and Volga regions. The macro-level approach, of course, has its own limitations because its statistical bases never fully represent micro-realities. For example, state statistics upon which macro-analysis is based usually ignored peasant nonagricultural economic activities and, especially, cottage industry. During the early post-emancipation decades, cottage industry, an important but often neglected topic among historians of the peasantry, heavily subsidized peasant household income, which, therefore, was significantly higher than indicated by state statistics. By the late nineteenth century, however, cottage industry was heavily challenged by industrial production, which underwent a sharp rise with each decade. As a result, many peasants who had formerly supplemented their income through various cottage industries lost these extra earnings. Coupled with population growth, this created problems for a large segment of peasants and spurred their migration to cities, which, by the way, in turn provided labor for further industrial growth. This crisis, it should be noted, had little to do with agriculture and affected only peasants who had formerly engaged in cottage industry (that is, produced goods for sale).

To balance the macro-level approach, a micro-level perspective is handy. Case studies of peasant poverty, based on local studies of peasant budgets and on-farm factors of peasant conditions, suggest that poverty in individual households was caused by many factors. For example, the failure to produce enough sons necessary for economic viability, illness, alcoholism, initial lack of resources, and family disputes all worked to impoverish families.[6] Regardless, case studies also reveal that poor peasant households had the potential for upward social mobility. In rural Russia, during the immediate post-emancipation decades, access to education was quite limited but by the late nineteenth century this began to change. Because of state and local government efforts, an extensive network of permanent rural schools was established. Peasants considered education in practical terms, as a form of preparation of children for adult life in the countryside. Although early on there had been some dispute among peasants about the usefulness of education, most scholars now agree that most peasants quickly came to view it as advantageous for their children and whenever possible sent them to schools. The influx of landless or land-short peasants into the cities allowed greater access to education. By 1911, 67 percent of urban youth were enrolled in primary schools. With population growth and the decline of cottage industries, many peasants moved to urban areas, becoming, by definition, urban youth.[7] Most of these peasants were members of communes, which legally had the right to restrict peasant mobility; even so, most communes refrained from using this measure. Indeed, it was in the interest of the commune to allow excess peasants to leave.

Peasant customs and material culture

As post-emancipation peasants faced vast changes in their lives, a natural question arises about how they lived, that is, in their everyday lives, in pre- and post-emancipation times. Since much of peasant life still centered on the village, much remained the same until the collectivization of the 1930s sharply altered significant aspects of village life (even then mores and habits often remained intact). One essential point is that no single identifiable Russian peasant way of life or material culture existed: the country was too vast and conditions too varied to allow for a single easily described culture. Peasants migrating to Siberia faced a vastly different reality than those of, say, Belarus, Ukraine, central Russia, or those in the Volga region or the deep south; peasant culture in each of these had its own specificities. Even so, the matter deserves attention.

A central issue concerns the peasant diet: what did peasants eat and drink? Although many peasant recipes are lost, a general picture can be recreated. Peasant diets centered on bread and other foods derived from cereals, on soups (perhaps the real centerpiece of the daily diet), and the ubiquitous every day (nonalcoholic) drink, *kvass*, made from lightly fermented rye and valued for its refreshing and rejuvenating qualities. As noted earlier, peasants preferred rye bread to wheat—it was tastier and healthier. Cereals (*kasha*) were eaten everywhere for breakfast and other meals: *kasha* could be made from wheat (*pshennaia*), oats (*ovsiannaia*), and many other grains. In the past, peasants made numerous types of *kasha* (the Russian poet Pushkin named twenty-five varieties prepared by peasants in the early decades of the nineteenth century), the recipes for many of which are long since lost or out of fashion. The most common soup was *shchi*—usually a cabbage soup (innumerable variants existed) seasoned with onions, garlic, dill, beef bones, and meat. Other common soups were *borsch* (a beet soup, also with endless variants), various vegetable soups, *rassol'nik* (a soup with numerous ingredients including beef or pork kidneys and pickles), mushroom soup, and so forth. Many versions of all these soups existed, according to family and regional custom. Peasants raised or collected vegetables, fruits and berries (from which preserves were made), honey, and, of course, mushrooms. Mushroom hunting in the woods and meadows was a popular occupation and recreation for children and adults: a whole lore surrounded the endeavor. The daily peasant diet did not center on meat, but peasants variously kept horses, pigs, goats, sheep, chickens, geese, rabbits, ducks, and so on. On holidays (which in the Russian calendar were innumerable), meat dishes occupied a prominent place on the table, as did other specialties, such as various cakes (Easter cakes), pancakes (*blinny*, also known as crepes, often rolled with various fillings), pies (*pirogi*, which could have meat, fruit, or vegetable stuffing), and gingerbread. Along with kvass, peasants made drinks from various fruits (infusions) and, during the winter, hot drinks (*sbiten*) made from honey and herbs. Not to be forgotten is *samogon'* (literally self-fire or home brew), a clear alcohol made from grain. (Brewing *samogon'* was illegal since Russian state finances depended heavily on the spirits tax, which home brewers escaped. Illegality did not deter the peasants on this matter.) Hot tea, sweetened with honey or fruit preserves, was also a common drink.

Traditional peasant clothing varied sharply from region to region. Peasants in the north used animal skins, whereas in the rest of Russia—woven clothes were made from linen, hemp, wool, silk (for special occasions), and later cotton. Most fabrics were produced by peasants themselves, whereas some were purchased at marketplaces or from traveling traders. Russian peasants hand painted fabrics and decorated them with elaborate embroidery and semiprecious stones. They had clothing for everyday and for holidays. Holiday dress was made from expensive fabrics and with elaborate decoration that varied from village to village and from province to province. Peasant women wore a headdress, such as the elaborate *kokoshnik* for holidays or a shawl for everyday wear. (As discussed in an earlier chapter, young children's clothing did not distinguish between boys and girls and were passed down from child to child.) Bast shoes (made from cane and hemp) were widespread among peasants well into the 1930s. Toward the end of the nineteenth century, peasants also commonly acquired readymade clothes, shoes, and boots.

As discussed earlier, Russian peasants shared similar ethnic and cultural roots. They also were mostly of the same religion. The vast majority of peasants were Russian Orthodox, although several other Christian denominations coexisted with Orthodoxy. The most notable among them were the Old Believers, an offshoot of Russian Orthodoxy, consisting of those who rejected the legitimacy of the Orthodox clergy and bishops; they also rejected the legitimacy of the emperors who they viewed as the anti-Christ. The Old Believers, sharp critics of serfdom, usually lived in isolation from other peasants and were often persecuted by the state. An even more radical offshoot of Orthodoxy was the Skopsty, who practiced castration (the term *skoptsy* refers to the procedure), a practice that sharply delimited the group's growth. Small congregations of Baptists, Roman Catholics, and other religions coexisted uneasily with Orthodoxy. In Ukraine, the Uniates (those who believed in merging the Roman Catholic and Orthodox churches) had a sizable following. Some large noble estates had a chapel, with a priest; Orthodox priests in rural areas were usually offspring of peasants (before emancipation either serfs or state peasants). Most villages did not have a church or priest so that peasants, if they wished, went to the nearest church, wherever located, for services (Sundays and religious holidays). A typical village church and its priest served several villages. For peasants, regular attendance was the exception rather than the rule. The nearest church was also the site of other religious services such as baptisms, weddings, funerals, and of cemeteries where peasants buried their dead. Funerals were performed by the Russian Orthodox priests, according to the religion's traditions.

In addition to the official religion, rich pagan and pre-Christian traditions survived in peasant culture. Pre-Christian Russian folk religion existed as a substratum, which as in other parts of the Christian world, underlay Orthodox practices and celebrations. Among the surviving vestiges of the pre-Christian folk religion were nature spirits, including the *domovoi* (house spirit), the *leshii* (wood goblin), and the *rusalka* (female water spirit), most of which were considered malevolent or mischievous, although they could be appeased by proper treatment and the offerings. Certain peasants, usually women, had the reputation of possessing knowledge of and being able to communicate with these spirits. Some of them functioned as popular healers. One of the most widely observed pre-Christian holidays, *Maslennitsa*, corresponded to Mardi Gras and featured feasting and various customary rituals, including the setting up of straw and wooden figures carried on carts. Russian folk art (wooden carvings, embroidery, paintings, and household items) widely reflected pre-Christian motifs.

Post-emancipation peasant experience

The peasants played a significant role in the industrialization and urbanization of Russia. Peasants, who could not make the redemption payments for their parcels of land, forfeited that land to the commune and migrated to the cities to seek employment in various industries. Peasant migrations heavily spurred urbanization and the growth of the city during the late imperial decades. It must be pointed out that temporary peasant migration also occurred before the end of serfdom and, as pointed out in previous chapters, migrants from the countryside represented a significant bulk of the urban population. After the emancipation, most imperial Russian cities of any size in effect became migrant cities.[8] Post-emancipation peasant social and territorial mobility obviously accelerated. Peasant migrants now outnumbered other types of urban residents.[9] Nevertheless, urban growth during these decades did not reflect peasant migration alone. Urban growth as a category also occurred because of the proto-industrial and entrepreneurial activities in many villages in the central non-black-earth provinces. By the late nineteenth century, many such villages acquired urban features and received the status of towns and cities (the transformation of Ivanovo-Voznesensk from village to city is described in an earlier chapter). Peasants' shifting between the city and the village had immense consequences for both spaces and for the peasantry itself. Peasant migrants brought back to the village new ideas and news, new fashion, and patterns of behavior, all of which fostered development and change in the village. From the countryside, they brought into the cities their familiar ways of popular culture and traditions, a process that helped preserve popular culture in an culturally diverse and complex environment. Peasants were not only producers and consumers of agricultural produce; they were producers and consumers of their home-made customer goods as well. After the emancipation, with the expansion of manufactured goods, peasants also became customers of city-made products. They actively bought various urban-produced articles, including musical instruments (accordions, harmonicas, etc.), samovars, manufactured garments, shoes, newspapers, and books. In many areas, glass-paned windows characterized peasant houses, a vast improvement over the sunless huts of the past. The city-village exchange had great potential for improving standards of living in the village and uplifting rural life as a whole (Figure 10.1).

Men usually prevailed among peasant migrants, whereas women peasant migrants constituted a smaller group. This reflects the significance of women's activities in the countryside and, presumably, the desire of male family members

Figure 10.1 Peasant migrants.

to control them. Even so, peasants often migrated into the cities with their immediate families: spouses and children. Sometimes the entire family worked in the same factory. Nevertheless, male peasant migrants most often worked in factories, whereas their female counterparts more commonly engaged in various nonindustrial activities: they became domestic servants, baby sitters, and even prostitutes.[10] The outmigration from the countryside to urban settings strongly impacted rural life and gender relations. If the 1861 reform freed peasants from their lords, migration liberated them from familial control. Young men were liberated from the authority of their elders within the family. Migrant women were able to earn their own wages. Young men had perhaps more advantages than unmarried women, who endured hardships and had to cope with patronizing, aggressive, or abusive men. Nevertheless, the new reality of out-migration from the countryside to cities, along with rapid economic development, created opportunities for both peasant men and women to liberate themselves from outmoded patriarchal structures and to create new forms of individuality. Even so, the decline of patriarchal control also had potential shortcomings for both men and women, often rendering them economically vulnerable, at least in the short run. In a long-term perspective, however, economic development and changes in the countryside created greater possibilities for peasant men and women to better their lives and those of their children.

The rapid economic development of the late nineteenth century gave rise to sizable middle and laboring classes. Most of the members of both classes had peasant backgrounds and not uncommonly still maintained ties with the countryside. Most Russian factory workers of the late nineteenth and early twentieth centuries were or had been peasant-migrants. As both classes grew in numbers, their influence in society also grew. Both classes formed numerous voluntary associations to pursue their economic and social goals. Both classes wanted political reforms and representation. During the late nineteenth century, there were several well-known attempts to push the government to carry out political reforms.

Other reforms of the 1860s also had a great impact on the lives of the Russian population. With the introduction of local government reform, the nonurban imperial population was divided into three groups: local nobility, peasants, and townsmen (residents of small towns). Each group elected its representatives to local *zemstvos* (local governments) for a three-year term. These local governments had complete autonomy over local affairs: local resources (land and finances), local taxes, communications, property insurance, commerce and industry, public health and education, appointment of the local bureaucracy.

In reality, these local *zemstvos* became a very significant factor in local life and provided an opportunity for the peasantry. Even so, the peasantry, the majority of the population, remained underrepresented in the zemstvos. For example, about 48 percent of *zemstvo* members came from the nobility; 40 percent from the peasantry; and 12 percent represented town residents: only the last representation reflected demographic reality. Nonetheless, in many instances, the peasantry responded positively to the local government reforms and actively engaged in local policy making. Contemporaries observed that the local assemblies, composed of nobles, peasants, and townspeople, operated with no trace of antagonism among the groups who met and carried out their deliberations on an equal basis. Contemporary observers recognized, often to their surprise, that peasant delegates were articulate, practical, and relevant: they arrived at *zemstvo* meetings prepared to take part in local governance. Although the reforms demarcated an enormous change in the way imperial Russia was governed at the local level, they clearly did not alter the fundamental political basis of rule at the nationwide imperial level. For example, the imperial Senate, supposedly a representative body for the empire, represented only the aristocracy and the monarch.

Even so, the emancipation era reforms reflected significant ongoing social and economic changes taking place in imperial Russia and revealed the state's attempt to adjust itself to these changes. The reforms signified the waning social basis for the existing estate structures and allowed for incorporating the actively developing civil society into the legal and state makeup. The reforms created a basis for the elimination of the old estate system and a foundation for the extension of popular participation in local and central government.

An important aspect of local government expansion associated with the *zemtsvos* was the construction over the next several decades of an enormous network of *zemstvo*-controlled local schools, libraries, and medical clinics throughout rural Russia, in addition to which *zemstvos* had responsibility for building and maintaining roads, bridges, canals, local jails, and so forth. The necessity to hire doctors, nurses, feldshers (nurse practitioners), teachers, statisticians, and other personnel for this extensive network of services, not to mention the construction of suitable premises, signified a decadelong process to bring the system into full function. Regardless, by the 1880s and 1890s millions of peasants had access to previously unavailable services and advantages on a very wide scale. Numerous young men and women who received their basic education at *zemstvo* schools then pursued further training at institutes of higher learning and even universities. By nature, these educated persons entered into the Russian intelligentsia (persons who wished to dedicate themselves to improving the life of the common folk), heavily increasing the participation of persons of peasant origins in various walks of Russian life, both urban and rural (Figure 10.2).

Another important aspect of local self-government was that numerous members of this new intelligentsia tended to enter into lives of service to the peasantry (and in urban areas to workers) through employment in the self-same *zemstvo* institutions that had been of benefit to them. The eventually vast *zemtstvo* network not only improved the lives of peasants through education, medical care, and other services but also served as centers of revolutionary propaganda. The premises of village schools and clinics also served as sites for revolutionary training and propaganda and for the distribution of literature critical of the regime. During the First World War, as we shall see in a later chapter, an analogous process occurred behind the fronts that stretched across Western Russia.

Simultaneously with the growth of the *zemstvo* system was the rise of a vast network of peasant-oriented cooperatives that spread across rural Russia after emancipation (a similar process occurred in urban areas). Peasants entering into a new financially independent way of life required and directly benefited from entry into rural cooperatives that gave them access to goods, equipment, seeds, and everything else that cooperatives offered. Like *zemstvo*

Figure 10.2 A. I. Morozov, Rural Free School 1865.

institutions, cooperatives also served as sites of revolutionary propaganda. On a most basic level, the *zemstvo* and cooperative networks had the effect of rapidly modernizing life for millions of Russian peasants. The end of the nineteenth and the beginning of twentieth century witnessed a decline of the Russian landed nobility, and, as we have explored in this chapter, a transformation of some of the former serfs into free farmers or workers, and an emergence of a new type of person, all processes well described in late nineteenth-century Russian literature. Anton Chekhov's *The Cherry Orchard*, cited in Chapter 7, may be useful here as well. *The Cherry Orchard* offers perhaps the clearest snapshot of these changes, providing a glimpse into the lives of nobles and their former serfs at a transformative moment. *The Cherry Orchard* is a play about an aristocratic woman, named Lyubov Andreevna Ranevskaya, who returned home to her estate with her family after living in France for several years. When they returned, the estate had been mortgaged and would soon be put up for auction to pay off debts long past due. By that time, Ranevskaya had spent her entire fortune and the main question facing her was how the family would prevent their beloved estate, with its famous cherry orchard, from being sold. Meanwhile, Yermolay Lopakhin, a former serf of the Ranevskaya estate, has become a successful merchant. A practical man, Lopakhin suggests to Ranevskaya that the way to save the estate involves chopping down the orchard and breaking up the land into individual lots to be sold as summer homes for a nearby growing industrial town. Ranevskaya and her family reject this idea because they can't bear to destroy the cherry orchard. Eventually the estate with its orchard is sold at auction, and in an almost cruel karmic turn, Lopakhin, the former serf, purchases the estate. "Just as the family leaves the home," writes Chekhov (himself the descendant of peasants), "one can hear in the distance the cherry orchard being chopped down."[11]

Lopakhin represented a new type of person being born during this post-reform era. Chekhov reminds us that Lopakhin was from the peasantry, and his father and grandfather were serfs for this once-wealthy family that had owned the cherry orchard. Chekhov illustrated the process of upward social mobility (or downward for some) described in earlier chapters, a process that intensified after 1861. By this process, Lopakhin and thousands like him turned themselves into wealthy and successful businessmen, so wealthy in fact that they were able to purchase the estates where their ancestors were serfs. Chekhov was able to demonstrate what former serfs felt about their present position. Most telling about Lopakhin was the intense emotion he felt after buying the estate:

"If only my father and grandfather could rise up from their graves and see all that's happened … I bought the estate where my grandfather and father were slaves."[12] For many former serfs like Lopakhin, owning the estate was more than just a demonstration of how powerful they had become; it was an emotional catharsis. Savva Purlevskii, another former serf who escaped from servitude by fleeing and transforming himself into a successful merchant, after hearing the announcement of the emancipation of the serfs in 1861, "returned from a church service, sat at a table and, without saying a word dissolved into tears…"[13] The fictional Lopakhin and the real Purlesvkii experienced the same sense of release.

It is impossible to estimate, much less exactly count, the number of such triumphant success cases among former serfs, but one should not underestimate the potential for social alteration launched by the emancipation. Although the reforms did not bring immediate improvement to the majority of peasant lives, they did create a foundation for further improvement. Even so, most peasants still confronted social and economic hardship caused by Russia's rapid industrial growth, urbanization, and population growth. One way or another, late imperial Russia addressed all these issues in early-twentieth-century reform and revolution.

Suggested readings

Black, Cyril, ed. *The Transformation of Russian Society: Aspects of Social Change since 1861*. Cambridge, MA: Harvard University Press, 1960.

Bradley, Joseph. *Muzhik and Muscovite: Urbanization in Late Imperial Russia*. Berkeley: University of California Press, 1985.

Brower, Daniel. *Estate, Class, and Community: Urbanization in Late Tsarist Russia*. Pittsburgh: University of Pittsburg Press, 1983.

Burds, Jeffrey. *Peasant Dreams & Market Politics: Labor Migration and the Russian Village, 1861–1905*. Pittsburgh: University of Pittsburgh Press, 1998.

Eclof, Ben. *Russian Peasant Schools: Officialdom, Village Culture, and Popular Pedagogy*. Berkeley: University of California Press, 1986.

Engel, Barbara. *Between the Fields and the City: Women, Work and the Family in Russia, 1861–1914*. Cambridge: Cambridge University Press, 1993.

Gorshkov, Boris B. *Russia's Factory Children: State, Society and Law, 1800–1917*. Pittsburgh: University of Pittsburg Press, 2009.

Wcislo, Frank W. *Reforming Rural Russia: State, Local Society, and National Politics, 1855–1914*. Princeton: Princeton University Press, 1990.

Wildman, Alan. *The Defining Moment: Land Charters and the Post-Emancipation Agrarian Settlement in Russia, 1861–1863. The Carl Beck Papers in Russian and East European Studies.* No 1205, September, 1996.

Worobec, Christine D. *Peasant Russia: Family and Community in the Post-Emancipation Period.* Princeton: Princeton University Press, 1991.

Peasants and the Russian Revolutions

According to Karl Marx, peasants do not constitute a revolutionary class. Yet in the case of the Russian revolutions of 1905, and February and October 1917, Russian peasants, in pursuit of desired political and economic changes, were enthusiastic actors in these revolutions. Peasants had aspirations to improve their lot through active involvement in politics and the revolutionary movement. Many became members and active supporters of political parties which developed at the beginning of the twentieth century. The period between 1905 and April 1918 witnessed remarkable peasant activism. Peasants created their associations, formed various committees, and convened congresses at the local and national levels. The revolutionary turn in 1917, however, ultimately brought about the Red Terror and civil war, leaving peasant aspirations for the time being only partially fulfilled: the early 1918 land law (to be discussed below) did pass the land to the peasants but then the state, faced with hunger in the cities, confiscated the produce of the land, often leaving peasants in a state of starvation. This chapter will explore the revolutions and developments associated with them, focusing on peasant experiences, various political parties' agrarian programs, and state policies regarding peasants.

The beginning of the twentieth century was marked by truly dramatic events: continuing economic reforms, industrialization, and calamities. Russia was undergoing a full-scale economic and industrial modernization. These processes were uneven and caused sharp social dislocations in the countryside and in the cities. Peasants used all legal channels to force the imperial, the provisional, and then the Soviet governments to hear their voices. Peasants in the communes and factories wrote petitions to the state authorities telling them that their rights were being violated by conditions in the factories and by the financial toll the redemption payments and taxes were taking on them. Peasants also joined various organizations that pushed for the economic and political rights of Russian peasants, including the All-Russian Peasant Union. At the same time, various political parties arose, which, striving to win support from peasants and workers, often called for radical reforms or methods. Still, the government usually paid only sporadic attention to the peasants' plight. The year of 1905 proved different. After Bloody Sunday, an early 1905 massacre of demonstrators outside the Winter Palace in St. Petersburg, unrest spread throughout Russian cities and rural areas. By fall of 1905 the situation became dire, threatening a complete loss of political control. At the advice of his chief minister at the time, Sergei Witte, Tsar Nicholas II, issued the "October Manifesto" (written by Witte), which ended the autocracy and established a constitutional monarchy, promising civil liberties, a broad electoral franchise with heavy peasant participation, and an elected national parliament, the State Duma, the first of which opened during the spring of 1906. It soon became clear that Emperor Nicholas and his supporters had a different vision of government under the new constitution than much of the rest of the population. Twice between 1906 and 1908, the emperor used the power given to him by the October Manifesto to dismiss the Duma before its term had run out and call for new elections, mainly because a majority of the deputies were sympathetic to the peasants' demands for the land and threatened to pass laws that were too radical for the government.

After the dissolution of the First Duma, the tsar appointed Peter Stolypin as prime minister, a strong leader who would attempt to both stem further civil disorder and, as we shall see, bring about reform that promised to transform peasant life. (It is interesting to note that for the position of prime minister the resentful Nicholas passed over Witte whom he distrusted for having advised him to issue the reforms that in fact saved his throne.) In any case, Stolypin took over the reins of day-to-day governance. One might call him "a man with a plan." But would the plan work?

At the beginning of the twentieth century, the agrarian question remained a crucial and unresolved issue. In 1905, 9.2 million peasant households in European Russia had 276 million acres of allotted communal land, plus 62 million acres of household plots. In addition, some 30,000 private owners, including the nobility, possessed over 188 million acres of land for an average of 54,627 acres of land per farm. The state owned 416 million acres of mostly forested land. It should be noted, however, that peasant allotted land consisted of arable land, meadows, and pastures (with a clear deficit of the latter), plus a small amount of nonarable land and almost no forest. Noble land included much forested land. Thus, according to the minister of agriculture, A. Ermolov, private owners of non-peasant origin had an estimated 94 million acres of arable land, and the state—no more than 16 million acres, while peasants owned 389 million acres of allotment and private land. Nevertheless, as discussed in the previous chapter, many peasants owned lands barely adequate or outright inadequate to sustain their lives. An average peasant household possessed about 39 acres of land.[1] Prime Minister Stolypin introduced a comprehensive plan of gradual agricultural reforms, which aimed, over a period of several decades, at transforming peasant communes into private farms. Stolypin's long-term goal was to eliminate the peasant commune, which he believed was outdated and likely to stir up disturbances, and to persuade peasants, gradually, to initiate individual farming. Additional reforms and policies of the new prime minister concerned government financial and logistic assistance of peasants, a program that included the introduction of peasant loans, education, military reforms, and government decentralization, giving local communities greater self-determination.[2]

Stolypin's agrarian reforms, in fact, largely followed proposed reforms which had been worked out, but not implemented, prior to the 1905 revolution by a specially appointed committee as a response to increased peasant insurrectionism, which had begun in 1900 and continued until 1907. This peasant unrest amplified during the spring of 1906 into full scale rebellion. Although the wave of peasant uprisings resulted first and foremost from unfulfilled peasant demands for land redistribution, it also reflected other social and economic dynamics in the countryside, such as population growth and the decline of cottage industry. Population growth created new demands for land and the decline of cottage industries in the countryside, as noted, deprived numerous peasants of needed income. Stolypin's dual objectives were to win over the peasantry and suppress the radicals. A conservative supporter of the monarchy, Stolypin believed that creating a mass of private peasant proprietors of land, that is, freeholders, would insure stability for the monarchy in the future.[3]

Starting in August 1906, the government introduced a series of decrees known collectively as the Stolypin Land Reform, which allowed the sale of public lands to peasants, eased the obtaining of peasant land credit, and proclaimed the right of individual peasants to consolidate their land allotments within the commune and to have title to these consolidated holdings as private property. (As part of the government's concessions to the peasantry, all remaining redemption payments for land peasants had received as a result of emancipation were cancelled.) Since the First Duma, whose makeup was far more radical than the government had expected, had been dismissed, pending the election of a new one, the government enacted these measures by means of article 87 of the constitution. This statute enabled the government to issue decrees when a Duma had been dismissed but with the obligation to seek the next Duma's approval of the decrees. The Second Duma, however, was even more radical than the

First and was also quickly dismissed—before it even had time to consider the new land reform (which in all likelihood it would have rejected). During the interim period after the Second Duma's dismissal and the Third's convening, the government issued decrees that restricted voting rights of peasants and nonwealthy urban dwellers, effectively ensuring a majority in the Third Duma for conservatives. Although the matter is not the focus of this study, it should be noted that the Fundamental Laws (Russia's new constitution) explicitly banned changing electoral formulas during the interim period between Dumas. In any case, elected under the new conditions of illegally restricted voting rights, the very conservative Third State Duma approved most of Stolypin's bills about the land and the peasantry. Meanwhile, spurred by peasant unrest and harsh economic conditions, the landowning nobility accelerated a process that began after emancipation by selling an additional 25 millions of acres of land over the next few years, mostly to peasant communes. On the eve of the February 1917 Revolution, about 43 million peasants still lived in peasant communes while, under the Stolypin plan, about 5 million peasants had become private farmers. Both categories together also rented about 94.5 million acres of land from mostly noble landowners in addition to the land they owned. Historians argue about whether the Stolypin land reform was successful or unsuccessful, although in reality it is hard to say. Stolypin himself had said that his program, which was gradualist by nature, would need forty years to reach full implementation. In reality, it was interrupted by the outbreak of war in 1914 and ended by the 1917 revolutions, far short of his time frame. One can only say that Stolypin had initiated a process of creating a layer of private peasant farms with unclear ultimate results (Figure 11.1).

If Prime Minister Stolypin's activities and actions as regards the peasantry had been restricted to his land reform, history might have turned out somewhat differently. In reality, he accompanied the initial steps of his land program with an exceptionally harsh policy toward peasant unrest, which was at a high peak when he took office. Under his direction, military units under the control of officers known for their stern attitudes headed out into the countryside to quell peasant unrest (one such officer reported just afterward to his superior: "I came, I punished, I left."). They entered rebellious villages, herded the inhabitants out into the fields, burned all structures, and hung those deemed as leaders of the revolts in front of the villages' peasants. These actions, taken without a hint of real judicial procedure, came to be known, infamously, as "Stolypin's neckties" (in reality, the hangman's noose). This was summary justice, minus the justice. The world-famed Lev Tolstoy, who had devoted much of his later life to the peasantry,

Figure 11.1 Peasant visitor to the State Duma.

whose customs and sense of justice he had come to admire, responded with the cry: "We cannot go on living this way!" Emperor Nicholas, until the day he lost the throne, continued to believe that the peasantry maintained their devotion to the "Little Father Tsar (*Tsar'-Batiushka*)." Where and when the emperor had lost that devotion is hard to say, but Stolypin's neckties and Bloody Sunday, the latter of which predated Stolypin's appointment as prime minister, certainly played their roles. During the following years, peasants maintained a certain quiet (before the storm?).

The First World War contributed to a deepening of peasant impoverishment and other woes. The outbreak of hostilities led to the drafting of vast numbers, mostly male peasants. By 1917 the numbers of landless peasants had grown. There were about 3 million landless households and about 5 million households with less than 13.5 acres in European Russia. In the Volga region, 11.2 percent of peasant households were landless; in the central non-black earth—9.4 percent, in northwest—7.2 percent, in the central black earth—5.7 percent. As a result of the war mobilization of resources, the government requisitioned horses on a wide scale. By 1917 about a half of peasant households had no horses and 47 percent had one horse. In the central black-earth region, two-thirds of peasant households had no horse. The overwhelming majority, about 85 percent, of peasant households were small and medium sized. They were self-sufficient but had to put up with mortgage debts, inadequate acreage of land, and even some remnants of serfdom. The wealthiest individual peasant farmers accounted for the balance, about 15 percent. In European Russia, the wealthiest farmers were concentrated in the Volga and Western Ural black-earth regions. Rich grain-producing farmers (mostly nobles and rich peasants) possessed the greater amount of land, about 67 percent. Some of these lands were rented out or leased on long terms. All these groups of farmers were interested in the agrarian reforms. Poor and average peasants dreamed about agrarian reforms that would eliminate noble agriculture and all types of private land ownership. They wanted to receive land free-of-charge and wanted it to be equally divided among families. With a somewhat different outlook, the wealthiest peasant farmers (the so-called kulaks) wanted the abolition of noble privileges, the expansion of agricultural credit, the further development of cooperatives, and more protections for private property.[4]

By 1917, in European Russia, most privately owned lands (a category that excluded peasant communal land) were mortgaged and had bank liens; over 80 percent of these mortgaged lands belonged to the nobility. Banks gave out credits of over 32 billion rubles in the form of land bonds, almost as much as they gave for industrial investment. Landlords from the nobility mostly spent the credits on their personal needs rather than invest in agriculture, just as they had been doing since the 1861 reforms. As of January 1, 1916, the outstanding debt of the nobility was 1.2 billion rubles. This tendency found a reflection in late-nineteenth to early-twentieth-century literature, especially in the works of Chekhov, as discussed in the previous chapter. The major part of mortgaged lands was located in areas where noble estates prevailed. For example, by province the following percentages of noble land were mortgaged: in Simbirsk province—85 percent, in Penza province—79 percent, in Saratov province—76 percent, in Voronezh province—75 percent, in Kazan province—74 percent, in Tula province—72 percent, and in Orel province—70 percent of noble lands. In the central non-black-earth region, over 30 percent of privately owned lands were under bank mortgages.[5] Often nobles were unable to redeem their land, which then eventually entered into the possession of the bank, which finally put it up for sale. Peasants as individuals, as communities, or as cooperatives, etc. purchased most of this land, although members of the middle class purchased a smaller percentage.

As noted, the war deepened the financial and other burdens on all major segments of Russian society and hastened the onset of revolution (historians disagree about whether or not a revolution would have occurred without the war, an unanswerable question). Regardless, some of the post-emancipation institutions put in place, with the best of intentions, by the tsarist regime played a role in the onset of the February Revolution. Readers may recall the network of local elected government organizations set up by the government after emancipation. These locally elected councils, known as *zemstvos* (land councils), had responsibilities for local education, health care, road and bridge maintenance and so forth. Simultaneously, a similar network took shape in cities and towns, where they were known as city Dumas (*gorodskaia duma*). Both networks collected taxes from local populations, functioned vigorously, and contributed significantly to the modernization of late tsarist society. Regardless, they had no authority over national policy—they were sternly restricted to local governance. Both networks hired many tens of thousands of educated individuals, men and women, of various occupations (doctors, feldshers, teachers, statisticians, lawyers, accountants, and many others) that could contribute to the councils' missions. By nature, such individuals were members of the Russian intelligentsia, educated people dedicated to improving the lot of laboring people, peasants and workers. Both networks, and especially the rural *zemstvos*, also served as sites of revolutionary propaganda and activity.

With the war's outbreak late summer of 1914, Russia found itself struggling on an enormous front that stretched from the Baltic to the Black Sea.[6] Her enemies included imperial Germany, the Austro-Hungarian Empire, and the Ottoman Empire. Maintaining the front, especially against the Germans, proved arduous. The Russian military effort proved inadequate, especially against imperial Germany, although the regime did succeed in establishing stable fronts after territorial losses. The government's focus on defending the military fronts themselves caused a drastic shortage of the infrastructure—personnel, equipment, and facilities behind the fronts—necessary to sustain the front itself. *Zemstvos* and urban Dumas on the home front voluntarily pitched in to help produce medical supplies, uniforms and ammunition. Even so, the armed forces continued to prove unable to set up and maintain a proper network of medical clinics, recuperation facilities, and dining halls behind the fronts. The gap was filled, again on a voluntary basis, by an enormous (and largely unstudied) network of facilities built and maintained by the *zemstvo*-city duma network, known in Russian as *zemgor* organizations (as noted above, in Russian a duma was called *gorodskaia duma* or city duma, thus *zemgor* or land-city organizations). These institutions found their personnel by means of voluntary service on the part of individuals qualified to perform the necessary tasks, especially medical personnel, cooks, and so forth. *Zemgor* personnel wore special uniforms and became an integral part of Russia's war effort. Unfortunately for the tsarist regime, this signified that many tens of thousands of individuals not friendly to the regime labored just behind the fronts and had the widest, most prolonged contact with Russia's millions of front soldiers, mostly peasants. Russia's soldiers had every reason to resent the regime that caused them such hardship: by 1916 the army commanders were aware of the anti-government propaganda among soldiers in *zemgor* institutions just behind the fronts but there was little they could do to correct the situation: arrested *zemgor* personnel were quickly replaced by new cadres just as hostile to the regime. By early 1917, Russia's fronts and urban garrisons contained millions of armed (mostly peasant) soldiers who were ripe for revolution.[7] The revolutionary disorders that began among workers and students in Petrograd (and elsewhere) in late February 1917 immediately won armed support from Russia's peasant soldiers, whether at the front or in urban garrisons. The tsarist regime fell and Russia's revolutions had begun.

By the time of the revolution, the question of agrarian reforms occupied a prominent place in most political parties' programs. The Stolypin reforms and the outbreak of the First World War spurred political parties to work out comprehensive and detailed programs and tactics in order to attract peasant support. During the February 1917 Revolution, the Provisional *Duma* Committee, representing liberal forces, acting with the agreement of the newly formed Petrograd Soviet, a body reflecting the interests of workers and soldiers and consisting mostly of socialists, formed the Provisional Government. This government was initially dominated by the Constitutional Democrats (Cadets), a party representing the educated upper middle classes, which desired constitutional government, as its title suggests. On March 3, the Provisional Government issued its first declaration, which proclaimed political freedom and the abolition of hereditary and estate privileges. Back in 1905, the Cadets had also advocated land seizures from nobles and land allocations to peasants in private or communal possession, depending on the local conditions. After the February Revolution, the party changed its agrarian program, which many members felt had been too radical. Now the party wanted to address the land question on the basis of recognition of property rights in order to benefit all interested groups (readers should keep in mind that on the contrary peasants wanted all noble and state lands). The Cadets now rejected the idea of land confiscation, which, they believed, would violate the principles of an economic and social system based on private ownership (capitalism). As proponents of capitalist development, the Cadets defended all agricultural productive structures, regardless of who owned them, nobles, peasants, or middle class. The party pushed for legal regulations of land tenure and ownership and the expansion of agricultural credit. It supported cooperatives and other measures that would stimulate agriculture. The Cadets, however, could not attract the majority of peasants, mainly because they supported the continuation of fighting in the First World War and, fatally, now opposed confiscation of the nobles' land.

In this respect, peasants tended to support socialist parties, primarily SRs and to a lesser extent the Marxist Social Democrats. SRs had formed as a party shortly after 1900 on the basis of bringing together members and followers of the previous populist parties of the 1860s–1880s, Russia's earliest revolutionaries. The populists had always advocated a revolution carried out by the peasants and the intelligentsia, and a transfer of all land to the peasants. SRs, under the leadership of its chief theoretician, Victor Chernov, himself the descendant of former serfs, worked out a program that called for a revolution carried out by three main groups—the peasants, the workers, and the intelligentsia. All land would go to the peasants and factories would belong to the workers. After the war broke out, SRs split into moderate and radical wings: the moderate wing (Right SRs) supported the government in the war and gradually softened its program as regards land confiscation, whereas the radicals (Left SRs) called for a revolution to overthrow the tsarist regime during the war. They also maintained their radical program on land confiscation and redistribution. By the time of the outbreak of the First World War, the Marxist Social Democrats had also long split into two groups. The moderate Mensheviks, many of whom supported Russia's war effort, felt that temporary cooperation with liberal middle classes would hasten a revolution and a gradual move toward socialism later. Their program espoused seizing noble lands and passing them to the control of local government bodies, an approach that had little appeal for peasants who wanted the land immediately. The radical Marxists, the Bolsheviks under the leadership of V. I. Lenin, like the Left SRs, wanted an immediate revolution and an end to the war. Unlike the Left SRs, the Bolsheviks espoused nationalization of all land, an approach which, like that of the Mensheviks, did not resonate among peasants. It should be noted that Marxists (both wings) by definition favored industrial workers as the basis of a revolution and expected little of the peasantry.

Initially, that is, just after the February Revolution, the peasants supported moderate socialists (mostly Right SRs) who were willing to compromise with the middle classes and the party that represented the middle classes, that is, the Constitutional Democrats. When it became clear that the moderates favored continuing the war and maintaining current land ownership practices, peasants, workers, and radical members of the intelligentsia gradually shifted their support to radical socialists, such as the Bolsheviks (the branch of the Marxist Social Democrats led by Lenin), and the Left SRs, who called for an immediate halt to the war and passing all land to the peasants. Thus, the Provisional Government, where the Constitutional Democrats had initially prevailed, quickly began to lose whatever broad popular support it had. For peasants, the central issue was always the land. The tensions and struggles that arose as regards the peasants throughout the first revolutionary year, as chronicled in the balance of this chapter, always revolved around this crucial issue.

In March 1917, the Provisional Government nationalized only the royal family land and introduced its first resolution regarding the land question that reflected the moderate position of the Cadets. The resolution recognized that the land question was foremost and that it would be the primary one at the upcoming Constituent Assembly. The government believed that all major decisions regarding land should be approved by the Constituent Assembly. The government's intention to maintain the inviolability of private land ownership until the Constituent Assembly was supported by most parties, except the Bolsheviks and Left SRs. Regardless, the Constitutional Democrats now supported the inviolability of private property, not a position likely to attract peasants.

Meanwhile, across much of Russia peasants began to seize the land of large noble estates. Peasants resorted to squatting, arson, and other attacks. The government decided to use force against the rebellious peasants and in the spring of 1917 sent troops to 20 counties. However, the soldiers did not use their weapons; their role was mainly to protect the estates and discourage peasants from attacking landlords' property. The government insisted that seizures could not resolve the land question. The Main Committee of the All-Russian Peasant Union, an organization that had had some popularity among peasants during the 1905–1907 era, issued an appeal, "To all peasants," widely published in leading newspapers. The appeal stated that the union encouraged farmers to support the new government, its commissioners and all public organizations recognized by the Provisional Government, and advised peasants to avoid attacks on other people's property and freedom. The Peasant Union strongly urged peasants to avoid the use of violence. These positions had the effect of delegitimizing the Union in the eyes of the peasantry, who wanted rapid revolutionary results. The Provisional Government ordered the Minister of Agriculture, the Cadet A. I. Shingarev, to develop propositions regarding the land matter. In April the ministry established land committees—the chief committee, provincial, district, and, at the request of peasants, village-level committees, which would take over noble land for later disposition. This moderate program, however, also did not attract broad peasant support. The government's agrarian program was supported mostly by the members of cooperatives, the Popular Socialists (a moderate offshoot of SRs) and the Trudoviks (a moderate group, also an offshoot of SRs) that arose in connection with the Duma which attempted to represent peasant interests; in June these two groups merged into a single party: the Labor Popular Socialists and provided political leadership for the All-Russian Peasant Union. By this time, however, the weight of peasant support was shifting to the left, leaving the new party and the Peasant Union with little influence. With each month, as the war continued and the land issue had not been solved, peasant support steadily shifted leftward.

Entering into the 1917 revolution, the Party of SRs was the most influential among peasants. SRs agreed with the Cadets on postponing the question of the inviolability of private land ownership until the Constituent Assembly and rejected force in resolving the issue of land tenure. Even so, SRs wanted to act in the interests of socialism and to struggle against bourgeois-proprietary principles. They believed that all arable lands under cultivation should belong to the working rural population. The party's views, worked out early in the 1900s by Victor Chernov, the grandson of a serf, echoed the ideas of the commune, labor, traditions, and forms of life of the Russian peasantry, especially, the almost universal peasant belief that the land "belonged to no one" and the right to use it belonged to these who worked it. SRs advocated a program called "land socialization," that is, the withdrawal of land from market circulation and turning it into public property—in reality, for exclusive use by those who worked it. According to the SR program, the land should be transferred for administrative purposes to local governments, that is, democratically organized rural and urban communities.

In light of this long held program, the March 1917 Regional Petrograd SR Conference advocated the abolition of private ownership of land and its transfer to the working people. But the conference avoided SRs' previous slogan— confiscation of the landed estates without compensation. Anticipating the development of a spontaneous peasant initiative from below, the conference's resolution condemned in advance any attempt to seize privately owned lands. According to the resolution, the land issue could only be resolved through legislation and the Constituent Assembly. The Petrograd Regional Conference position on the land issue was supported by the Moscow and other provincial SR conferences.

In April 1917, an All-Russian Congress of Soviets adopted the Social Revolutionary resolution on the land question, which called for confiscation of land without compensation.[8] Delegates demanded the termination of all land transactions, including purchases, sales, donations and pledge of land and the termination of peasant separations from communes (an anti-Stolypin measure). At this point, the Bolshevik party, which would take power in October 1917, had no real agrarian program. Only at its April 1917 conference did the party promulgate a program, which called for immediate confiscation of all noble, state, church, and middle class land and the nationalization of all land, that is, all land would belong to the state. The Conference called for the establishment of soviets of peasants' deputies, peasants' committees, and other bodies of local self-government, which would function independently from the nobility and officials. (The rise of peasants' soviets had already begun with the collaboration of SRs.) At the conference, the party leader V. I. Lenin suggested the possibility of renting out the nationalized land and the prohibition of subleasing. But Lenin's proposal to transform all confiscated landed estates into large model farms, which would be maintained by councils of deputies from agricultural landless laborers, gave neither practical nor tangible benefits to the overwhelming majority of peasants who lived and worked on traditional peasant communes. These peasants had expected noble land to pass to them. In addition, and even more seriously, the program was unclear about the fate of peasant lands. Thus, the Bolsheviks' agrarian program gave their opponents strong grounds for criticism and accusations that they failed to understand peasant needs. At local peasant gatherings (usually congresses of local peasant soviets held during the spring of 1917 in the central provinces), the Bolsheviks were represented only by a tiny minority of delegates. Peasants' land concerns were most fully addressed in the SR agrarian program, which led to vast peasant support for that party.

Meanwhile, in April 1917 peasants virtually broke the social estate system of government. The Cadet newspapers noted that the revolution swept away institutions reflecting social estates. Peasants were implacable in their hatred for these local bodies, because they had been disenfranchised in these institutions. The Minister of Justice Alexander F. Kerensky, formerly an SR and now a member of the Trudoviks, a peasant aligned group somewhat more conservative than SRs, noted in April that the old local government institutions had disappeared without a trace to be replaced by news ones. In Vologda province, for example, most of the district committees, about 75 percent, were created solely on the initiative of the peasants themselves, whereas only 25 percent arose on the orders of officials. In other provinces the situation was similar. Spontaneity and quick change in institutions reflected the urgent yearning on the part of peasants for new government bodies in the countryside and the need for peasant self-organization. The new government, however, considered peasant committees as provisional, which should be soon replaced with newly formed *zemstvos* that would represent all social estates on proportional basis. This position was shared by all the parties, except the Bolsheviks and Left SRs, although a number of peasant congresses spoke against these new *zemstvos*, fearing the reestablishment of nobles' authority.

Peasant county executive committees were officially nonpartisan, although many members had sympathies for SRs, and proceeded to take the initiative in reorganizing local rural life and politics. In March–May 1917, peasants of the central provinces of Russia engaged in conflict with landowners more than 1780 times. The Provisional Government wanted land disputes to be settled in mediatory chambers, where the landowners still had an advantage over the peasants. Naturally, peasants did not trust these chambers. Landowners complained to the Provisional Government that peasant committees considered themselves to be the supreme executive authority, appointed by the revolution. On their orders, land, meadows and forests were taken away from landowners, which eliminated rents and would quickly bankrupt the landowner. The committees' actions were directed not only against landlords from the nobility, but also against the kulaks, wealthy villagers, and individual settlers (persons with separated land holdings under Stolypin reforms). In March–May 1917, most peasant committees approved decisions of enforced rent of land and fixed rent prices. Formally, these actions did not abolish private ownership of land, but eventually significantly limited it. Peasant committees controlled the land market and tried to prevent land accumulation in the hands of rich peasants (the kulaks) in favor of passing it into the possession of poor and middle peasant. They also prohibited land transfer to large-holding tenants. This constituted an attack on private land ownership, carried out allegedly because the revolutionary state need to expand the acreage of cultivated land in a situation in which private land owners often refused to plow and sow all their land. However, many committees pursued policies that placed landowners in a situation in which they could not cultivate all their land. For example, peasant committees prohibited the use of hired workers, requisitioned agricultural tools, and then seized the land of these private landowners who, deprived of tools and workers, could not plow their land in a timely fashion. The committees did not acknowledge that their actions toward private farmers contradicted the requirement of the Provisional Government to plow all fallow land.

The Provisional Government attempted to resist the policies of the peasant committees. In May 1917, new Minister of Agriculture, Cadet A. I. Shingarev, called for all district and village peasant to prevent any violence against the property of local landowners, villagers, and peasants. The Interior Minister Prince G. E. Lvov issued a circular to the provincial commissioners, stating that the committees' decisions that in effect restricted the rights of land owners were unacceptable. In June 1917, the interior minister suggested that the Provisional Government needed to introduce an executive order entirely banning local peasant committees. However, the government, fearing the peasants' reaction to such a ban, refrained from dissolving organs of local peasant self-government.

The rural policies of the Cadets in the Provisional Government were mostly supported by the Menshevik and SR leadership of the Petrograd Soviet. Peasant committees customarily turned to the Soviet when they needed assistance and help. For example, in June 1917, a committee that represented the poor peasants of a village in Vologda province, most of whom lived by renting lands, asked the Soviet about what legal policies it could pursue in order to plow and sow privately owned lands. The Soviet responded in this and many similar cases that the rights of private owners should not be violated and that peasants must pay rent until the Constituent Assembly reached its decisions on the land. In a way, this revealed the desire of peasant committees to follow a lawful path. It clearly reflected a legal culture that had developed in the Russian countryside. The Petrograd Soviet of Workers and Soldiers Deputies condemned arbitrary seizures of landed estates as an act harmful to people's freedom and made it clear that the land, livestock, equipment, buildings belonged to the owners since neither the Provisional Government nor the Soviet had as yet abolished private property.

In their activities, peasant committees normally followed the provisions of peasant congresses that convened more and more frequently as the year progressed. In March–May 1917, twenty-nine provincial and sixty-seven district peasant congresses convened in European Russia. The congresses issued 229 land decisions during these months. Thousands of peasants attended these gatherings. For example, the Tambov provincial congress had 300 peasant delegates, the Simbirsk congress—400, the Moscow and Voronezh—600 each, and Penza, Yaroslavl, Nizhny Novgorod—1,000 peasant delegates each. All these conventions, with the exception of one county (Shlisselburg in Saint Petersburg province), supported the Provisional Government and the SR-Menshevik idea that the land tenure and ownership questions should be settled at the Constituent Assembly. Nevertheless, peasant farmers unanimously demanded the confiscation of the treasury, crown, church, monastery, and landlords' land without compensation. Via peasant provincial and local congresses, communal peasants determined the system of transitional measures for land utilization that peasant committees should follow until land laws were enacted by the Constituent Assembly. While retaining private property rights, transitional measures adopted at these congresses restricted land utilization by the nobility and large landowners. Peasant committees were charged with locating and recording unused lands and supervising the renting out of these lands to local needy peasants. These measures also set fixed rent prices on land, approximately ¼ of the prewar rate. Peasant congresses forbade all transactions involving purchase or sale of land, regulated employment, and distributed war prisoners, who were sent to agricultural work. In general, the transitional measures adopted by the Congress of Peasants' Soviets, reflected the aspirations of peasant communes.

In May 1917, peasants convened their first all-Russian congress, represented by 1,353 delegates from 70 provinces and regions of Russia. Most delegates identified themselves as SRs (537); there were also 136 nonpartisan delegates, 103 Mensheviks and 20 Bolsheviks, confirming, as mentioned above, that the

Socialist Revolutionary Party enjoyed the widest support from the peasantry, although it should be noted that not a few of SRs were leftists. In political matters, the Congress followed the Right SRs, expressing confidence in the Provisional Government and support for war effort. Regarding the land question, two trends developed: one, radical left, which reflected the ideas and aspirations of the lower segments, poor peasants and soldiers, and the second, liberal-reformist, which reflected the interests of peasant land owners. The left trend demanded that the All-Russian Peasant Soviet or the All-Russian Soviet of Workers, Soldiers and Peasants immediately transfer all the land to the peasants, which, they thought, the Constituent Assembly would later formalize by law. This demand, however, was unacceptable for the Congress's SR leadership because on May 6 they entered the Provisional Government in a coalition with the Cadets and feared that any such radical move would destroy this coalition. Many peasant delegates wondered why the congress could not nationalize the land immediately. Their main argument was that most owners land had enormous bank debts and would not be able to retain their land in any case. Their opponents, however, insisted that land nationalization would undermine the economy of the country and the credibility of Russia abroad. The leader of SRs, V. M. Chernov, argued that neither the Peasant Congress nor the Provisional Government had the power to abolish private property; only the Constituent Assembly could take this step.

As a result, the congress approved a compromise resolution. The resolution confirmed that the land question be settled at the Constituent Assembly and without exception all lands were placed under the jurisdiction of the local land committees, in effect, although not in word, legitimizing land seizures. These land committees were given broad authority over cultivation, seeding, harvesting, mowing the meadows, and the like, as well as the right to manage all agricultural machinery, tools, horses, and so forth on a voluntary and cooperative basis. The committees were also given the right to regulate the leasing of land, control the harvesting and storage of grain, etc., as well as exercising control over prohibition of purchase, sale, donation, transfer and bequest of land until the Constituent Assembly. The second most important decision of the All-Russian Congress of Peasants was the adoption of "Regulations on the Soviets of Peasants' Deputies." According to these regulations, the Congress gave the peasant soviets the right to protect the interests of peasant farmers and to represent them in government and public organizations. Among the tasks delegated to the peasant soviets were the implementation of measures that could be put into effect before the Constituent Assembly, preparation of the peasantry for the Constituent Assembly elections, control over the actions and monitoring of the authorities, so that they would not depart from democratic principles, and the representation of peasant interests in all government and public institutions. By mid-July, the Soviets of Peasants' Deputies were organized in 50 provinces and 371 districts throughout Russia. Most of these soviets were led by SRs.

The new coalition in the Provisional Government abolished the Stolypin land management committees in June 28, 1917. All their cases were transferred to the jurisdiction of the newly created land committees, associated with the Provisional Government's ministry of agriculture led by Victor Chernov, the most prominent SR leader. In July 1917, the government prohibited transactions involving the purchase or sale of land until the Constituent Assembly. Nevertheless, in many instances, peasants continued to seize land, especially if the land had not been cultivated by the current owners. Having secured support (for the time being) of the Peasant Soviets, the Provisional Government unleashed a campaign against unsanctioned seizures of land. Already on July 17, the interim minister of internal affairs, the Menshevik Irakli Tsereteli, sent out a circular letter with the requirement to maintain the integrity of the land fund and immediately stop the arbitrary actions of the land committees. Tsereteli demanded that Provisional Government commissioners strengthen the fight against peasant arbitrariness and follow strictly the policy of the government in preventing seizures of property and land.

When peasants in the communes realized that it was virtually impossible to induce the Provisional Government to release unused land to peasants, they shifted their attitudes to the left, which signified growing support for the Left SRs (the left wing of the Socialist Revolutionary Party) and, to a lesser degree, the Bolsheviks. Thus, in June–August 1917, 34 provincial and district congresses of peasants demanded immediate land transfers to peasant land committees. The Minister of Justice Pavel Pereverzev, a moderate SR, became concerned about the rise of peasant organized and politicized activism and noted that this activism hardly coincided with the government's intentions. The ministry estimated that in June–July, 46 percent of peasant actions (regarding land and so forth) were organized, and the growth of their organization was influenced by the peasant congresses which wanted to expedite the solution of the agrarian question, without waiting for the Constituent Assembly convention.

In the meantime, facing new challenges, Russia's landowners from all social segments began to consolidate their efforts in order to protect their interests. The idea of creating a landowners' union arose as early as 1906, but at that time it did not receive support from landowners. After the February Revolution, a charter of the newly formed All-Russian Union of Land Owners reflected a broad-minded spirit in that all landowners, regardless of the size of their private property, religion, and so forth, were eligible for membership. In May 1917, the Cadets organized a founding congress of the All-Russian Union of Land Owners and Farmers. The union represented former noble landowners, farmers, individual settlers, tenants, and other categories of land owners from thirty-one provinces of Russia. The purpose of the union was clear: to protect the interests of private property as an indispensable part of the state system. Although the initiative for the creation of the union came from the nobility, most of its members by the summer of 1917 were proprietors-farmers. The union also had its local organizations. It convened local congresses, where most delegates were peasants. At the Saratov congress, for example, of 150 attendees, 135 were peasant farmers, mostly of above-average size farms. Peasant farmers also dominated the management of the local unions.

A considerable part of individual peasant farmers (as opposed to commune members) joined the landowners' union. The unions' branches typically filed petitions and complaints to the government, requesting protection of their interests as landowners from the actions of land committees. For example, by September 15, in Penza province there were 456 land violations, of which 307 were against peasants landowners. At the orders of land committees, peasant communal committees seized from noble landlords and rich peasants (kulaks) 25 percent of arable land, 45 percent of forests and 49 percent of meadows, reaching a sum of 285,600 acres. The cost of landowners' loss was estimated at 1,288,567 rubles. At the same time, 35 percent of losses belonged to well-to-do peasant farmers. Although the actions of land committees affected less than 1 percent of villagers and individual settlers, the fear of losing their land pushed the majority of them to unite with noble landlords. In June 1917, the union of landowners of Penza province included 350 large landowners and more than 10,000 individual peasant farmers. Peasant landowners were the majority of the union members in Samara, Kazan, Simbirsk, Smolensk, and other provinces of the European part of Russia and in the Ukraine. Most delegates of congresses of the local Union of Land Owners were peasants, who possessed from about 121 to 405 acres of land and operated strong capitalist farms. They rejected the agrarian program of the socialists and advocated instead the Cadet program. But these Stolypin peasant farmers were in the minority.

In May 1917, SRs confirmed the immutability of the main provisions of their long-term agrarian program, which included the abolition of private ownership of land, the confiscation of the landlords' land, the equalizing redistribution of land, and the prohibition of hired labor, rent, etc. These principles formed the basis for the party's agricultural reforms. The Cadets firmly maintained their original premise: the protection of private property as the foundation of the country's economy. Meanwhile, the Bolsheviks, who had never had a strong peasant following, began to promote the idea of immediate land seizures by peasants. At the same time, the left wing of SRs, the Left SRs, began to advocate the organized seizure (that is, by local soviets or other local committees) of land (as opposed to individual seizures advocated by the Bolsheviks) from nobles and wealthy middle-class landowners for use by peasants until the Constituent Assembly. These party disparities and tensions prevented reaching agreements on both the main and specific matters in land reform legislation.

In late August 1917, during the famous monarchist rebellion of General L. G. Kornilov, the Chief Land Committee held its third conference. In a special resolution, the conference expressed its firm opposition to "counter-revolutionary attacks." Delegates called for alterations in "indecisive" government policy regarding land relations. In its closing session, the representatives of the land committees affirmed that the situation in the countryside was desperate and that the country was edging toward civil war. From January to October 1917, there were over 15,000 incidents of peasant unrest and insurrections in European Russia, including 3,500 in Central Russia during September–October, 1670 uprisings in the Volga provinces, and 1349 in the central non-black-earth region. Especially in the Volga region and South Russia, landowners initiated an armed campaign to retake land seized by peasants, which naturally further heightened the atmosphere of conflict.

The autumn period witnessed a sharp change in peasants' actions. If from March through August, peasants used various economic means to attain their goals but often respected private ownership of noble and *kulak* land, in the fall, peasants routinely used violence, armed seizures, beatings, arson and terror. A tragic event occurred in the village Sychevka of Tambov province in September, which ignited peasant resistance verging on peasant war. Earlier, the local SRs managed to keep the peasants from lootings and seizures of landed estates. But on September 7 in the village, guards hired by "kulak" Romanov wounded two peasants who had trespassed on his property. As a response, local peasants ransacked and burned Romanov's estate and killed Romanov himself. The next night, peasants set fire to landed estates in all neighboring villages. Within a week, the disturbances had spread to fourteen counties of the province. As a result, seventy landed estates were destroyed. More than 30 percent of the victims of this violence were peasant landowners. The district commissioner reported to the police and authorities, specifying that the violence was caused by the unclear land policies of the government which produced a fear among peasants that they would not receive the land. In September–October, there were 193 peasant insurgencies in Tambov province alone, of which 136 resulted in the devastation of estates. The Tambov events had wide implications. Provincial and county commissioners from Ryazan, Voronezh, Tula, Orel, Penza, Saratov, Nizhny Novgorod, and other provinces reported to the ministry of internal affairs that the peasant movement had expanded under the influence of the Tambov events, as well as because of the general discontent with the agrarian and food policies of the Provisional Government. The reports affirmed a strong peasant move to the left politically and asserted that as the peasant movement grew, it became nearly impossible to suppress it. The ministry recommended the use of police and military forces. The peasant uprisings eventually spread to 79 counties of several provinces in Central Russia. In a sense, this manifested a revolt of the poor peasants. It destroyed the private property not only of landlords but of well-to-do peasants: the same rage was shown against both. Pogroms aimed at individual settlers and peasant proprietors were particularly widespread in the Volga provinces, where peasant violence aimed at landlords and rich peasant farmers. Peasants organized themselves into fighting armed squads. In response, local land owners' unions appealed to the Provisional Government for help.

In September, the government introduced some measures aimed at coping with peasant insurgencies, including strengthening local police forces, increasing funding for the local police, and expanding the number of combat officers. The government considered a draft resolution to give provincial commissars (a term initiated by the Provisional Government and later widely used by the Communists) extraordinary power to deal with the revolutionary outbreaks in the countryside. The government declared that all local power should be concentrated in hands of the Provisional Government commissars. On October 20, the government approved a resolution proposed by the Mensheviks to create "committees of public organizations" for consolidated measures against the revolutionary movement in the countryside. In September–October, military force against peasants was used 112 times in the central provinces. The new government of revolutionary Russia was waging war against the revolution. Regardless, soldiers, most of whom were themselves of peasant origins, increasingly refused to shoot at the peasants and often deserted to their side (repeating what had happened during the last months of the tsarist regime). Thus, among peasants, as among other mass social groups, a sociopolitical background for another revolution had been prepared.

Suggested readings

Badcock, Sarah et al., eds. *Russia's Revolution in Regional Perspective, 1914–1921.* Bloomington, IN: Slavica Press, 2015.

Pallot, Judith. *Land Reform in Russia, 1906–1917.* Oxford: Clarendon Press, 1999.

Retish, Aaron B. *Russia's Peasants in Revolution and Civil War: Citizenship, Identity, and the Creation of the Soviet State, 1914–1922.* Cambridge: Cambridge University Press, 2008.

Realpolitik: From the Red Terror to the New Economic Policy

Figure 12.1 Armed Tambov peasants as a part of resistance to the Bolshevik government.

The Bolshevik rise to power in October 1917 had dramatic consequences for the Russian countryside and the peasantry. The Bolsheviks' War Communism policy, conducted from 1918 to 1921, led to strong dissatisfaction with the new government among much of the population and, ultimately, civil conflict. The forceful food requisitioning campaign in the grain-producing areas led to mass starvation, high mortality, immense homelessness among children, and armed resistance in the countryside. In the end, in order to preserve and consolidate their power, the Bolsheviks were forced to end this course in 1921, and to announce the start of the New Economic Policy (NEP). War Communism itself began in the spring of 1918 and, according to one of its initiators, the Chairman of the Council of Peoples Commissars, V. I. Lenin, was a measure necessary to deal with the various economic crises that arose after the Bolsheviks' assumption of power. This policy was in fact logical and normal from the Bolshevik point of view, arising from their widely articulated goals. The civil war that resulted from the policies of War Communism contributed to the further development of the idea that War Communism was a desirable set of measures, given the reality of civil opposition: in other words, these developments fed on and intensified one another. This chapter will recount the principal events of the October Revolution and its immediate aftermath focusing on issues of significance for the peasantry and will then explore in detail the situation in the countryside during War Communism (1918–1921) and NEP (1921–1928), a set of policies that marked a sharp retreat from War Communism.

The Second Congress of Soviets, long delayed by the moderate SRs and Mensheviks, who feared radicalized local soviets would send leftist delegates to the congress and shift power at the center to radicals, finally opened on October 25, 1917, a fateful day in Russian and world history. The congress's makeup indeed differed sharply from that of the First Congress (Spring 1917) with its enormous moderate SR and Menshevik majorities. This time the Bolshevik and Left SR delegations, who often cooperated closely, outweighed the previously predominant SR-Menshevik bloc. For purposes of this study, the major issue is that the 2nd Congress, voting along party lines, overthrew the Provisional Government and proclaimed Soviet power. Some Bolsheviks and the Left SRs had considerable reservations about the sharpness of the break between themselves and the moderate socialists but, as the saying goes, the die was cast and, with incalculable results, Russia entered into a new phase of the revolution. On the whole, Russian society had few regrets about the passing of the Provisional Government, whose inaction had worn out its welcome, and yet none of the post-February 27 exuberance broke out at this point. Even workers and soldiers maintained silence. The Left SRs joined several prominent Bolsheviks in a prolonged attempt to induce Bolshevik leaders to compromise with the moderate socialists to create an "all-socialist" government, a position espoused by almost all workers, soldiers, peasants, and radical intelligentsia: the popular slogan of the day was *odnorodnoe sotsialisticheskoe pravitel'stvo* (a government of all socialists). The reluctance of Lenin and the moderate socialists to form an all-socialist bloc government (by this time, the two sides were quite hostile to one another) defeated this effort, after which the Left SRs, who had a large following in many soviets, joined the Bolsheviks in the new government in a minority position. The Left SRs' main goal was to head the Commissariat (the new revolutionary term for Ministry) for Agriculture, which they achieved, along with several other posts of varying significance. With these plans in mind, the Left SRs finally split from the main SR Party, which adamantly opposed the new government.

The new government head, V. I. Lenin, quickly proceeded to issue two new decrees of vast significance for the peasantry. He issued the Decree on Land, which nationalized all land but otherwise closely followed the SR land program in allowing the peasants to subdivide and utilize land along lines suitable to them. He also declared an armistice at the front, effectively ending the war for Russia, although the actual peace treaty was signed several months later. The result was that millions of peasant soldiers abandoned the fronts and internal garrisons to return to their villages for the great land subdivision (in Russian, *velikii peredel*) centuries in the waiting. These two measures for the first (and last) time won considerable support for the Bolsheviks among the peasantry, who still showed primary allegiance to their long-term preference—the SRs, Left or Right.

Of note is that the 2nd Congress of Soviets that brought the Bolsheviks (and Left SRs) to power was entirely a workers' and soldiers' affair, although, of course, most soldiers and many workers were peasants. The Congress of Peasant Soviets, which convened in Petrograd during November, shortly after the workers' and soldiers' congress, witnessed an epic struggle between the Right SRs under Victor Chernov's leadership, and the Left SRs, whose principal spokesperson was Maria Spiridonova, who in 1906 had shot a general responsible for a punitive expedition against the peasantry. Released from hard labor in Siberia by the February Revolution, she won enormous popularity among laboring classes in Russia. The forces supporting Chernov and Spiridonova at the congress were almost even, although the leftists had a few more votes, leading the moderate wing under Chernov's leadership to abandon the congress. The Left SRs then led the peasant soviets to unify with the workers and soldiers soviets at the national level. Given Russia's demographics, this seemed to put the peasants in a leading position in the new revolutionary state. Left SRs then entered the Soviet government and, as noted, assumed the Commissariat for Agriculture and other posts along with the predominant Communists (post-October the Bolsheviks adopted the term "Communists" as correctly representing their identity).

Later in November 1917, the long-awaited Constituent Assembly elections occurred, with massive participation and results that also seemed to bode well for the peasants—and the moderate wing of the SRs. The SRs swept most rural constituencies, while the Communists did very well in cities. Notable was the collapse of support for the Mensheviks, whose earlier heavy worker support had shifted to the Communists. Russia's liberals, the Constitutional Democrats, saw their support delimited to wealthy urban areas—they had failed to identify significant worker, peasant, or intelligentsia constituencies. Regardless, the moderate SRs, under Chernov's leadership, would have a solid majority of seats at the body that all major political forces had awaited as the ultimate arbiter of Russia's political future. In reality, the SR victory was not as solid as it seemed. The party's local election lists had been compiled long before the SR-Left SR split, so that peasants had voted for "SR" delegates, without being able to choose between Right and Left SRs. Election results to peasants soviet throughout Russia during late summer and fall showed that, if they had a choice, they would often support Left SRs over moderate SRs as shown by the peasant soviet congress during November. These and other realities of revolutionary Russia during late 1917 and early 1918 did not bode well for the SRs and the long-awaited Constituent Assembly, which opened under Victor Chernov's chairmanship early in the new year of 1918. It had one session, during which it began to draw up SR-oriented agrarian legislation for the new state, and then was shut down on Lenin's orders by armed guards. The message was clear: Soviet Russia would not be guided by "outmoded" standards of liberalism.

Immediately after the closing of the Constituent Assembly, the Third Congress of Workers, Soldiers, and Peasants Soviets opened. Its goal was to serve as a symbolic replacement for the Constituent Assembly and to write a new land law reflecting the ideals of the two parties in power, the Communists and Left SRs. Negotiations at the congress and behind the scenes were tense: Lenin's Land Decree had compromised by granting peasants the right to dispose of nationalized land as they wished; regardless, many Communists were not happy with this arrangement and strived to increase state control over land, agriculture, and, ultimately, the peasants. Even so, the Left SRs maneuvered in such a way that they were able to formulate the new land law entirely in the SR spirit, which granted peasants almost complete leeway in land utilization. The Left SRs felt that this would ensure peasant support for them and allow them to govern at least on an equal basis with the Communists.

During the brief Left SR-Communist (peasant-worker) honeymoon that ensued, peasants across Russia, with the involvement of local Left SRs, Communists, and Anarchists hastened to divide up the enormous noble, middle-class, state, and church lands among peasants. Peasants could utilize this land in traditional redistributional communes, pure communes (all members worked all the land in common and divided the proceeds equally), and even as private farmers (continuing the Stolypin reform), and so forth. The Left SRs were enthusiastic backers of communal farming of all types and spoke of new Soviet Russia as a "vast commune from the Baltic to the Black Sea." But they also felt that it was improper to force land policies on peasants: thus the survival of individual farmers, to which the Communists were deeply opposed. How all of this might have turned out under different circumstances is impossible to say, but the reality was that the severe economic crisis of 1917, abetted by the continuing war until November, and then worsened by Communist policies of nationalizing banks, transportation, fuel, industry, and large-scale commerce, led to rampant inflation, severe crop shortages, and the beginnings of hunger in the cities. By April, all other efforts having failed, the Leninist government urged workers to form armed groups to go out into the countryside to seize grain, not a policy that encouraged good relations with the peasants (see below for further discussion). Leninist policies as regards food seizures led to sharp disputes with their uneasy partners in the government, the Left SRs, who bitterly opposed these and other Leninist measures. By late spring 1918, the Left SRs left the government, hoping that mass peasant support for them would ultimately bring them back into the government on an at least equal basis with the Communists. Freed from Left SR constraints, Lenin announced the "food dictatorship," which set low extremely prices for grain and made any normal city-countryside relationship impossible (see below).

The final state-level Left SR-Communist confrontation came at the Fifth Congress of Soviets in early July 1918. (The Fourth Congress in April had met to vote on the Brest-Litovsk Peace Treaty with Germany, which the Left SRs opposed because of its exceptionally harsh terms toward Russia). Based upon data from local soviets, the Left SRs believed they would have a majority at the Congress. As the congress opened, the Left SRs carried out the assassination of the German ambassador to Soviet Russia, in the hopes that this would break the Brest-Litovsk Treaty, which was extremely unpopular in Russia (they also banked on Germany's defeat at the hands of the Western allies). Nothing turned out as planned: the Communists invited extra (illegal) delegates to the congress to ensure their majority; Germany did not reopen hostilities; and the Communists arrested the entire Left SR delegation, including Maria Spiridonova, and called for all soviets throughout Russia to expel Left SRs. The one-party state, in reality much preferred by Lenin, had arisen. Now unhindered by Left SRs, the Fifth Soviet Congress introduced the policy of the "committees of the poor" in the villages, designed to organize the poorest peasants and local Communists, who would then seize all grain in the possession of peasants. This disastrous policy, to be further analyzed below, led to open conflict between the state and the peasantry, starvation in the countryside, and many other problems. One might call it, "just letting the Bolsheviks be Bolsheviks."

Prior to the revolution, Bolshevism, like Marxism itself, had been vague about what society and the economy would be like after the revolution. They believed that the expropriation of capital would ultimately create a classless society, but provided little detail about the road to this ideal society. Even so, it would be wrong to assume that the Bolshevik Party was solely Marxist in its ideology. The ideology of Bolshevism in power was a mixture of Marxism, Leninism, and realpolitik. That is, ideologically the new Bolshevik government desired to create a state according to their vision of Marxist-Leninist ideals, but, when push came to shove, it followed the methods of realpolitik in order to maintain power. The Bolsheviks believed that they would be able to create a functioning nonmarket society, although no such economy had existed in the modern world. These beliefs reflected their ideals. In order to achieve the ideals, it turned out that they needed terror, repression, and a certain set of conditions: the total submission of the state to their will, the concentration of power solely in their hands, and total control over all state institutions and resources. These became their realpolitik instruments. All too often Bolshevik realpolitik prevailed over Marxist-Leninist ideology, which sometimes seemed to serve primarily to obscure the actual (realpolitik) harsh policies. After the October Revolution, the new government began to implement their policies immediately. They took under control not only the sphere of production, but also consumption. War Communism policies, aspects of which in reality began immediately after the October Revolution or during the spring of 1918 before serious civil conflict had begun, included the nationalization of private enterprise and banks, the introduction of the food dictatorship, the abolition of free trade, and the introduction of compulsory labor. All of this produced a sharp reaction among broad population segments. Thus it was that precisely War Communism set in motion the civil war and vice versa: War Communism deepened civil conflict which ultimately culminated in civil war, with government, state, and party melded into a single entity waging war against much of the population. But the policies failed to function and immediately met popular resistance; the new government then faced enormous difficulties in holding onto the power they had taken in October. Underlying this resistance were massive unemployment and galloping inflation, which quickly reached 200,000 percent, signifying that money had become worthless and that people, if they could, lived by barter. This was a genuinely unforeseen circumstance with potentially horrendous consequences: a country the size of Russia with as complicated an economy as the nation had could hardly switch to a barter system, for which there was no model in the modern age, without catastrophe. Yet, the ideology of the new government rejected private property and capital. Consequently, it rapidly nationalized private property in the realm of production and expropriated all capital using War Communism (that is, realpolitik) methods.

At the center of Bolshevik practical activities regarding the peasantry rested Lenin's understanding of the social and class structure of the Russian peasantry, that is, the idea of peasants as a class in capitalist society. Since the revolution was proletarian, according to the Bolsheviks, only the poor, that is, proletarian, semi-proletarian, and small peasant farmers, who lived completely or partly by hiring themselves, represented the base of the revolution in the village. These layers of the peasantry, especially those who hired out their labor at least part of the time, constituted a significant proportion of the village population and, in Lenin's view, after the liquidation of the landlords and rich peasants (the kulaks) these portions of the peasantry should join the side of the proletarian revolution. Even so, the Communist government figured that a small number of the peasants (kulaks) would always move in the direction of free trade, that is, to the side of the bourgeoisie. In the Bolsheviks' understanding, the kulaks were exploiters because they used hired workers. For them, the kulaks represented an element of the bourgeoisie and, it follows, were class enemies of the revolution. On the one hand, in the broadest sense for Marxists the liquidation of the kulak class was an historical mission of the socialist revolution. On the other, Friedrich Engels, Marx's close associate, had written that it would be wrong to appropriate the kulaks' property, because they also were involved in work and therefore earned part of their product by their own labor. In theory, Engels's position was shared by Lenin, but in practice Lenin did not always follow Marxism.

During 1918–1921 the government carried out forced food requisitions from peasants in order to supply cities suffering from hunger and the Red Army. This policy, known as the *prodrazverstka* (food procurement or food levy) campaign, affected primarily grain-producing black-earth soil areas—Orel, Voronezh, Tambov, and, especially, the Volga provinces.[1] Attempts to introduce a delimited version of *prodrazverstka*, in fact, had been undertaken earlier, in 1916, by the tsarist government as the means to feed the Russian Army and urban areas, although it applied only to grain. The tsarist and later the Provisional Government ministry of food supply fell short in their responsibilities to provide the army and urban areas with grain. In both cases, the respective governments attempted to combine moderate grain requisition and state grain market regulation models. Nevertheless, these earlier policies of food procurement had never been fully implemented or realized: when peasants refused to give up their grain, the respective governments simply backed down. Consequently, urban areas still experienced grain shortages throughout 1916–1917. Under the new Bolshevik government, during 1918–1920 all food supplies in the countryside become objects of procurement and, in this case, the policy was vigorously executed.

The campaign had started well before it was officially introduced in January 1919. By early 1918 rampant inflation in the face of severe shortages of all supplies and goods led to the total devaluation of the ruble. In March 1918, the government issued a decree "On the organization of exchange of goods," believing that the economy could function without money (it should be noted that there was a strong element of utopianism in this view since significant examples of this "moneyless" exchange in modern societies are lacking). In any case, no real exchange of goods between the city and the village occurred. This decree was accompanied with Commissariat for Food Supplies instructions which totally banned any sale of grain in the countryside, except for the cases when the area handed over an amount of grain that had been predetermined by the government. In such cases, peasants could exchange their surplus grain and other foodstuffs for industrial goods (presumably produced in the cities). Furthermore, the whole process of this exchange was organized in such a way that the local authorities, that is, Communist functionaries, who were in charge of *prodrazverstka* in their respective areas, received the main portion of the goods supposedly scheduled for exchange and kept them for themselves. (Images of Communists eating luxury foods—caviar, sturgeon, and other delicacies—while others starved quickly entered into the folklore of the period.) Not surprisingly, the peasant response was to hide their grain harvest and other foodstuffs from the procurement authorities. Peasants, even the poorest ones, began to sabotage the policy and used any means to retain their food. By mid-1918, it became clear that the main task of early War Communism had failed—the planned exchange of manufactured goods for food had not occurred. Moreover, the situation was further exacerbated by clear signs of famine in many cities (food supplies quickly dwindled when no new shipments arrived from the countryside). Most cities, including major ones, received only 10–15 percent of what they needed. Most people in the cities obtained bread and foodstuffs from petty traders, known as *meshochniki*, or literally "sack carriers," that is, people who travelled by any means of transportation they could find to bring grain to populated areas in hopes of exchanging it for goods. The activities of these *meshochniki* were illegal and the government considered them as "speculators," whereas in reality, they were typically independent farmers, including the poor ones, who of their own volition came to the city with their produce, which they usually exchanged for other goods. Paradoxically, the sack carriers, who in reality saved hundreds of thousands of people from starvation, became a subject of ruthless prosecution by the newly created VChK, the All Russian Extraordinary Commission to Combat Counterrevolution, Sabotage and Speculation.

When the government had realized that it was virtually impossible to obtain foodstuffs from peasants peacefully, it created (mid-summer of 1918) a special force, the brigades of *Kombedy* (committees of the poor) to supplement the already existing Food Brigades (*Prodovolstvennye otriady*), which arose several months earlier. These brigades launched real terror in the village. Formally, their activities were to be directed against the kulaks, whereas in practice their activities affected most peasants, because it was almost impossible to distinguish the rich from the poor. Most peasants in the villages were neither poor nor rich, but rather middle peasants (*seredniaki*) and most existing grain was in their possession. In May 1918, the government introduced an executive order which gave the Commissar of Food Supplies extraordinary powers to procure food in the countryside. The order prescribed that any peasant who failed to provide the required levy of food provisions was considered as *kulak*. This order was in a way a declaration of war against about 60 percent of the population, factually pushing the country toward a civil war.

In the spring of 1918, Lenin, in a letter to the Commissar for Food Supplies, wrote that "in light of the critical situation with food we must not spread our forces too thin, but concentrate them on the central provinces where it is possible to take a large amount of grain."[2] Orel, Penza, Samara, Saratov, and Tambov provinces were defined by the government as possible areas for procurements. The grain levy defined by the government was often twice as high as some areas had ever produced. For example, the grain levy for Saratov province was 31,100,000 *pud* (1 *pud* equals 16 kg), while the estimated cereal surplus of the 1918 harvest was 22,143,000 *pud*. The levy for Tambov province was 36,000,000 *pud*, whereas the estimated cereal surplus was 16,157.000 *pud*.[3] When the first grain requisition decrees were discussed in local soviets during the summer of 1918, the Bolsheviks always demanded that they be fulfilled; in the words of one local Bolshevik leader, "the requisitions must be carried out at any cost."[4] In order to pursue the goal of working out the best method of collecting grain, during late summer of 1918 the entire personnel of the Commissariat for Agriculture, under the leadership of its head S. P. Sereda, disembarked from Moscow to Orel province (to the southeast of the capital) to work out the procurement procedures.[5]

Nevertheless, in many instances, these food procuring brigades performed their duties reluctantly and were hard to control. Overall, they collected a little over 450 million kg of grain, which, within the contest of vast Russia and its large population, was very little. Additionally, corruption among the members of the brigades was widespread. They themselves often traded the procured grain on the black market (one might call them "state bagmen"). Thus, after several months of their activities, the government was already discussing a possible elimination of the food procurement brigades because they aggravated the situation. In December of 1918 the Bolshevik Party Congress eliminated the committees of the poor. The elimination of the *kombedy* was a pragmatic move. By that time, the country was plunged into civil war and, under those circumstances, the government felt that it needed to avoid the total alienation of the peasants (in reality, as future months and years would show, the new government had already alienated most peasants.)

Meanwhile the urban population suffered from starvation, disease, and compulsory labor obligations. The government policies devised to supply cities, towns, and industrial centers largely failed. In November 1918 the government introduced a new executive order "On the procurement organization." The order gave the Commissariat for Food Supplies the exclusive monopoly over food provisions, including obtaining foodstuffs and redistribution. All other food distributors were banned. This meant that any private sale of foodstuffs, including the activities of the sack carriers, became illegal and the transgressors were subjected to arrest and punishment. Their goods were confiscated in favor of the state. Meanwhile, the Commissariat for Agriculture continued its food requisitioning in Orel province, with the help of local party members, numerous armed brigades that arrived from urban areas, and local committees of poor peasants. The end result was that the province was stripped bare of grain (most of it went to feed Moscow), leaving, according to local Communist leaders, city and village in a state of starvation.

During early 1919 a congress of Food Supply and Agriculture personnel convened in Moscow and officially approved the method worked out in Orel province. This was the official state-wide procurement method used beginning in January 11, 1919, when the government introduced a decree which formally established *prodrazverstka*. This policy essentially meant the seizure of nearly all foodstuffs produced by the peasantry in exchange for manufactured city goods. As regards the so-called exchange, this was largely a dream, which in practice never came true. It was impossible to achieve the desired result in practice because of the total absence of manufactured goods: as cities starved, peasant-workers, many with ties to their villages, simply disembarked for their home villages and provinces. As bad as conditions were in the countryside, at least some food was available there. Factories either shut down or ceased producing sufficient goods to trade. In effect, industry had been almost completely destroyed within a year of the birth of the Bolshevik government and was unable to offer anything substantial to the peasantry. The peasants avoided selling grain (the only thing they possessed to keep themselves alive) and tried to hide it. Even the small amount of consumer goods officially intended for exchange with peasants remained in the hands of the members of food procuring agencies (members of committees of the poor, armed detachments from cities, and local party officials). Consequently, the situation worsened month by month, arousing fury among peasants. Outright insurgencies soon resulted. To complicate the matter further, the government introduced compulsory labor service. Initially, this policy applied to the bourgeois and rich elements but it was quickly extended to all citizens of 16–50 years of age.

As a result of the food procurement campaign and other War Communism measures, almost all of which were energetically opposed by all other political parties and groups, including the Left Socialist Revolutionaries (earlier on the Bolsheviks' closest allies), the country's government became a one-party dictatorship, with all power concentrated in the hands of the Bolsheviks. The government created a nonmarket economy, fully controlled by the state, in which private capital was completely obliterated. The Bolsheviks wanted complete control of all resources of the country. This aggravated the contradictions between the workers and peasants. In their pursuit of total control, the Bolsheviks went too far. They totally destroyed private trade, leaving only the state in control of food supplies, but the problem was that the state had virtually nothing to offer to the population. Long established urban supply systems based upon trade with the village were shattered. Consequently, the civil war became a multifaceted conflict, where the "reds," "whites," and "greens" all fought one another. The third color represented the peasantry, who defended its own interests. The Greens could hardly see much difference between the Whites (supporters of the tsarist regime) and Reds and vigorously resisted both. Farmers used all available means of peasant warfare against Bolshevik politics in the village.

In 1920, the Red Army, which consisted predominantly of peasants, was also drawn into the struggle against the government. Peasant discontent demoralized the army, caused mass desertions, rebellion, and the refusal to carry out punitive actions. One of the major military revolts occurred in Zavolzhsko-Ural region in the summer of 1920 and was called by the government *Sapozhkovshchina*.

The leader of this rebellion was a commander in the Red Army, A. S. Sapozhkov, who had fought against the White Army and himself descended from peasants of Samara province (Novouzensk County). He was a Left Socialist Revolutionary and had commanded the Red Army's 9th division, which had been replenished with peasants recruited from certain counties of Samara province. These peasant-soldiers were dissatisfied with food procurement, compulsory labor, and other burdens placed upon peasants by War Communism. Many of their families had suffered from food confiscations. In July 1920, Sapozhkov wrote an appeal "To all workers and the Red Army," stating that in Soviet Russia, which called itself a government of workers and peasants, "the power of workers and peasants has long ceased to exist." The opinion of these groups, supposedly the backbone of the revolution, was not being taken into account and the government instead used soldiers "to take everything from the people in order to keep itself in power." Sapozhkov took control over an area in Samara province and reorganized his forces into what he called the "First Red Army of Truth." By July 15, the army had about 30,000 men.

Soon the uprising spread to other grain producing regions of the Volga, including parts of Samara, Saratov, Tsaritsyn, and Orenburg provinces, all of which had suffered heavily from the state's food requisitioning policies. Being familiar with the area, Sapozhkov was able to resist a considerable force of the Red Army dispatched to fight against him. Lenin had requested a quick and resolute containment of the Sapozhkov rebellion in order to isolate the rebels from the rest of the population. Lenin insisted that every manifestation of sympathy with the rebels be suppressed. He also demanded the arrest of all suspected perpetrators and the taking of hostages in order to prevent the possibility of assistance. By September the rebellion finally was defeated and the rebels tried and sentenced to death. Some escaping rebels formed guerrilla groups and continued to fight against the Reds but were eventually crushed during the spring of 1922. This episode did not, however, end armed peasant resistance against the Communist regime.

By early winter 1920, the young Soviet Republic had plunged into disaster. Government actions had put the rural population under the direct threat of famine because people could get foodstuffs only from their own dwindling reserves or from the sack carriers. Famine became real and spread across many regions. The food procurement campaign was a major cause of famine in the Volga basin region in 1921–1922. The campaign led to chaos and spurred popular protest in the countryside. By the end of 1920, the scale of the peasant anti- Bolshevik movement further increased. Uprisings occurred, among others in Ukraine, in Western Siberia, in Tambov province, and in the Volga basin region. The largest uprising of all occurred in Tambov province. Up to 50,000 peasants under the leadership of A. S. Antonov, also a Left SR, now turned against the regime and participated in the anti-Bolshevik resistance, which became known as the *Antonovshchina*. The government sent one hundred thousand troops against the Tambov peasants and more to other regions. In the spring of 1921, about 200,000 people in the countryside were directly involved in armed protest. As a response to peasant resistance to the *prodrazverstka*, the local VChK, food procurement enforcement agencies, and the Red Army frequently arrested whole families of the rebelling peasants, including children and elders and placed them all together in prisons. One government official's report noted that Moscow's "concentration camps" (this was the origins of the term) held children who had been brought with their parents from Tambov province.[6] Meanwhile, millions of homeless children, sent by their starving parents to search for food for survival's sake, were roaming train stations and marketplaces throughout European Russia looking for anything at all to eat.

The year 1920, the third of peasant resistance against the Bolshevik regime, witnessed some changes in organization and methods of fighting on both sides. Peasant resistance expanded geographically, became more ordered and alert. A few respected peasant leaders emerged who created military formations and widely used methods of guerrilla warfare. Peasants put forward political slogans that rejected the one-party dictatorship and called for the restoration of free democratic elections. The peasantry opposed the Bolsheviks' social experiments and called for the liquidation of state farms, protested against the state's monopolization of land, and demanded an end to food procurement and forced labor obligations. Although 1920 may have been the year of heaviest peasant resistance, the year 1921 witnessed further uprisings in Western Siberia, upon whose grain the new state by that time depended for survival (food requisitions, uprisings, and war had effectively ended any possibility of acquiring sufficient grain in central and southern provinces).

It is almost impossible to estimate the numbers of casualties among the peasant population during the food procurement campaign and the civil war. The Soviet state became quite cautious about releasing demographic statistics. Thus, in Soviet historiography no serious attempt to estimate the losses occurred. Some émigré sources suggest figures of over 10 million deaths, including over 8 million civilians. Whatever the exact numbers (some estimates reach 12,00,000), high mortality resulted from civil war, War Communism, including the Red Terror and *Prodrazverstka*, and, most of all, famine and disease epidemics.

Considering that the Red Army by that time was exceedingly weak, the mass insurgencies in the countryside and the swelling worker protest in cities were a very serious threat to the government. The crisis only deepened when on March 1, 1921, sailors of the Kronshtadt naval base near Petrograd rebelled against the Soviet regime. Among the demands of the Kronshtadt rebellion, which, it should be noted, included local Bolsheviks, Left SRs, Anarchists, and SR-Maximalists, all groups that had ardently supported the October Revolution, were new fair elections and the election of a new multiparty government. Only by using extreme measures did the Bolshevik government manage to suppress the various revolutionary episodes (Kronshtadt, the Antonovshchina, the West Siberian rebellion). The Kronshtadt uprising especially shocked the ruling party because since early 1917 the huge naval base and its personnel had been one of the foreposts of the revolution. It became apparent that a change in approach and policies was necessary or the regime would collapse. On the one hand, Lenin realized that the Bolshevik government must learn to coexist with the original driving forces of the revolution, the proletariat and the peasants, whose interests and outlooks were not as divergent as the Bolsheviks had thought. On the other, Lenin also firmly adhered to the necessity of creating a powerful single-party system and destroying any vestiges of organized political opposition. In one respect, War Communism policies had fulfilled certain primary tasks, that is, creating absolute one-party dictatorship through terror, but, in the end, the policy failed in other basic tasks of statecraft such as creating a functioning economy with real popular support. Thus, in order for the government to survive, War Communism had to be brought to a hasty end.

Consequently, in 1921, shortly after the Kronshtadt rebellion, the Bolshevik government introduced NEP, which in essence offered a combination of considerable economic liberalization and continued strict political control. NEP lasted from spring of 1921 to 1928. It represented an attempt to pull the country out of the crisis and to give some impetus to economic and agricultural development. The NEP configuration was worked out at the 10th Bolshevik Party Congress, which also made decisions regarding the Kronshtadt rebellion and which banned opposition parties, thus officially instituting the one party system (until then some leftists parties had continued a semi-legal existence). Regarding NEP, a series of decrees replaced food procurement with a food tax, permitted free trade in agricultural goods and the creation of cooperatives, privatized certain industries, legalized private trade, allowed private entrepreneurs to lease state-owned enterprises, and permitted private capital to create enterprises, including industrial ones, with up to twenty hired workers (ten workers for mechanized companies). Of direct concern to the peasants, in October 1922 the government introduced a new land code (for further details, see below), which affirmed most of the early 1918 law but which permitted the renting of land and the use of agricultural wage workers to cultivate land, almost all of which was now in the hands of peasants. (To successfully work their land, peasants often hired other peasants at certain crucial times and, when appropriate, hired themselves out to other peasants.) One might justifiably conclude that the peasantry, at great cost, had won this round of the struggle.

The ideological father of NEP, Lenin, believed that the policy was a temporary but necessary measure: it was a time to dampen the pressure on the peasantry and to make peace with this crucial segment of the population. Later, Lenin acknowledged that NEP would last until the right time to end it and that the government would return to terror, including the economic one, when it was deemed appropriate. For the time being, however, Lenin aimed to establish a union (*smychka*) between the peasantry and the working class. Thus, beginning in March 1921, the Bolshevik leaders adopted a policy aimed at loosening centralization and curtailing the use of terror. Compulsory labor was replaced with a labor exchange facility, because unemployment had reached extraordinarily high rates. The existing ration card system of food distribution was abolished. Instead, the government paid close attention to management and cooperation. NEP was able to alleviate the collapse of commerce and retail trade almost instantly. Remarkably, by the end of 1921, private merchants, called *nepmen*, controlled 75 percent of retail and 18 percent of wholesale trade. Even so, the state maintained control of the so-called commanding heights of the economy: finance, heavy industry, communications, transportation, power production, and fuel.

As mentioned, the NEP decrees abolished food procurement and introduced a food tax, at approximately 20 percent of production. As noted above, in October 1922, the government introduced the new land law with provisions about issues of concern to the peasants. The code retained the abolition of private property on land, minerals, forests and water resources. A significant difference, however, was that it legitimized hired labor in the countryside, which the government had forbidden during War Communism. Land rent was permitted for a period of no more than one rotation, that is, with the three-field system for three years and with the four-field system—four years. No one was allowed to rent more land than the labor capacity of the renter's household. Hired labor was permitted only if the employers also worked on a par with wage workers and if the employer was unable to perform all necessary work. In 1923 the tax in kind was replaced with a single agricultural tax and in 1926 with a cash tax. These provisions, however, provided for higher tax rates on rich peasants. Thus, on the one hand, peasants were given the opportunity to improve their well-being and, on the other, they were not motivated to expand their activities excessively because of higher taxes. As a result, the number of average households grew at the expense of rich and poor peasants, whose numbers decreased. Nonetheless, the Russian peasantry gained an opportunity to breathe more freely, as some of their acute problems had been addressed. The government also attempted to introduce an equal exchange between the countryside and industry. This miniature liberalization of the agricultural economy alleviated the crisis for both the village and the city: by 1926 food supply in Soviet Russia had improved significantly. Also noteworthy is that throughout the NEP era the full range of agricultural associations that arose during 1918–1919—pure communes and cooperatives—functioned legally, alongside traditional redistributional communes and even individual farms of the Stolypin type (these farms enjoyed a significant revival after the introduction of NEP much to the chagrin of the Communist government).

Although during the NEP era the country rapidly overcame the previous economic devastation and agriculture quickly reached pre–First World War levels, NEP was not a successful economic model for the long run, nor did it eliminate the exploitation of peasant labor by the state. While, the situation was dramatically different from the previous several years of Bolshevik rule, a large part of the produce created by peasants was alienated from them by high taxes and other regulations, which, in essence, equaled a capitalist-style exploitation of their labor, supposedly anathema to Marxists. Additionally, the state controlled prices. It lowered prices on agricultural goods and maintained high prices on manufactured goods. Thus, the commodity exchange between the village and city was unfair and resulted in the so-called scissors crisis.[7] (If one plotted the prices of agricultural goods and industrial goods separately on a graph, the prices of agricultural goods remained low, whereas those of industrial goods rose, with the two crossing one another on the graph like an open scissors.) In this situation, peasants could not afford industrial goods. Therefore, there was little incentive for the development of the industry (peasants couldn't afford the goods) and peasants had little motivation to produce more than they could consume. During 1923–1924 peasants essentially worked almost for no income. The intricate regulations were designed in a way that over half of what peasants produced, they were forced to sell for almost nothing, whereas they could sell only 30 percent of what they produced at a market price. Thus, the state's free market manipulation (one might call it "malfunction") turned into an instrument of peasant exploitation. Approximately one half of what peasants produced was purchased by the state for money, whereas the rest was literally plundered (a return of forced requisitions under another guise). Despite some attempts at alleviation by the state, the NEP system produced corruption, the disproportionate growth of state and local bureaucracy, and widespread theft of state property—a reality that plagued the USSR throughout its existence. NEP provided insufficient inducement for the economic development the party had envisioned. The depressed level of agricultural production could not meet the country's fast-growing urban needs (peasants who had fled to the countryside returned to cities to reemploy themselves in newly reopened state-owned industrial concerns and small businesses owned by nepmen) and the needs of the state for a high level of exports (to provide funds to expand industrial production).

In 1926, at the 15th Party Conference Josef Stalin (whose real name was Dzhugashvili Josef), who was emerging as a new leader after the death of Lenin in 1924, expressed the opinion that NEP had become outdated and that the country needed a new impetus for further economic and industrial development. Although few realized it at the time, this marked the start of the abolition of NEP. During the years of 1926–1927, supplies of grain exceeded the prewar era and reached 160 million tons for the first time. But rich peasants, about 10 percent of the population, still avoided selling grain to the state, retaining about 2.5 million ton of grain. Logically, peasants were unwilling to sell grain at a low price because of inflated prices on manufactured goods such as agricultural tools, machinery, and other manufactured goods of use to them. The problem was not in food production but in the ability of the state to acquire the grain for use in the cities or for export. As time went on, food supplies for major cities declined and by the autumn of 1927, cities and industrial centers faced serious food shortages; the rise in food prices in cooperative and private stores led to popular discontent. This was coupled with a bad harvest in 1927. As an emergency measure, the government introduced a rationing system, that is, rationing of food consumption. In order to ensure grain procurement, in many areas of the USSR, the authorities returned to the food requisitioning policy and established fixed prices on grain. During 1928–1929, the state used various repressive and sometimes violent policies in order to obtain grain. Meanwhile industry experienced no growth. Ultimately, Stalin, who had quietly assumed the reins of power, decided to end NEP and introduce a new set of agricultural and industrial policies. The Soviet Union's peasants, like the rest of the population, faced a new way of life.

Suggested readings

Badcock, Sarah et al., eds. *Russia's Revolution in Regional Perspective, 1914–1921.* Bloomington, IN: Slavica Press, 2015.

Figes, Orlando. *Peasant Russia, Civil War: Volga Countryside in Revolution, 1917–1921.* Oxford: Clarendon Press, 1989.

Lih, Lars T. *Bread and Authority in Russia, 1914–1921.* Berkeley: University of California Press, 1990.

Melançon, Michael. "Trial Run for Soviet Food Requisitioning: The Expedition to Orel Province, Fall 1918." *Russian Review*, vol. 69, no. 3 (July 2010): 412–437.

Melancon, Michael. "The Hammer and the Sickle: Lenin, the Left Socialist Revolutionaries and Soviet Russia's First Land Laws," in *Russia's Century of Revolutions: Parties, People, Places: Studies Presented in honor of Alexander Rabinowitch*, Michael S. Melancon and Donald J. Raleigh, eds. Bloomington, IN: Slavica Publishers, 2012, pp. 59–88.

Retish, Aaron. *Russia's Peasants in Revolution and Civil War: Citizenship, Identity, and the Creation of the Soviet State, 1914–1922.* Cambridge: Cambridge University Press, 2008.

Peasant Life during Collectivization

By 1927–1928 the Soviet government faced continuing crises in grain procurements, in great part because of the endemic problem of imbalanced prices for agricultural versus industrial goods (the scissors crisis discussed in the previous chapter). Under Joseph Stalin's growing control, the state embarked upon new measures as regards the peasants, the sole producers of grain and other agricultural products. Early public discussions of the issue (in newspapers and in party and Soviet institutions) focused mainly on methods, supposedly voluntary, of inducing the peasants to increase their crops and bring grain and other products forward for sale to the state. In other words, the state portrayed the matter primarily as a procurement issue. With much fanfare, Stalin embarked on a trip through the Urals and Western Siberia (both heavy grain-producing regions) to set the example for grain procurement methods. Newspapers regularly reported on the alleged success of the campaign, with Stalin at the center of the effort, and described the entire enterprise as the Uralo-Siberian Method of grain procurement.[1] Later the Uralo-Siberian campaign took on a different, more sinister coloration: peasants rudely ordered to give up their grain or suffer severe consequences. Lists were compiled of those who did not comply, and many were rounded up and never heard from again. Another oddity of the Uralo-Siberian campaign was that at various locales along the route Stalin's speeches, published in local newspapers, hardly mentioned "grain procurement." Stalin's speeches instead focused almost entirely on a new theme: persuading the peasants to give up their traditional communes in order to join "collective farms" (*kolkhozes*). All of this signified a new turn in Soviet life which would alter it and the peasants' lives forever.

Perhaps no state has imposed an agrarian policy that resulted in such disastrous consequences (dispossession, mass resistance, forced relocation, famine, and devastating mortality) than the Soviet Union's collectivization and nationalization of agriculture. The program began in 1928 and, with stops and starts, reached its completion by 1934 (after-effects continued much longer).

Following realpolitik principles and methods, the Bolsheviks and their new leader, the increasingly dictatorial Joseph Stalin, ruthlessly executed the plan which at first had not been fully revealed to the Soviet public. Collectivization, as the policy came to be called, had a devastating impact on the lives of millions of Soviet citizens; peasants were deprived of their land and property; and many perished in labor camps or in wilderness areas of the far north where people were brought and left without any means of survival. Although the Bolshevik government had shown awareness of ecological concerns as regards preservation of wilderness areas and related issues, in this case it displayed scant knowledge of or attention to ecological concerns: consideration of local or regional environmental circumstances simply played no role. Agriculture of all regions of the geographically diverse USSR was to be collectivized, regardless of its status or type in any given region or whether any other factors existed. Although the geography of collectivization was state-wide, the areas that endured the direst weight of the policy were the black-earth regions of the south, the Volga region, Ukraine, and Western Siberia, that is, the major grain-producing areas. The long-term consequence of collectivization, as the future would reveal, were decades of stagnation, decay in the Russian village, and endemic food shortages. From a major food and grain exporter, Russia ultimately became one of the world's largest grain importers. Food shortages on the home front were common throughout the remaining history of the USSR, an absurdity for country with enormous food-producing potential. This chapter explores the collectivization policy, focusing on state and local government activities and their implications for the peasantry.

As discussed in previous chapters, after emancipation Russia had developed a substantial sector of private agricultural farms (mostly peasant and noble), alongside the more numerous traditional peasant communes, and maintained its position as one of the major global exporters of grain. The October Revolution brought about the end of noble estates, which, along with other land (church, state, imperial, middle class), passed primarily into the hands of the peasantry for usage; some noble estates became state-run farms with labor hired on a factory-like basis. Under duress during the civil war and food dictatorship, peasant smallholders (private farmers) mostly reentered peasant communes. With the introduction of the NEP in 1921, however, many smallholders reemerged, that is, with the complicity of peasant communes and local party and Soviet leaders, smallholders reoccupied their status as independent farmers. This type of farming was especially common in northern regions suitable for mixed crops and animal husbandry, as opposed to grain farming in the south, where large-scale operations had an economic advantage. The later fate of these smallholders, in Russian *edinolichniki* or "those who go it alone," is unclear although many seem to have survived until collectivization and even beyond. It should be noted that recent research by Russian scholars of agriculture and peasant life suggests that during the early and mid-1920s local officials were willing to turn a blind eye to *edinolichniki*, even allowing them to officially enroll in peasant communes while continuing in reality to "go it alone." Their actual numbers probably exceeded official statistics which showed them as less than 2 percent of peasants by 1926.

In any case, the unexpectedly poor harvest of 1927 caused a food crisis in cities and sharply lowered grain exports, which in turn delimited the government's strivings to expand heavy industrial investment. Successful agriculture required intensive methods of production and stability, neither of which was forthcoming in Stalin's Soviet Russia. Some voices within the party leadership supported the idea of continuing NEP and investing in the production of consumer goods in order to lower prices (with wider availability) on these goods (see below for further discussion). Stalin, however, believed in another approach: he wanted to take all agriculture under direct state control in order to achieve several goals. This would supposedly create a supply of state-owned agricultural goods and grain reserves, eliminate the class of private producers and middlemen, and exterminate the class of the so-called kulaks (wealthier peasants on communes and, presumably, private farmers), whom he blamed for withholding grain from sale to the state. According to the architects of collectivization, as the program was called, the main problem the Soviet state faced was the fragmentation of the agrarian sector, because it was in peasant hands with overreliance on manual labor, low productivity, and the consequent failure to produce enough to satisfy the growing demand of the urban population and produce surpluses for export, the profit from which the state could invest in heavy industry. The state also expected these measures to lower the prices of agricultural goods by eliminating chains of intermediaries (*nepmen*), which bourgeoned during the NEP, and to promote mechanization of agriculture, which would increase productivity. The Bolshevik leadership fully expected that total collectivization (to be explained further below) would bring about an abundance of grain and other foodstuffs sufficient to provide for a rapidly increasing urban population.

Feeding the urban population, however, was not the only concern of the Soviet government. The state leadership desired a vast industrial expansion. Industrialization required substantial funds that could supposedly be obtained only through exports of grain. By the autumn of 1927, the Communist Party grew increasingly frustrated with existing peasant agriculture. Under these conditions, Stalin decided that the only way to ensure a guaranteed grain supply would be to accelerate the imposition of collective farming. The collectivization of agriculture was conceived by Stalin as a last resort to be used to solve the problems noted above. Thus, the major reason for mass, expedited collectivization of agriculture was the 1927 grain procurement crisis, and the state's desire to take the peasant agrarian sector under its control in order to finance further industrialization.

The first attempts at collectivizing peasants had been undertaken by the government during civil war era, soon after the revolution. The government encouraged the creation of cooperative farms that could have various types of land tenure and organization. Among these types were "associations for joint land cultivation," designed as a first step to further the transition to "collective state farms." This policy, however, had not been enforced and peasants could choose for themselves their preferences for agricultural activities. Nevertheless, these first attempts to create large state-controlled farms, based upon voluntary principles, failed badly. The total number of peasant farmers who gave their property into the public domain was less than 1 percent, even though the state offered tractors and fertilizers as incentives. By July 1927, there were about 15,000 collective farms of this type and their productive capacity was mediocre. The hundreds of model farms run by the state (based upon confiscated large noble farms) with proletarianized labor were even less productive and were widely perceived as utter failures.

In March 1927, the Soviet of People's Commissars issued a resolution "On the collective farms," which emphasized promoting farming *tovarishchestvo* (cooperatives) and collectives of farms (*kolkhoz*), plus so-called machine associations for mechanized farm equipment (whose equipment would be rented out to collective farms as needed). The resolution encouraged the participation of wide numbers of peasants, especially among the poor. Simultaneously, in order to stimulate the development of these units of production, the government granted them with privileges, while imposing new restrictions on peasant communes, individual farmers, and *kulaks*. In this period the government significantly increased taxes on peasant communes. In the 1928 "General principles of land use and land management," collective farms were given priority in obtaining land and credits, as well as in receiving tax breaks. In June 1929, the government organized Machine-Tractor Stations in order to provide collective farms with agricultural machinery. These were the first steps on the way toward total collectivization of agriculture. The office of central planning still retained the peasant commune as predominant in the agricultural economy during the first five-year economic plan, 1928–1932. Meanwhile, the 26th Party Conference, April 1929, defined "kulaks" as an enemy of socialism and projected increasing kolkhoz farms to equal 20 percent of the total over the next five years. By the spring of 1929, however, only 4 percent of the agricultural sector was under the kolkhoz system. Thus, at least at the beginning of collectivization, the government portrayed collectivization as a gradual process, which, it should be noted, met widespread peasant indifference. During this period, there were still some possibilities for discussion and alternative opinion within the Bolshevik party. Led by Nikolai Bukharin, close associate of Lenin, a group within the party politburo opposed Stalin's forced collectivization and other forms of extreme pressure on the peasantry. Given the lack of government grain reserves, Bukharin suggested slowing down the pace of industrialization, giving up the mass creation of collective farms and repressing kulaks. Instead, he suggested returning to the free sale of grain and raising its price by a factor of 2–3. Bukharin even urged importing grain, if necessary. Stalin rejected these ideas, believing that collectivization must be continued and that grain shortages could be compensated for by the grain-producing regions of Siberia, which were less affected by poor harvests. In reality, Bukharin's group did not control Soviet administration and thus had no influence on the party leadership's decisions. Stalin gradually assumed almost total control over the party and the government.

Similarly, in March 1927, the Soviet government introduced a regulation "On the state farms," or *sovkhoz* (Soviet Enterprise). As noted above, farms of this type had been established on confiscated and nationalized large noble estates after November 1917. They had used the labor of hired workers: one might simply call them farm workers. The first state farms were highly specialized according to a food product, an industrial crop, or livestock breeding. These "Soviet enterprises" were supposedly managed by the state, but in reality the state provided no guidance, no fixed assets, and no personnel. Due to mismanagement, inefficient use of resources, and peasant laborers' indifference, many of these farms had ceased operating by the mid-1920s. Now the government desired to revive this kind of farm as well. According to the regulation, *sovkhoz* farms were exempt from rent for the land, all loans were written off, and they were awarded further funding in the amount of 6 million rubles. The wages of workers on *sovkhozs* increased and were closely associated with labor productivity growth and the economic strengthening of the farm. In contrast to the kolkhoz, which was allegedly "a free cooperative association of farmers" at the expense of and for the potential profit of its members, a *sovkhoz* was a state enterprise. These Sovkhoz workers, like those of the early 1920s, were hired employees. They received a fixed cash wage, earned retirement, and qualified for other state-provided benefits, unlike members of kolkhozes.

For Stalin, the process of setting up of kolkhozes appeared to lag; he wanted more rapid collectivization.[2] At the April 1929 Plenum of the party's Central Committee, he stated that the "agricultural sector is the main and only cause of economic crisis." The pace of collectivization of agriculture in fact had increased sharply compared with the earlier plan. The original moderate plan of reforms, proposed by the State Planning Committee, was revised upward. The Kolkhoz Center, a central management body, received additional powers. To spur an increased tempo, thousands of industrial workers were sent to the village, along with numerous party activists and even OGPU (secret police) members, certainly a unique turn in Russian and world agrarian life. By spring 1929, mass collectivization had begun. The realpolitik of forced collectivization involved all possible measures to expedite the process: from brigades of the Communist Youth Union, who agitated among peasants, to police, who arrested recalcitrant peasants. In villages the continuing forced grain procurement, accompanied by mass arrests and devastation of farms, led to riots: hundreds of such disorders among peasants had occurred by the end of 1929. Peasants had no desire to give up their land, livestock, and tools (much of which on peasant communes belonged to them personally) to the kolkhozes and collectives; instead, they slaughtered livestock (they often arranged vast feasts to consume the slaughtered livestock) and sharply reduced sowing. Many people decided not to raise grain at all, while others resorted to violent acts of resistance. Some desperate people tried to hide their grain by burying it. The situation in the village approached civil war. As a counterintuitive response, the party confronted this resistance with the decision to enact immediate statewide collectivization in November of 1929.

The use of coercive measures did achieve a sharp increase in persons signed on to kolkhozes. By autumn, collective farms totaled 7.5 percent of all agricultural types. In November 1929, the party newspaper *Pravda* (No. 259) published an article by Stalin entitled "The Year of Great Change." Stalin praised the early results of collectivization and called for total collectivization. Stalin's ideas became the basis for of the resolution of the plenum of the party Central Committee (November 1929). The resolution stated that the country had started the construction of large-scale socialist agriculture in the village. It also set goals for complete collectivization of all agriculture in certain regions. The plenum also decided to send 25,000 industrial workers as managers for newly created collective farms. Later, the number of these urban kolkhoz managers increased to 73,000. One can only imagine peasant farmers' reaction to the arrival of urban workers, party functionaries, police, and armed units in their midst (Figure 13.1).

The most active period of collectivization occurred between January and March 1930. In January 1930, the Central Executive Committee of the Soviets and the Central Committee of the Bolshevik Party made a decision about accelerated total collectivization, which, according to the new plan, should be accomplished in one to two years.[3] This decision established several special regions where the reform should proceed to completion as soon as possible and created a special commission to develop a collectivization schedule. The regions of North Caucasus and the Volga were scheduled to complete collectivization in one year, by the spring of 1931. Other grain-producing regions were to complete collectivization by the spring 1932. The rest of the country should finish the process in five years. According to the 1930 decisions, all peasants' field land plots, including the land of the earlier created cooperatives, were to be established as publicly owned and transformed, on the given concern, into a single land area. Also, all working animals, livestock, seed, feedstocks, and tool outbuildings were to be socialized. Household facilities, dairy cattle, small agricultural tools, etc., could be retained for peasants' personal utilization.

Figure 13.1 Peasant women from a collective farm. Propaganda photo.

General community meetings were to approve membership in the kolkhoz. Kulaks and persons deprived of their voting rights because of various violations were not accepted. By late February 1930, 50 percent of agriculture was in collective farms throughout the Soviet Union, which doubled the official five-year plan for collectivization.

As discussed in previous chapters, all major previous agrarian reforms in the imperial period, such as the abolition of serfdom in 1861 or the Stolypin reform, and even the agrarian programs of major political parties, were clear and detailed. Furthermore, as the general hypothesis of this book suggests, peasants possessed an ecological mentality, that is, they worked the land and raised livestock with consideration of detailed ecological possibilities. In this regard, the Bolshevik state displayed only an adapted version of Marxism and realpolitik. Stalin's collectivization of agriculture had no detailed instruction for its realization. The party decision defined the regions and time frame, but said nothing about how this could be accomplished. The rhetoric of the central authority was dominated by phrases such as "we must achieve" or "we must accomplish" but turned a blind eye on how to turn numerous peasant communes, with their individualized land utilization, into kolkhoz collectives in one to two years. In fact, realpolitik dominated the implementation of this agricultural experiment by the Bolshevik government. Perhaps the only specific instruction that the leadership provided was the call for the "elimination of kulaks as a class," which also fits well into the category of realpolitik since the term quickly came to signify any peasant who resisted collectivization. With the absence of clear instructions, local party and Soviet authorities accepted this call as a signal to change radically their policies toward peasants.

Whatever they may have thought, local party workers supported the new course. The leaders of large agricultural areas praised rapid collectivization. This artificial speeding up in the collectivization process led to enormous violations of the supposedly voluntary principle of joining collective farms and in reality ruthlessly forced peasants to comply. The local party and Soviet authorities began to take steps on their own to solve the puzzle of the party's commands (they clearly understood the imperative to fulfill the plan or else). And almost everywhere they reduced the process of "voluntary organization of kolkhozes" to violence. Peasants were forced to join the collective farms, under threat of harsh sanctions, arrest, and imprisonment. These methods inevitably spurred opposition and various forms of resistance. The peasants' unwillingness to work in kolkhozs severely affected fieldwork. It led to poor cultivation of fields, indifference, and sharp declines in yields.

The collectivization of agriculture led to the reality that the affluent and medium wealthy peasant population, now labeled as "kulaks," virtually disappeared from the village. Those peasants who had been forced onto collectives naturally displayed little concern for the final outcome of their labor. Additionally, the state essentially confiscated a large part of what was produced. Peasants realized that regardless of how much they increased productivity, exclusively at the cost of their heightened labor efforts, the state would take away almost everything. In kolkhozes, farmers received no cash payment for their work except for the low amount prescribed by the so-called workdays (*trododen'*). Thus, members of collective farms got little money or produce to sell for extra sorely needed income. During later years, after terrible hunger broke out in many food-producing areas, they were allowed to retain enough to barely sustain their families. Special mention should be made of the fact that during collectivization and well beyond, the Soviet Union introduced another measure, fully deserving the title realpolitik that is, the internal passport for *kolkhozniks* (members of collective farms); collective farm members were not able to leave their kolkhoz without special permission. As a result, a *kolkhoznik* could not go live elsewhere because they had no documents. In fact, collective farm members were tied to the place where they were born. Although in some respects similar, this was hardly a revival of serfdom, but it did introduce obligatory unpaid work, a type of labor that has hardly ever been productive.

In the fall of 1929, the harvesting campaign took violent forms as all market mechanisms fell away. Not surprisingly, the first collectivization results were dismal. During the first five years of the kolkhoz experiment, the volume of agricultural production decreased by 14 percent, compared to the prewar years. There was a decline in grain production by 10 percent, a decline in the number of cattle by one third, and the number of sheep decreased even more. Similar declines were observed in all areas of agriculture. In the future, this negative trend was to some degree gradually overcome but during collectivization's initial stages, the effect was overwhelming. At the same time, state food procurements doubled, some of which was exported, obviously one of the principal causes of hunger during 1932–1933 in many agricultural regions of the Soviet Union (the Caucasus, the Volga region, the Ukraine and Kazakhstan in particular). Authorities registered cases of cannibalism in many starving areas. According to various sources,[4] the famine claimed the lives of between 3 and 5 million people. These developments were the direct results of the Bolshevik government's policies (realpolitik). In spite of the weak harvest in 1931–1932, the government sold abroad almost the entire stock of grain, leaving almost nothing for the domestic market. This homicidal sale was done for the sake of industrialization. Industrialization intensified at the price of millions of peasant lives.

Collectivization immediately spurred sharp peasant resistance.[5] All kinds of violent acts took place, from the burning of crops as a means of slowing the process to the hanging of local authorities in their areas. Some villages even compared the administration that was in place to the antichrist and suggested that they were entering the end times. There were also many peasants who looked at the restrictions that were placed on them as a second installment of serfdom. These factors clearly suggest how much the peasants hated the idea of collectivization. Although Stalin saw his methods as a success for the Soviet Union as a nation, the majority of the peasants disagreed. The peasants did everything they could to try to end the transformation taking place. In the early 1930s, many peasants tried to peacefully protest collectivization, both through writing letters to the government and by speaking out at local meetings. However, when these attempts were not taken seriously, the peasants turned toward more violent acts. According to various statistics, there were 346 insurgencies in January 1930, which were joined by roughly 125,000 people. Already in February 1930, the number of protest actions grew to 736 with 220,000 people. During the first two weeks of March 1930, 595 riots took place joined by 230,000 peasants. In March 1930, the authorities reported 1,642 insurgencies in Belarus, the central black-earth region, the Lower and Middle Volga regions, the North Caucasus, Siberia, the Urals, Leningrad, Moscow, West, Ivanovo-Voznesensk, Crimea, and Central Asia. The insurgencies involved about 750,000–800,000 people. There were over a thousand insurgent villages in the Ukraine in March 1930 alone.

By March 1930, the disastrous results of the early stages of forced collectivization (realpolitik) finally alarmed Stalin. In a famous (or better infamous) article titled "Dizzy with Success," published in the party newspaper *Pravda*, Stalin blamed the local authorities for the extremes of collectivization.[6] Stalin accused local leaders of imposing the unreasonable pace of collectivization with the goal of impressing the government with high numbers and their willingness to use of force. He also now urged careful consideration of the diversity of geographical conditions of the vast USSR when determining the pace and methods of collective-farm development, a first belated nod toward ecological circumstances.

In reality, this "dizzy success" had been achieved with the use of violence and by total neglect of the ecology of local conditions. For example, 70 percent of the Tyumen region of Western Siberia had been collectivized by March 1930. This region, with its arctic and subarctic climate, was not agricultural; its peasants engaged in some subsistence agriculture, fishing, and deer herding. Nonetheless, completely inappropriate collectivization was ruthlessly pursued by the OGPU (secret police) and prosecutorial power, plus that of specially assigned plenipotentiaries to identify the "criminal activity" of kulaks and all prosperous elements. Peasants everywhere sent thousands of letters of complaints, stating that they were all the same and all hungry.

Despite mass terror, this forcefully created collective farm system began to disintegrate already in the spring of 1930; by May 1930, only 20 percent of farms remained as kolkhozes. But this in fact only represented a government breathing space, spurred by Stalin's "Dizzy with Success" commentary. The party reaction followed immediately. On March 14, 1930, the Central Committee of the Communist Party (Bolsheviks) issued a resolution "On the Fight against Misrepresentation of the Party Line in the Collective-Farm Movement." After this criticism, many artificially created collective farms began to collapse. The process of collectivization slowed down, but did not end. For example, severe repressions quickly were resumed in the Tyumen region and elsewhere, where the original collectivization campaign had not yet occurred. According to a decision of the local Tyumen Bolshevik party committee, 3,200 households were to be deported to GULAG (prison camp) settlements in February 1930 and 750 households in March. In June the local party committee demanded the arrest of 290 households, deemed in violation of collectivization norms, to be sent to construction sites and peat works. The key issue seems to have been whether or not an area had experienced the first stage of collectivization; if it had not, the campaign could proceed, even during the party's "retreat" in other areas.

The first victims of the collectivization campaign were kulaks, especially these who used hired labor. Alongside collectivization, the Bolshevik government decided to liquidate the kulaks. For example, in February 1928 the newspaper *Pravda* published an article "Exposing the Kulaks." The author attacked kulaks and reported that rich peasants dominated rural areas, exploited the labor of their hired workers, and had even entered local party organizations (cells) and led some of these cells. Soviet party controlled media started publishing reports about kulaks' malicious activities. Thus, stigmatization and exposure of "enemies" had begun. The Soviet authorities advocated and promoted forceful expropriation of grain stocks, at first as a "temporary" emergency measure. These forcible seizures of grain discouraged farmers from expanding production and, as a result, it hurt poor peasants, who lost work opportunities (hiring their labor to other better-off peasants). The temporary emergency measure soon turned into the dynamic ruthless policy of "eliminating the kulaks as a class." As mentioned, the original concept of a kulak, wealthy peasant, was soon expanded to mean any peasant who opposed collectivization. From a social category it underwent a transformation to a political one (realpolitik).

As mentioned earlier, during the late 1920s there was still opposition within the party. The so-called right opposition led by Bukharin was against forced and expedited collectivization. This faction believed that the state should support individual peasant farms. A member of the opposition, A. I. Rykov, criticized the dispossession of kulaks and other "War Communism" methods. He believed that the party should in fact stimulate the development of individual farmers and that the state should assist their clustering in productive areas. But for Stalin, who had assumed control over the party and the state, kulaks were ideological enemies and an obstacle for creating a socialist economy.

Stalin personally formulated the policy of eliminating the kulaks as a class. He assumed that kulaks should be destroyed in open battle and deprived of their livelihood, including the use of land, tools, and the right to lease land and machinery and to employ laborers. Thus, the elimination of kulaks, or *dekulakization*, had started and intensified during 1928–1932 with the suppression of anti-kolkhoz peasants and kulaks. In January 1930 the party issued a resolution "On Measures of Liquidation of Kulak Farms in the Areas of Complete Collectivization." The government divided kulaks into three categories, which included counterrevolutionary peasants and organizers of terrorist attacks and uprisings, the richest kulaks, and a third quite sinister category, "the rest of the kulaks." These categories were obviously and deliberately vague: any peasant risked being deemed a kulak. The heads of families of so-called counterrevolutionary and terrorist kulaks were arrested and their cases were transferred to the so-called *troika* (a Russian term signifying a group of three), a special tribunal of three members, representing the police, regional party committees, and the prosecutor's office. The alleged kulak's family members, as well as the kulaks themselves, were subject to eviction to remote areas of the USSR, mostly to Western Siberia. Members of the third ambiguous category, "the rest of kulaks," were settled within their province on a specially allocated area, outside the kolkhoz lands, where they operated, under mysterious circumstances and unknown ultimate fate, as *edinolichniki* (private farmers) (Figure 13.2).

The resolution demanded that the first category of kulaks, counterrevolutionaries and organizers of terrorist attacks, should be liquidated by immediate imprisonment in concentration camps. At this point some parallels with the Nazi Germany may be valid. As a repressive measure, the OGPU (political police) proposed to send to concentration camps 60,000 kulaks of that category

Figure 13.2 Trial of kulaks, 1929.

and to evict 150,000 kulaks and family members of the second category. The deported peasants (kulaks of the other categories) were placed in specially created settlements in uninhabited or sparsely populated areas. The concentration camps and special settlements operated under the authority of GULAG, one of the instruments of the Bolshevik realpolitik, founded in April 1930 (the new Soviet state, had opened its first concentration camps as part of the Red Terror during the fall of 1918, after an assassination attempt on Lenin). The state confiscated all property of the deported peasants, giving each a one-time payment of 500 rubles.

The government categorized people and punishment clearly, at least in the statutes, but how to identify a counterrevolutionary or how to differentiate a rich peasant from a peasant farmer with an average income was not spelled out. There was absolutely no criterion for determining a "kulak." Consequently, most peasants who merely objected to collectivization were designated kulaks or even counterrevolutionaries. There were instances in which even local poor villages were dispossessed. Most peasants who suffered from collectivization and the related repression were hardly suspect of anything. They merely fell victims to Bolshevik realpolitik.

As mentioned in the previous chapter, Bolshevik policies caused mass homelessness among children in food-producing areas of the countryside during the civil war food procurement campaign (1918–1921). Now, anew, a wave of homeless children emerged to an alarming extent in Western and Eastern Siberia, where collectivization victims were often sent. During 1932 classified letters and telegrams from Siberia informed the central state authorities that homelessness and beggary among the region's children had taken on a mass character, particularly in Omsk, Novosibirsk, and Tomsk, widely spread areas of Siberia. Classified telegrams from local authorities urged the central government to deal with the growing problem. Children's homeless grew alarmingly in other areas heavily affected by collectivization as well.[7]

The arbitrariness of the campaign is striking. The OGPU (secret police) regularly formulated in advance plans to arrest a certain number of kulaks in any given period of time. For example, one OGPU operation order from February 6, 1930, planned to arrest 60,000 kulaks of the "first category." Already on the first day of the operation, February 9, 1930, approximately 16,000 peasants were arrested by the political police and 25,000 members of their families were deported to GULAG special settlements. According to classified police records, by April 15, 1930, during the first operational period, 140,724 suspects under the first category had been arrested, of whom 79,330 were kulaks, 5,028—clergymen, 4,405—former landlords and industrialists, and 51,961 were, simply, "anti-Soviet" elements. During the second period, between April 15 and October 1, 1930, 142,993 suspects were arrested, including 45,559 kulaks and 97,434 anti-Soviet elements. In one month alone, in January 1931, the OGPU arrested 36,698 people, most of who were classified as kulaks. During 1930–1931, the political police sent 381,026 families consisting of 1,803,392 persons to GULAG or OGPU special settlements. According to the OGPU registers, between January 1930 and September 1931, 517,665 families of 2,437,062 persons were registered as "special settlers" of OGPU settlements. The campaign against kulaks melded into a general political repression, with unclear boundaries between them.

The campaign for collectivization of agriculture generally achieved its goals. The great majority of peasants entered collective farms. The collectivization campaign did provide some short-term benefits for the Bolshevik government. It was able to export a considerable portion of what was produced in the highly ineffective and mismanaged kolkhozes and *sovkhozs*. *Sovkhoz* workers received an underrated cash wage and kolkhoz members received cash according to calculated labor days (*trudodni*) and a tiny fraction of the harvested crop. Such policies also resulted in a massive theft of grain and other produce from the fields and farms, for which accused persons could receive up to ten years of imprisonment and the exile to the GULAG. Most of these people were not kulaks but merely starving people who simply took necessary measures for survival.

As mentioned, food-producing areas were especially stricken by famine. Entire villages ceased to exist in the Volga provinces, the Ukraine, and Kazakhstan. The state's long-term objectives, whether benign or malign, had been achieved as well. The most industrious and entrepreneurial people had been eliminated and the rest, scared by repression and hunger, meekly worked on the farm in exchange for meager payment. The state extracted from the village all the resources it wanted (all that were available to take). The state achieved complete control of agriculture and the meager profit it produced.

In summary, the immediate impact of collectivization was a dreadful famine and the consequent deaths of millions, mass imprisonment of innocent men, women, and adolescents, a new wave of as yet unquantified and barely noted children's homelessness, and the total destruction of independent peasants, whether real kulaks, *edinolichniki*, or simply industrious persons, willing and able to work. Agriculture had fallen under total state control: nationalized and unproductive. Long-term consequences were decades of stagnation of Russian agriculture, the decay of the Russian village, and an end to the peasantry as it had been known. For the remainder of the Soviet Union's existence, members of kolkhozes tried their best to receive permits to leave the farm permanently. Young men, who had been released from kolkhozes to serve in the military, preferred not to return to the village after their service and legally resettled elsewhere. Young men and women strived

Figure 13.3 Propaganda poster.

Figure 13.4 Propaganda photo.

to enter institutions of higher learning to escape kolkhoz life. From an exporter of foodstuffs, the USSR became one of the major importers of grain and meat products.

In conclusion, I would note that for some historians, Stalin was a great manager, able to mobilize society to carry out great achievements. But to this story must be added the reality that these achievements, to the extent they occurred, were based on terror, violence, and extreme hardship. They were also based on manipulation of public opinion, the encouragement of denunciation of others, enflaming social hatred, and dividing society along predetermined, often artificial, sociocultural lines.

Suggested readings

Brandenberger, David. *National Bolshevism: Stalinist Mass Culture and the Formation of Modern Russian National Identity, 1931–1956*. Cambridge, MA: Harvard University Press, 2002.

Davies, R. W. *The Soviet Collective Farms, 1929–1930*. London: Macmillan, 1980.

Fitzpatrick, Sheila. *Everyday Stalinism: Ordinary Life in Extraordinary Times: Soviet Russia in the 1930s*. New York: Oxford University Press, 1999.

Fitzpatrick, Sheila. *Stalin's Peasants Resistance and Survival in the Russian Village after Collectivization*. New York: Oxford University Press, 1994.

Viola, Lynne. *Peasant Rebels under Stalin: Collectivization and the Culture of Peasant Resistance*. New York: Oxford University Press, 1996.

Volin, Lazar. *A Century of Russian Agriculture*. Cambridge, MA: Harvard University Press, 1970.

Conclusion: Demise of the Russian Peasantry

This brief excurse through the history of the Russian peasantry can hardly relate their whole history and the abundance of their experience. Instead it seeks to explore the moments and developments that have great historical value. It emphasizes peasant ecological mentality largely to help explain peasant economic behavior, about which there has been much misunderstanding, often with a belittling edge. We have seen that the ecological paradigm has worked well in explaining peasant agriculture and economy during the imperial period. Most peasants, even during serfdom, managed their economic activities themselves, virtually without state or landlord intervention. Peasants made their decisions about what crops they should grow and when they should cultivate the fields. They decided what volume of labor they should spend, and what agricultural techniques and tools they should use. They even calculated the amount of foodstuffs that would be required for them to accomplish the needed labor. The agricultural economy depends strongly on the environment and peasants understood this, and successfully adapted their activities and tools for their specific ecological settings. In areas not quite suitable for agriculture, peasants developed crafts and cottage industries. Many villages in the central non-black-earth region turned into towns and cities even before the emancipation. There was a natural process and pace for economic development of a geographical area, with the peasant population at the center. An examination of peasant nonagricultural endeavors shows peasants of the central non-black-earth region to have been important and active societal agents. They were not simply subject to external determining factors, as all too often claimed, but instead had an active position in making their own history.

Far from isolating themselves in the village, peasants actively searched for contacts with the outside world and inserted themselves into and reshaped various economic and social networks. Thus, they constantly stretched the limits of existing laws, which often seemed to respond to peasant pressures rather than vice versa. Peasants interacted with other social groups on the broadest scale—urban, rural, and all points in between. The self-motivated integration of the peasant into the economic and social networks of imperial Russia suggests greater societal flexibility and dynamism than the previously predominant arrogant and elitist historiographical approach to the peasant would typically admit. Recently, a number of historians, including myself, have challenged the old paradigm (dark, ignorant masses isolated in the village).

Even a brief exploration of the peasantry will discover that peasants had a multitude of interests that extended far beyond their villages. Peasants were aware of and responsive to major political events of national and international importance. Peasants learned about news and information from official sources, rumors, and hearsay and subjected these to their own interpretation and often shrewd assessment. Peasants identified themselves with their villages and provinces but also with the nation and Christianity. Although peasants certainly created their own system of utopian social views and ideals, in order to protect their economic and social interests they were always ready to use existing legal channels and concrete laws and rules, all of which manifested their surprising awareness of the world outside the village. In the early twentieth century, Russian peasants actively engaged in revolutionary activities, joined political parties, and acted consciously, hoping to better their lives. This pertained to peasants of the Volga region and the south as much as to those of the central provinces.

Although the October Revolution had the potential for improving peasant living standards, to which numerous peasants responded by forming agricultural endeavors of various kind, its efforts ran afoul of what we have called here Bolshevik realpolitik. Marxist ideology also played a role in that it systemically belittled the peasant way of life and peasant awareness (consciousness) of the outside world: Marx himself had spoken of the "idiocy of the village." Bolshevik realpolitik found its first violent expression in various forceful food procurements of 1918–1920, followed by the brutal expedited collectivization of 1929–1932, all of which created the groundwork for the demise of the peasantry as social class. Soviet collectivized and nationalized agriculture was not able to sustain the peasant population. The countryside was impoverished and people lived in miserable conditions. Peasants responded to this harsh political and social environment in their own elegant way: they realized that nothing they could do would change the circumstances and so they left the village. One might say that the Soviet countryside literally "gave up the ghost." Villages literally ceased to exist. Despite restrictions on their mobility, peasants used every means at their disposal to leave the Soviet countryside and village. Numerous kolkhozes were forced to close down, because there was no one left there to work. The younger generations left and the older died.

The continuous mass migration from the countryside to the cities created an enormous problem with housing and general urban overpopulation throughout the existence of the Soviet Union. Many people in cities lived in unbelievably overcrowded apartments. The density of urban population attained very high levels, an acute problem to this day, which in turn creates ecological problems.

After the demise of the Soviet system, Russian agriculture further declined somewhat as it experienced setbacks reflecting the "shock therapy" economic changes of post-1990 Russia. Only enormous food imports sustained the population. Nevertheless, within a number of years agriculture began to revive. The government now tries to be an agent of agricultural development by attracting financial resources. The 2002 land code encouraged domestic investment in agriculture. The former collective and state farms have been privatized and turned into corporate farms that operate as common stock companies with various organizational forms. In addition, there is a growing sector of individuals' plots and farms. Today private farms and individually owned plots control about 20 percent of agricultural land and 48 percent of cattle, and account for over a half of all agricultural production. In northern regions, farming includes mainly livestock raising, whereas in southern areas and Western Siberia, farms produce grain. Russia has once again become an exporter of grain and foodstuffs, a sharp turn from the constant vast Soviet-era imports of foodstuffs. Regardless, Russian agriculture is still in the process of a transformation that has proceeded slowly. Bolshevik policies succeeded in making the agricultural sector repellent to most young people. Today in Russia most people have no desire to work in agriculture. The Russian peasant hardly exists. The agricultural sector occupies about only 9 percent of total employment. Of course, economic modernization displaces the peasant way of life everywhere. Corporate farms are not villages or small farms. Yet many parts of the world made and are still making the transition, painfully but without the acute use of force. The communist methodology for modernization was marked by an extreme violence and contempt which has left its imprint on Russian life to this day. Let us at least recall, as did the great Russian poet Pushkin, that the peasant in the village was the carrier of Russian language and culture.

Notes

Introduction

1   Boris B. Gorshkov, *A Life under Russian Serfdom: The Memoirs of Savva Dmitrievich Purlevskii, 1800–1868* (Budapest and New York: Central European University Press, 2005), 66.

2   James C. Scott, *The Moral Economy of the Peasant: Rebellion and Subsistence in Southeast Asia* (Yale University Press, 1977).

3   Samuel Popkin, *The Rational Peasant: The Political Economy of Rural Society in Vietnam* (Berkeley: University of California Press, 1979).

4   Richard Pipes, *Russia under the Old Regime* (New York: Scribner, 1974); and idem, *The Russian Revolution, 1899–1919* (London: Knopf, 1990). For further discussion of similar interpretations see also Martin Malia, *Alexander Herzen and the Birth of Russian Socialism* (Cambridge, MA: Harvard University Press, 1961); and idem, "What Is the Intelligentsia?" in Richard Pipes, ed., *The Russian Intelligentsia* (New York: Cambridge University Press, 1961).

5   Orlando Figes, *A People's Tragedy: A History of the Russian Revolution* (New York: Viking, 1996), 89.

6   For discussion, see Alexander Gerschenkron, "The Rate of Growth of Industrial Production in Russia since 1885," *Journal of Economic History* VII (1947): 144–174; idem, *Economic Backwardness in Historical Perspective* (Cambridge, MA: Belknap Press of Harvard University Press, 1962); idem, "The Early Phases of Industrialization in Russia: Afterthoughts and Counterthoughts," in W. W. Rostow, ed., *The Economic of Take-Off into Sustained Growth* (New York: St. Martin's Press, 1963); idem, "Problems and Patterns of Russian Economic Development," in C. E. Black, ed., *The Transformation of Russian Society, Aspects of Social Change since 1861* (Cambridge, MA: Harvard University Press, 1967); and idem, *Europe in the Russian Mirror, Four Lectures in Economic History* (New York: Cambridge University Press, 1970).

7   See Arcadius Kahan, *Russian Economic History: The Nineteenth Century*, Roger Weiss, ed. (Chicago, 1989); and idem, "Continuity in Economic Activity and Policy during the Post-Petrine Period in Russia," *Journal of Economic History* 25.1 (1965): 61–85.

8   For discussion, see William Blackwell, *The Beginnings of Russian Industrialization, 1800–1860* (Princeton, NJ: Princeton University Press, 1968)

and Olga Crisp, *Studies in Russian Economy* (New York: Palgrave Macmillan UK, 1976), 17.

9   See, for example, Tom Kemp, *Industrialization in Nineteenth-Century Europe*, 2nd ed. (New York: Routledge, 1985), ch. 5; Sidney Pollard, *Peaceful Conquest: The Industrialization of Europe* (Oxford University Press, 1981); Peter Stearns, *The Industrial Revolution* (Westview Press, 2012).

10 For discussion of peasant multi-occupational economy, see Judith Pallot and Denis Shaw, *Landscape and Settlement in Romanov Russia, 1613-1917* (Oxford, 1990), 221. Although Pallot and Shaw point out that the cottage industry was widespread in the Russian province, agriculture was their main concern in this book.

11 For discussion, see Leopold H. Haimson, "The Problem of Social Stability in Urban Russia, 1905-1917," *Slavic Review* 23 (1964): 619-642 and 24.1 (1965): 1-22; idem, "Social Identities in Early Twentieth Century Russia," *Slavic Review* 47 (1988): 1-21; idem, "Civil War and the Problem of Social Identities in Early Twentieth-Century Russia," in Diane P. Koenker, William G. Rosenberg, and Ronald Grigor Suny, eds., *Party, State and Society in the Russian Civil War: Explorations in Social History* (Bloomington, 1989), 24-47.

12 For discussion, see Gregory L. Freeze, "The *Soslovie* (Estate) Paradigm in Russian Social History," *American Historical Review* 91 (1986): 11-36.

13 David Moon, "Reassessing Russian Serfdom," *European History Quarterly* 26.4 (1996): 483-526, 515.

14 Elise Kimerling Wirtschafter, *Social Identity in Imperial Russia* (Dekalb: University of Northern Illinois Press, 1997), 102. See also idem, *Religion and Enlightenment in Catherinian Russia: The Teachings of Metropolitan Platon* (DeKalb: Northern Illinois University Press, 2013).

15 Boris B. Gorshkov, "Democratizing Habermas: Peasant Public Sphere in Pre-Reform Russia," *Russian History/Histoire Russe* 31 (Winter 2004); and idem, "Serfs on the Move: Peasant Seasonal Migration in Pre-Reform Russia, 1800-1861," *Kritika* 1.4 (Fall 2000).

16 Baron August von Haxthausen, *Studien über die innern Zushtände [das Volksleben und insbesondere die ländichen Einrichtungen] Russlands* (Berlin, 1852).

17 V. I. Lenin, *Polnoe sobranie sochinnii*, 5th ed., vol. 50 (Moscow: Politizdat, 1965), vol. 6:. 25.

18 Nikolai Alekseevich Polevoi, *Istoriia russkogo naroda*, 6 vol (Moscow: Tipografiia Avgusta Semena, 1829-1933).

19 Soliviev, Sergei Mikhailovich, *Istoria Rossii s drevneishikh vremen*, 6 vol (St. Petersburg: Tovarishestvo 'Obshchestvennaia pol'za, 1851-79).

20 Afanasii Prokof'evich Shchapov, *Sochineniia*, 3 vol (S. Petersburg: Izd. M. B. Pirozhkova, 1906-1908); V. O. Kliuchevsky, *A History of Russia*, transl. by C. J. Hogarth (New York: Russell & Russell, 1960).

21 Pallot and Shaw, *Landscape and Settlement in Romanov Russia, 1613-1917*.

22 Kahan, *Russian Economic History*, 7.

23 Leslie E. Anderson, *The Political Ecology of the Modern Peasant* (Baltimore: Johns Hopkins University Press, 1994).

Chapter 1

1 This chapter derives from my published studies: *A Life under Russian Serfdom* (Budapest, Hungary: Central European University Press, 2005); "Democratizing Habermas: Peasant Public Sphere in Pre-Reform Russia," *Russian History/Histoire Russe* 31 (Winter 2004); "Serfs on the Move: Peasant Seasonal Migration in Pre-Reform Russia, 1800–1861," *Kritika* 1.4 (Fall 2000); and "Serfdom: Eastern Europe," in Peter N. Stearns, ed. in chief, *Encyclopedia of European Social History from 1300 to 2000,* 6 vols (New York: Charles Scribner's Sons, 2001), 2: 379–388.

2 Moon, "Reassessing Russian Serfdom," 515; idem, *The Russian Peasantry, 1600–1930: The World the Peasants Made* (London and New York: Addison Wesley Longman, 1999); and idem, *The Abolition of Serfdom in Russia, 1762–1907* (London: Longman, 2001).

3 Inna Ivanovna Ignatovich, *Krest'ianskoe dvizhenie v Rossii v pervoi chetverti XIX veka* (Moscow: Izdatel'stvo sotsial'no-ekonomicheskoi literatury, 1963), 16; Vladimir Aleksandrovich Fedorov, *Pomeshchich'i krest'iane tsentral'nogo promyshlennogo raiona Rossii kontsa XVIII pervoi poloviny XIX veka* (Moscow: Izdatel'stvo Moskovskogo universiteta, 1974), 3.

4 Gorshkov, "Serfs on the Move," 633.

5 Carol S. Leonard, *Reform and Regicide: The Reign of Peter III of Russia* (Bloomington: Indiana University Press, 1993), 46.

6 Boris Mironov, "concequences," 468.

7 For more discussion of serf marriages, see John Bushnell, "Did Serf Owners Control Serf Marriage? Orlov Serfs and Their Neighbors, 1773–1861," *Slavic Review* 52 (1993): 419–445.

8 Marina Mikhailovna Gromyko, *Mir russkoi derevni* (Moscow: Molodaia gvardiia, 1991), 167–176.

9 For more discussion about gender roles and labor obligations, see Chapter 3.

10 Steven Hoch, *Serfdom and Social Control in Russia: Petrovskoe, a Village in Tambov* (Chicago: University of Chicago Press), 1986.

11 Gorshkov, "Serfs on the Move," 645.

12 Boris B. Gorshkov, "Serfdom: Eastern Europe," in Peter N. Stearns, ed. in chief, *Encyclopedia of European Social History from 1300 to 2000* (New York: Charles Scribner's Sons, 2001), 2: 384.

13 Vladimir A. Fedorov, *Krest'ianskoe dvizhenie v tsentral'noi Rossii, 1800–1860* (Moscow, 1980), 48–50.

Chapter 2

1   For more discussion about the Time of Trouble, see Chester S. L. Dunning, *Russia's First Civil War: The Time of Troubles and the Founding of the Romanov Dynasty* (Penn State Press, 2001).

2   David Moon, *The Russian Peasantry, 1600–1930: The World Peasants Made* (London and New York: Addison Wesley Longman, 1999), 21–22, 49.

3   Moon, *The Russian Peasantry*, 43.

4   Ibid., 34.

5   Leonid V. Milov, *Velkorusskii pakhar' i osobennosti rossiiskogo istoricheskogo protsessa* (Moscow: Rospen, 2001), 38.

6   Milov, *Velkorusskii pakhar'*, 40.

7   Ibid., 59–60.

8   Wayne S. Vucinich, ed., *The Peasantry in the Nineteenth Century Russia* (Stanford: Stanford University Press, 1968), xvi; Francis M. Watters, "The Peasant and the Village Commune," in Wayne S. Vucinich, ed., *The Peasant in the Nineteenth Century Russia* (Stanford: Stanford University Press, 1968), 133 and 152; Theodore H. Von Laue, "The State and the Economy," in Cyril Black, ed., *The Transformation of Russian Society* (Cambridge, MA: Harvard University Press, 1960), 298 and 301; Hugh Seton-Watson, *The Russian Empire 1801–1917* (Oxford: Clarendon Press, 1967), 514–517; Sidney Harcave, *The Russian Revolution of 1905* (London: Collier Books, 1970), 19–20; Richard Robbins, *Famine in Russia 1891–1892* (New York: Columbia University Press, 1975), 3–10 and Alexander Gerschenkroni, "Agrarian Policies and Industrialization: Russia 1861–1917," in H. J. Habakkuk and N. Postan, eds., *Cambridge Economic History of Europe*, vol. 4, part 2 (Cambridge: Cambridge University Press, 1965), 776.

9   Gorshkov, "Serfs on the Move," 650–651.

10 Fedorov, V. A. *Krast'ianskoe dvizhenie v tsentral'noi Rossii, 1800–61* (Moscow: Izdatel'stvo Moskovskogo Universiteta, 1980), 33.

11 Fedorov, *Krast'ianskoe dvizhenie v tsentral'noi Rossii, 1800–61*, 34.

Chapter 3

1   The discussion in this chapter is based on Chapter 1 of my book *Russia's Factory Children: State, Society and Law, 1800–1917* (Pittsburg: University of Pittsburg Press, 2009).

2   One of the major questions in childhood studies is the origins and development of childhood as a social concept. Starting with Philippe Aries, scholars have widely viewed childhood as a cultural invention of modern times. Aries asserted

concept that premodern Europe did not distinguish childhood from other stages of life. Following Aries scholars have argued that medieval and early modern society did not see children as persons in a unique and separate stage of life but rather perceived them as miniature, underaged adults. Accordingly, this suggests that peasants did not separate children from other persons of other ages. This study follows the most recent scholarship, plus the findings of Russian-language ethnographers and anthropologists. For discussion of this issue, see T. A. Bernshtam, *Molodezh v v obriadovoi zhizni russkoi obshchiny XIX - nachala XX v* (Leningrad: Nauka, 1988), 24–25; Clark Nardinelli, *Child labor and the Industrial Revolution* (Bloomington and Indianapolis: Indiana University Press, 1990), 51–57.

3   I. I. Shangina, *Russkie deti i ikh igry* (St. Petersburg: Iskusstvo, 2000), 7.

4   Shangina, *Russkie deti i ikh igry*, 7.

5   Bernshtam, *Molodezh*, 25.

6   Ibid., 57.

7   Ibid., 56.

8   Gromyko, *Mir russkoi derevni*, 108.

9   Shangina, *Russkie deti i ikh igry*, 7.

10   Gorshkov, *Russia's Factory Children*, Chapter 1.

11   Shangina, *Russkie deti i ikh igry*, 53.

12   G. S. Maslova, *Narodnaia odezhda v vostochnoslavianskikh traditsionnykh obychaiakh i obriadakh XIX - nachala XX veka* (Moscow: Nauka, 1984), 106.

13   Philippe Aries, *Centuries of Childhood: A Social History of Family Life*, transl. by R. Baldick (New York: Knopf, 1962).

14   Bernshtam, *Molodezh*, 122–123.

15   Ibid.

16   Bernshtam, *Molodezh*, 25, 122.

17   For discussion of peasant seasonal migration before 1861, see Gorshkov, "Serfs on the Move," 627–656.

18   N. A. Minenko, *Russkaia krest'ianskaia sem'ia v Zapadnoi Sibiri, XVIII - pervoi poloviny XIX v* (Novosibirsk: Nauka, 1979), 120.

19   Gorshkov, *A Life under Russian Serfdom*, 64.

20   Kh. Chebotarev, *Istoricheskoe i topographicheskoe opisanie gorodov Moskovskoi gubernii s ikh uezdami* (Moscow: Tipografiia Gippiusa, 1787), 119–348.

21   M. M. Gromyko, *Traditsionnye normy povedenia i formy obshchenia russkikh krest'ian XIX v.* (Moscow: Nauka, 1986), 109.

22   E. N. Baklanova, *Krest'ianskii dvor i obshchina na russkom Severe, konets XVII– nachalo XVIII v.* (Moscow: Nauka, 1976), 23.

23   Baklanova, *Krest'ianskii*, 23, 41–42; Bernshtam, *Molodezh*, 123; V. A. Aleksandrov, *Sel'skaia obshchina v Rossii, XVII–nachalo XIX v* (Moscow: Nauka, 1976), 206–207; Vladimir Il'ich Lenin, *Razvitie kapitalizma v Rossii* in V. I. Lenin, *Polnoe sobranie sochinenii*, 55 vols (Moscow: Izd. Politicheskoi literatury, 1967–1970), 3: 325.

24 Baklanova, *Krest'ianskii*, 22, see Table 6.

25 B. N. Mironov, *Sotsial'naia istoriia Rossii*, 2 vols (St. Petersburg: D. Bulanin, 2000),
    1: 20, 129, 180.

26 Mironov, *Sotsial'naia*, 199–200; Baklanova, *Krest'ianskii*, 23.

27 Wanda Minge-Kalman, "The Industrial Revolution and the European Family:
    The Institutionalization of 'Childhood' as a Market for Family labor," *Comparative
    Studies in Society and History*, 20.3 (July 1978): 454–468; Bernshtam, *Molodezh*,
    57–58; Gromyko, *Mir russkoi derevni*, 107; Minenko, *Russkaia*, 51–52.

28 Gorshkov, *A Life under Russian Serfdom*.

29 A. N. Martynova, *Otrazhenie deistvitel'nosti v krest'ianskoi kolybel'noi pesne. Russkii*
    folklor. Sotsial'nyi protest v narodnoi poezii (Leningrad, 1975), 15:152; B. A.
    Romanov, *Liudi i nravy Drevnei Rusi* (Moscow and Leningrad: Nauka, 1966), 155.

30 This data is based on the 1717 census of 1,064 families of serfs and monastery
    peasants of the Kubenskii region of Vologda province, northern Russia, cited in
    Baklanova, *Krest'ianskii*, 22.

Chapter 4

1   N. Boiarkin, "*Vzgliad na selo Ivanovo*," *Moskovskii telegraf* 17 (Moscow, 1826), part
    XI, 114–115.

2   M. I. Tugan-Baranovsky, *The Russian Factory in the Nineteenth Century*, transl. by
    Arthur and Claora S. Levin (Homewood, IL, 1970), 2.

3   Parts of this chapter are drown on my article "Serfs on the Move: Peasant Seasonal
    Migration in Pre-Reform Russia".

4   V. A. Fedorov, *Pomeshchichii krest'iane tsentralinogo promyshlennogo raiona Rossii
    kontsa XVIII pervoi poloviny XIX veka* (Moscow, 1974), 4.

5   N. M. Druzhinin, *Gosudarstvennye krest'iane i Reforma P. D. Kiseleva* 2 (Moscow,
    1958), 296–390.

6   G. S. Isaev, *Rol' tekstil'noi promyshlennosti v genezise i razvitii kapitalizma v Rossii,
    1760-1860* (Leningrad, 1970), 41.

7   Gorshkov, "Serfs of the Move," 632.

8   A. K. Korsak, *O formakh promyshlennosti voobshche I o znachenii domashnego
    proizvodstva v Zapadnoi Evrope I v Rossii* (Moscow, 1861).

9   I. V. Meshalin, *Tekstil'naia promyshlennost' krest'ian moskovskoi guberni v XVIII i
    pervoi polovine XIX veka* (Moscow, 1950), 25.

10 Isaev, *Rol' tekstil'noi promyshlennosti*, 53; L. V. Ternoborskii, *O proizvoditel'nykh
    silakh Rosii* 2 (Moscow, 1858), 2: 136.

11 "Ob uluchshenii vydelki l'nianykh poloten v Rossii," Jurnal manufaktur i torgovli 11
    (1830): 6–10.

12 Ibid., 10.

13 Chebotarev, *Istoricheskoie i topograficheskoie.*

14 Ibid.; Kh. Chebotarev, *Trudy Vol'nogo Ekonomicheskogo Obshchestva* (St. Petersburg, 1767), 7: 75–82; ibid. (1769), 11:119; RGADA (Russian State Archive of Ancient Acts), *fond* 1355, *opis'* 1, *dela* 9 and 26 and *Topograficheskoe opisanie kaluzhskogo namesnechestva* (St. Petersburg, 1785), 19–20.

15 Isaev, *Rol' tekstil'noi promyshlennosti,* 56.

16 Chebotarev, *Istoricheskoie i topograficheskoie,* 110–360.

17 Gorshkov, "Serfs on the Move," 632.

18 Ibid., 634.

Chapter 5

1   I. F. Tokmakov, *Istoriko-statisticheskoe opisanie sela Grebneva Bogorodskogo uezda* (Moscow: Gorodskaia tiporgafiia, 1903), 10–16.

2   RGIA, *fond* 18, *opis'* 1, *delo* 156, *listy* 302–304.

3   Ibid., *delo* 22, *listy* 113–114.

4   *Zhurnal manufaktur i torgovli* 1 (1828): 100.

5   RGIA, *fond* 18, *opis'* 1, *delo* 131, *listy* 75-75a.

6   L. Samoilov, *Atlas promyshlennosti Moskovskoi gubernii* (Moscow: Gorodskaia tiporgafiia, 1845), 73–75.

7   "Nadezhdy shelkovoi promyshlennosti," *Moskovitianin* 14 (Moscow, 1850): 132–133.

8   For general discussion of the general economic growth of Russia during the first half of the nineteenth century see Tugan-Baranovsky, *Russian Factory*; Blackwell, *The Beginnings of Russian Industrialization*; Olga Crisp, *Studies in the Russian Economy*, 5–73; and Arcadius Kahan, *Russian Economic History.*

9   For discussion of some aspects of trading peasants activities before 1961, see Crisp, *Studies in the Russian Economy*, 73–95; Blackwell, *The Beginnings of Russian Industrialization*; Jerome Blum, *Lord and Peasant in Russia from the Ninth to the Nineteenth Century* (Princeton: Princeton University Press, 1961); Alfred J. Rieber, *Merchants and Entrepreneurs in Imperial Russia* (Chapel Hill: University of North Carolina Press, 1982), 45–52; Gregory Guroff et al., eds. *Entrepreneurship in Imperial Russia and the Soviet Union* (Princeton: University of Princeton Press, 1983); and Anne Lincoln Fitzpatrick, *The Great Russian Fair: Nizhnii Novgorod, 1840–90* (New York: Macmillan, 1990).

10 Samoilov, *Atlas Promyshlennosti*, 19; S. Tarasov, *Statisticheskoe obozrenie promyshlennosti Moskovskoi gubernii* (Moscow, 1856).

11 *Trudy Komissii po peresmotru ustava Fabrichnogo i remeslennogo* (St. Petersburg, 1863), 1: 51–62.

12 *Iz istorii fabrik i savodiv Moskvy i Moskovskoi gubernii: konets XVIII nachalo XX veka, Obzor dokumentov* (Moscow, 1968), 45. Also see *Istoria Moskvy* 3, *Period razlozheniia krepostnogo stroia* (Moscow, 1954), 302.

13 For further discussion of serf-entrepreneurial activities see Tugan-Baranovsky, *Russian Factory* and Blackwell, *The Beginnings of Russian Industrialization*.

14 Blackwell, *The Beginnings of Russian Industrialization*, 205.

15 Tarasov, *Statisticheskoe obozrenie*, 28.

16 Ibid., see Volokolamskii and Klinskii districts.

17 Ibid., see Bronnistkii and Bogorodskii districts.

18 In her study, Linda Edmondson rightly pointed out that "one can do little more than guess" about the relationship between feminism and women's economic status in Russia because of the absence of research on the economic history of Russian women. See Linda H. Edmondson, *Feminism in Russia, 1900–17* (Stanford: Stanford University Press, 1984), 12. Although several studies on this topic appeared since 1984 when Edmondson's book was published, most focus on female workers in the late nineteenth and early twentieth centuries. Women's economic role in Russia in the pre-reform decades and particularly women entrepreneurs still remain a neglected subject.

19 *Trudy Vol'nogo Ekonomicheskogo obshestva* (St. Petersburg, 1783), 83:157.

20 *Zhurnal manufaktur i torgovli* 6 (1830), 2: 14–15, 53–85.

21 *Zhurnal Ministerstva vnutrennikh del* (1844), 7: 132–133.

22 *Zhurnal manufaktur i torgovli* 7–9 (1855), 3: 59–63; *Vladimirskie gubernslie vedomosti* 26 (1856): 205.

23 Isaev, *Rol' tekstil'noi promyshlennosti*, 162.

24 Meshalin, *Tekstil'naia Promyshlennost' Krest'ian*, 108–109.

25 *Opisanie Pervoi vystavki rossiiskikh manufakturnykh izdelii* (St. Petersburg, 1829), 136–150.

26 *Zhurnal manufaktur i torgovli* 1–3 (1844)1: 349.

27 A. Shipov, *Khlopchatobumazhnaia promyshlennost' i vazhnost' ee snacheniia v Rossii* (Moscow, 1857), 1:50–51.

28 *Moskovskie vedomosti* 121 (Moscow, 1843), 719.

29 The calculation of this number is based on the figures taken from Kazantsev, *Rabochie Moskvy*, 16 and from Meshalin, *Tekstil'naia Promyshlennost' Krest'ian*, 208.

30 *Obzor Razlichnikh Otraslei Manufakturnoi Promyshlennosti Rossii* (Moscow, 1863), 2: 449.

31 *Vestnik Promyshlennosti* (Moscow, 1860), 13: 226.

32 RGIA, *fond* 18, *opis'* 5, *delo* 1543, *list* 6.

33 *Vladimirskie gubernskie vedomosti* 25 (Vladimir, 1856), 196.

34 N. Ponomarev, *O bumagopriadil'nykh fabrikakh v Rossii* (Moscow, 1839), 64–71.

35 RGIA, *fond* 18, *opis'* 2, *delo* 30, *listy* 78–79.

36 Ibid.

37 Ibid., *fond* 18, opis' 1, *delo* 3, *listy* 482– 486, 487, 558.

38 N. I. Fil'kovskii, *Moskva v istorii tekhniki* (Moscow, 1952), 293– 294.

39 Cited in Isaev, *Rol' tekstil'noi promyshlennosti*, 186.

40 *Zhurnal manufaktur i torgovli* (Moscow, 1854)1: 146.

41 M. Vasil'ev, "Selo Ivanovo," *Vestnik promyshlennosti* 3 (Moscow, 1859), 57.

42 V. S. Prugavin, *Promysly Vladimirskoi gubernii* 1 (Moscow, 1882), 6–7; *Statisticheskii vremennik Rossiiskoi imperii*, 3rd ed., 121–123, 150.

43 *Moskovskii vestnik* 3 (1827): 309–311; ibid., 5 (1827): 109–110.

44 RGIA, *fond* 18, opis' 2, *delo* 636, *listy* 237–238.

45 Isaev, *Rol' tekstil'noi promyshlennosti*, 197–198.

46 The Russian State Public Library. The Manuscript department, *fond* 332, *karta* 75, *delo* 27.

47 Ibid.

48 Ibid., *fond* 332, *karta* 77, *delo* 21, *list* 1.

49 S. G. Strumilin, *Ocherki ekonomicheskoi istorii Rossii* (Moscow, 1960), 437.

50 Kazantsev, *Rabochie Moskvy*, 33; *Moskovskie gubernskie vedimosti* 45 (Vladimir, 1848)

Chapter 6

1 For detailed discussion of manorial and possessional workers, see Tugan-Baranovsky, *The Russian Factory*, 82–131; Blum, *Lord and Peasant in Russia*. See also PSZ, 2nd ed., vol. X, no. 7816; cited in Tugan-Baranovsky, 92.

2 For discussion of workers' unrest in these factories, see Reginald E. Zelnik, *Labor and Society in Tsarist Russia: The Factory Workers of St. Petersburg, 1850-1870* (Stanford: Stanford University Press, 1971).

3 TsGIAM, *fond* 17, opis' 97, *delo* 119, l. 30; see also "Otchet Moskovskogo Oberpolitseimeistera za 1846 god," "Vedomost' narodonaseleniia v Moskve za 1846," no. 5, 1846.

4 These figures are taken from Isaev, *Rol' tekstil'noi promyshlennosti*, 118–169.

5 Kazantsev, *Rabochie Moskvy*, 54–76.

6 *Materialy dlia statistiki Rossii, sobiraemye po vedomstvu Ministerstva gosudarstvennykh imuschestv*, 1st ed. (St. Petersburg, 1858), 43; Kazantsev, *Rabochie Moskvy*, 66.

7 *Obozrenie glavneishikh otraslei manufacturnoi promyshlennosti v Rossii* (St. Petersburg, 1845), 134.

8 RGIA, *fond* 18, opis' 2, *delo* 1927, *listy* 212, 213; TsGIAM (Central State Archive of the city of Moscow), *fond* 14, opis' 1, *delo* 3266, *listy* 2–38; ibid., *fond* 2354, opis' 1, *delo* 41, *listy* 197a–199, 228.

9 Soviet historians usually took the opposite view, claiming that the "proletarianization" of the Russian worker occurred already during the first half of the nineteenth century. See discussion in P. G. Rydziunskii, "Voprosy istorii Russkoi promyshlennosti v XIX v," *Istoriia SSSR* 5 (Moscow, 1972): 40–58.

10 A. B. Zaks, "Delo Krest'ian Fabriki Mertvago.(Bor'ba Fabrichnykh Krest'ian za Svoe Osvobozhdenie v 1857-1859 gg," *Revoliutsionnaia Situatsiia v Rossii v 1859-1861* (Moscow, 1960), 207.

11 *Moskovskie vedomosti* (December 7, 1846).

12 "Otchet Moskovskogo Oberpolitsmeistera za 1846 god," 80–81.

13 Kazantsev, *Rabochie Moskvy*, 77–78.

14 For more discussion about child industrial labor in Russian factories, see Boris B. Gorshkov, _Russia's Factory Children: State, Society and Law, 1800-1917_ (University of Pittsburgh Press, 2009).

15 TsGIAM, *fond* 17, *opis'* 34, *delo* 48, *list* 244.

16 Tugan-Baranovsky, *Russian Factory*, 164.

17 Ibid., 167.

18 von Haxthausen, *Studien über die innern Zushtände*, vol. I, pp. xiii, 170–71, 326; vol. III, pp. 584, 586. Cited in Tugan-Baranovsky, *Russian Factory*, 167.

19 B. N. Kazantsev, "Zakonodatel'stvo Russkogo Tsarizma po Regulirovaniiu Krest'ianskogo Otkhoda v XVII-XIX vv," *Voprosy Istorii*, 1970, no. 6.

20 PSZ, 2nd collection, vol. X (1835), no. 8157; N. S. Kiniapina, "'Rabochii vopros' v politike tsarizma vtoroi chetverti XIX veka," *Istoria SSSR* 1 (1967): 39–40; Kazantsev, *Rabochie Moskvy*, 98; Tugan-Baranovsky, *The Russian Factory*, 132–146.

21 Kiniapina, "'Rabochii vopros' v politike tsarizma vtoroi chetverti XIX veka," 40; Tugan-Baranovsky, *Russian Factory*, 136.

22 Kazantsev, *Rabochie Moskvy*, 99.

23 Tugan-Baranovsky, *Russian Factory*, 139.

24 PSZ, 2nd ed., vol. X, 1835, no. 8157. Also see Kiniapina, "'Rabochii vopros' v politike tsarizma vtoroi chetverti XIX veka," 39–40; Kazantsev, *Rabochie Moskvy*, 109–133; Tugan-Baranovsky, *Russian Factory*, 132–146.

25 Isaev, Rol' tekstil'noi promyshlennosti, 266–267.

26 Little is written on the associations of peasant-migrants in pre-reform Russia. The existing scholarship which addresses certain aspects of the associations usually concentrates on the late nineteenth-early twentieth centuries. For discussion of *zemliachestva* and *arteli*, see Christine D. Worobec, *Peasant Russia: Family and Community in the Post-Emancipation Period* (Princeton, 1991); J. Burds, "The Social Control of Peasant Labor in Russia: The Responses of Village Communities to labor Migration in the Central Industrial Region, 1861–1905," in Esther Kingston-Mann and Timothy R. Mixter, eds., with the Assistance of Jeffrey Burds, *Peasant Economy Culture and Politics in European Russia, 1800–1921* (Princeton University Press, 1991); Robert R. Johnson, *Peasant and Proletarian: The Working Class of Moscow*

in the Late Nineteenth Century (Rutgers, 1979); Zelnik, *Labor and Society in Tsarist Russia*. Cited in Zelnik, *Labor and Society*, 147.

27 There are major differences between *zemliachestva* and *arteli*: *zemliachestva* were organized in urban areas or at large enterprises, and usually were stationary and large in membership. *Arteli* were often small groups of peasant-migrants who jointly sought temporary or seasonal work.

28 For discussion, see Worobec, *Peasant Russia*, 33; Burds, "The Social Control of Peasant Labor in Russia," 97–100.

29 Johnson is perhaps too quick to conclude that *zemliachestva* "constituted a world apart ... that outsiders had great difficulty in penetrating"; see Johnson, *Peasant and Proletarian*, 161.

30 The earliest known incidents of labor protest took place at possessional and manorial factories where the labor force was not free.

31 TsGIAM, *fond* 16, *opis'* 34, *delo* 48, *listy* 1–25.

32 Johnson, *Peasant and Proletarian*, 68.

Chapter 7

1 This right was given to serf peasants in 1848. See Gorshkov, "Serfs on the move," 650.

2 PSZ 2, vol. IV (1832), no. 5648.

3 *Svod zakonov* (1842) vol. XI, part II, *Ustavy torgovye*, 50, nn. 317–323.

4 *Svod zakonov* (1857) vol. IX, *Zakony o sostoianiakh*, 228–230, nn. 1137–1146; and ibid. (1842), vol. XI, part II, *Ustavy Torgovye*, 2–50, nn. 4, 5, 211–232, 266–269, 317–325.

5 PSZ 2, vol. XXIII (1848), no. 22042.

6 *Svod zakonov* (1842), vol. XI, part II, *Ustavy torgovye*, 35, no. 220; and ibid., vol. XI, *Ustavy gosudarstvennogo blagoustroistva*, parts 1, 2 and 3.

7 TsGIAM, *fond* 16, *opis'* 6, *vol.* 1, *dela* 123, 367, 373, 398, 572, 699, 1204.

8 A. Shipov, "Vliianie na promyshlennost' svobodnago I obiazatel'nogo truda," *Vestnik promyshlennosti* 2, part 3 (May, 1859): 65.

9 In 1840, Prokhorovs spent about 17,000 banknote rubles, in 1842—25,845; see L. V. Koshman, "Fabrichnye shkoly v Rossii v pervoi polovine XIX v.," *Vestnik Moskovskogo Universiteta. Istoria* 2 (1976): 20–23.

10 TsGIAM, *fond* 17, *opis'* 97, *delo* 61, *tom* V, *list* 171.

11 V. Zel'tser, "Rabochie i khoziaeva 'Trekhgorki' v pervoi polovine XIX v.," Istoriia proletariata SSSR (Moscow, 1933), 1–2: 194.

12 Kazantsev, *Rabochie*, 103.

13 RGIA, *fond* 560, *opis'* 38 (1844), *delo* 499, *list* 23; and ibid. (1846), *delo* 530, *list* 112.

14 A. P. Chekhov, *Izbrannye proizvedenia v trekh tomakh*, 3 vols (Moscow, 1967), 3: 594–595.

15 C. M. Ioksimovich, *Manufakturnaia promyshlennost'*, 1–36; Tugan-Baranovsky, *Russian Factory*, 77.

16 Meshalin, *Tekstil'naia promyshlennost' krest'ian*, 122.

17 Ibid.

18 *Vestnik promyshlennosti* 3 (1859) section *"Smes"*, 74; N. B. Varadinov, *Istoriia Ministerstva vnutrennikh del*, 3 vols (St. Petersburg, 1861), 2: 436.

19 Isaev, *Rol' tekstil'noi promyshlennosti*, 51.

Chapter 8

1 This chapter is drawn on my article "Democratizing Habermas: Peasant Public Sphere in Pre-Reform Russia. For other studies, see Adele Lindenmeyer, *Poverty Is Not Vice: Charity, Society, and the State in Imperial Russia* (Princeton: Princeton University Press, 1996); Gary Thurston, *The Popular Theater Movement in Russia, 1862–1919* (Evanston, IL: Northwestern University Press, 1998); David Wartenweiler's, *Civil Society and Academic Debate in Russia, 1905–1905* (Oxford: Clarendon Press, 1999) and Cathy A. Frierson, *All Russia Is Burning! A Cultural History of Fire and Arson in Late Imperial Russia* (Seattle: University of Washington Press, 2002).

2 For further discussion, see Jean L. Cohen, and Andrew Arato, *Civil Society and Political Theory* (Cambridge, MA: MIT Press, 1992).

3 For feminist critique of Habermas's exclusion of women from the public sphere, see Seyla Benhabib, "Models of Public Space: Hannah Arendt, the Liberal Tradition and Urgen Habermas" in Joan B. Landes, ed., *Feminism, the Public and the Private* (Oxford: Oxford University Press, 1998): 65–99. See also Craig Calhoun, ed., *Habermas and the Public Sphere* (Cambridge, MA: MIT Press, 1992). Scholars, such as Geoff Eley, Nancy Fraser and others, consider the possibility of inclusion of subordinate social strata into the public sphere. See Calhoun, *Haermas and Public Sphere*. See essays by Eley, Fraser and Mary P. Ryan.

4 Gorshkov, "Serfs on the Move."

5 For a detailed discussion of peasant seasonal migration before 1861, see Gorshkov, "Serfs on the Move." For a discussion of laws on peasant migration, see also David Moon, "Peasant Migration, the Abolition of Serfdom, and the Internal Passport System in the Russian Empire, c. 1800–1914," in David Eltis, ed., *Coerced and Free Migration: Global Perspectives* (Stanford: Stanford University Press, 2002), 324–357.

6 See, for example, Blackwell, *The Beginnings of Russian Industrialization, 1800–1860* and Crisp, *Studies in the Russian Economy*. See also Ivan V. Meshalin, Tekstil'naia promyshlennost' and Isaev, *Rol' tekstil'noi promyshlennosti*.

7   See Milov, *Velkorusskii pakhar'* (Moscow: Rospen, 2001); Gorshkov, "Serfs on the Move"; Moon, *The Russian Peasantry*; Elise K. Wirtschafter, "Legal Identity and Posession of Serfs in Imperial Russia," *Journal of Modern History* 70 (September 1998): 561–597; Gromyko, *Mir russkoi derevni*; A. V. Kamkin, "Ppavosoznanie gosudarstvennykh krest'ian vtoroi poloviny XVIII veka," Istoriia SSSR 2 (1987); V. I. Krutikov, "Pravosoznanie krest'ian i ego otrazhenie v krest'ianskom dvizhenii," in *Sotsial'no-politicheskoe i pravovoe polozhenie krest'ianstva v dorevoliutsionnoi Rossii* (Voronezh, 1983); D. I. Raskin, "Ispol'zovaniie zakonodatel'nykh aktov v krest'ianskikh chelobitnykh serediny XVIII veka," Istoriia SSSR 4 (1979); Vladimir A. Fedorov, "K voprosy ideologii krepostnogo krest'ianstva" in *Voprosy Agrarnoi istorii Tsentra i Severo-Zapada RSFSR* (Smolensk, 1972).

8   On rumors about abolition of serfdom see GARF, f 1165, op. 1, dd. 86, 88, 90, 92, 98. Also see Golikova, 176–177; Chistov (1969); Gromyko, *Mir russkoi derevni*, 221.

9   Savva Dmitrivich Purlevskii, "Vospominaniia krepostnogo," Russkii Vestnik 130 (July 1877), 339; Russkii arkhiv 6 (1898), 132.

10 For discussion, see Kamkin, "Ppavosoznanie,"; Krutikov, "Pravosoznanie krest'ian."

11 See, for example, Gromyko, *Mir russkoi derevni*, 241; Raskin, "Ispol'zovanie,"180–182; Kamkin, "Ppavosoznanie," 163–173; Krutikov, Pravosoznanie krest'ian," 177–185; See also Wirtschafter, "Legal Identity." For archival evidence, see files of peasants' legal dealings with the office of Moscow governor in TsIAM f. 16, op. 6 (tom 1), dd. 123, 367, 373.

12 Gromyko, *Mir russkoi derevni*, 212.

13 RGIA f. 1286, op. 19 (1858 g.), d. 603, ll. 2–6. See also discussion in Vladimir A. Fedorov, "Trebovaniia krest'ianskogo dvizheniia v nachale revoliutsionnoi situatsii, do 19 fevralia 1861 g." in Militsa V. Nechkina, editor in chief, *Revoliutsionnaia situatsiia v Rossii v 1859–1861 gg.* (Moscow, 1960), 133–147.

14 Gromyko, *Mir russkoi derevni*; Fedorov, *Krest'ianskoe dvizhenie*.

15 Iakov I. Linkov, *Ocherki krest'ianskogo dvizheniia v Rossii v 1825 - 1861 gg.* (Moscow, 1952), 57.

16 Fedorov, *Krest'ianskoe dvizhenie*, 97.

17 Cited in Linkov, *Ocherki krest'ianskogo*, 97.

18 Fedor S. Gorovoi, Padenie krepostnogo prava na gornykh zavodakh Yrala (Perm', 1961), 114.

19 GARF, f. 109 "Sekretnyi arkhiv," op. 3, d. 1375, ll. 69–74.

20 Linkov, *Ocherki krest'ianskogo*, 4; I. I. Ignatovich, "Krest'ianskie volneniia pervoi chetverti XIX v.," Voprosy istorii 9 (1950), 48–49.

21 For discussion, see Fedorov, *Krest'ianskoe dvizhenie*.

22 K. Tikhonravov, "Ofeni Vladimirskoi gubernii," Zhurnal Ministerstva vnutrennikh del [St. Petersburg] 9 (1854); Pavel I. Iakushkin, Putevye pis'ma; Materialy dlia statistiki Rossii sobiraemye po vedomstvu Ministerstva gosudarstvennkh

imushchestv (Sankt Petersburg, 1858), 57. See also citations in Gorshkov, "Sers on the Move," 628, 652, 654.

23 Here nastroenie means a range of ideas, views, attitudes, opinions, interests, etc. See Bol'shoi Tolkovyi Slovar' Russkogo Iazyka (St. Petersburg, 2003), 602.

24 GARF, f. 109, "sekretnyi arkhiv," op. 3 d. 78 (a message of S. Bezobrazov to Aleksandr II, 1857); ibid, d. 73 (a message of K. Aksakov to Aleksandr II, 1855).

25 GARF, f. 109, "sekretnyi arkhiv," op. 3, dd. 3197–3246; f. 109, 4-aia ekspeditsiia, d. 199; f. 815, d. 224; ibid., f. 16, op. 48 (1858), d. 244; f. 815, op. 1, d. 144.

26 Linkov, *Ocherki krest'ianskogo*, 57.

27 Gorshkov, "Serfs on the Move," 633–34, 641, 650–651, 655.

Chapter 9

1 Most Soviet scholars of serfdom have offered an economic explanation of serfdom's decline. These historians traditionally emphasized the "crisis of feudalism" which, they believe, accelerated during the first half of the nineteenth century. *Revoliutsionnaia situatsiia v Rossii v 1859–1861 gg.* Militsa V. Nechkina, editor in chief (Moscow: Izdatel'stvo Akademii Nauk, 1960).

2 For this interpretation, see W. Bruce Lincoln, *The Great Reforms: Autocracy. Bureaucracy, and the Politics of Change in Imperial Russia* (DeKalb, IL: Northern Illinois University Press), 1990.

3 Aleksandr Kazemirovich Korsak, *O formakh promyshlennosti voobshche i o znachenii domashnego proizvodstva kustarnoi i domashnei promyshlennosti* (Moscow: V Tip. Gracheva, 1861).

4 Gorshkov, "Democratizing Habermas," 348.

5 Ibid., 385.

6 D. I. Shakhovskoi, *Velikaia Reforma* (Moscow: Sytina, 1911), 105

7 Shakhovskoi, *Velikaia Reforma*, 108.

8 V. A. Fedorov, "Trebovania krest'ianskogo dvizhenia v nachale revoliutsionnoi situatsii, do 19 fevralia 1861 g.," in M. V. Nechkina, editor-in-chief, *Revoliutsionnaia situatsia v Rossii v 1959–1861 gg.* (Moscow: Izd. Akademii nauk SSSR, 1960), 133–147.

9 For a discussion about the peace arbitrators, see Roxanne Easly, *The Emancipation of the Serfs in Russia: Peace Arbitrators and the Development of Civil Society.* Routledge Series on Russian and East European Studies (Routledge: London and New York, 2009).

Chapter 10

1   A. A. Kornilov, *Kurs istorii Rossii XIX veka*, reprint (Moscow: Vysshaia shkola, 1993), 335; and N. P. Oganovskii, *Zakonomernost' agrarnoĭ evoliutsii* (Saratov: Ėlektro-tipo-litografiĭa B.L. Rabinovich, 1909-1911).

2   Kornilov, *Kurs istorii Rossii XIX veka*, 336; D. I. Rikhter, "Zadolzhennost' chastnogo zemlevladenia" in *Vliianie urozhaev i khlebnykh tsen na nekotorye storony russkogo narodnogo khoziaistva* (St. Petersburg, 1897), 379–380; I. Shakhovskoi, "Vylupnye platezhi" in *Velikaia reforma* (Moscow: Sytina, 1911), 6:, 106; and Oganovskii, *Ocherki po istorii*, 445–446.

3   Kornilov, *Kurs istorii Rossii XIX veka*, 336–337; Oganovskii, *Ocherki po istorii*, 450–451.

4   Kornilov, *Kurs istorii Rossii XIX veka*, 337; Oganovskii, *Ocherki po istorii*, 446.

5   For more discussion about agrarian crisis, see G. T. Robinson, *Rural Russia under the Old Regime : A History of the Landlord-Peasant World and a Prologue to the Peasant Revolution of 1917* (London; New York; Toronto: Longmans, Green and Co, 1932); Lazar Volin, *A Century of Russian Agriculture. From Alexander II to Khrushchev* (Cambridge, MA: Harvard University Press, 1970); among recent studies that emphasize agrarian crisis is Stephen Wheatcroft's "Crises and the Condition of the Peasantry in Late Imperial Russia," in Esther Kingston-Mann and Timothy Mixter, eds., *Peasant Economy, Culture, and Politics of European Russia, 1800–1921* (Princeton, NJ: Princeton University Press, 1991), 128–172.

6   For this interpretation see Christine D. Worobec, *Peasant Russia: Family and Community in the Post-Emancipation Period* (Dekalb: Northern Illinois University Press, 1995).

7   For more discussion of peasant schools see Ben Eclof, *Russian Peasant Schools: Officialdom, Village Culture, and Popular Pedagogy* (Berkeley: University of California Press, 1986).

8   Jeffrey Burds, *Peasant Dreams & Market Politics: Labor Migration and the Russian Village, 1861–1905* (Pittsburgh: University of Pittsburgh Press, 1998).

9   For more discussion about Russian urbanization during the late imperial decades, see Daniel Brower, *Estate, Class, and Community: Urbanization in Late Tsarist Russia* (Pittsburgh: University of Pittsburgh Press, 1983); and Joseph Bradley, *Muzhik and Muscovite: Urbanization in Late Imperial Russia* (Berkeley: University of California Press, 1985).

10 For more discussion about peasant women migrants see Barbar Engel, *Between the Fields and the City: Women, Work and the Family in Russia, 1861–1914* (Cambridge: Cambridge University Press, 1993).

11 Laurence Senelick, trans., *Anton Chekhov's Selected Plays* (New York: W.W. Norton & Company, 2005), 315.

12   Senelick, *Anton Chekhov's Selected Plays*, 361.

13   Gorshkov, trans., *A Life under Russian Serfdom*, 114.

Chapter 11

1   T. V. Osipova, *Rossiiskoe krestianstvo v revoliutsii i grazhdanskoi voine* (Moscow: Strelets, 2001), ch.1.

2   For more discussion about Stolypin reforms, see Judith Pallot, *Land Reform in Russia, 1906–1917* (Oxford: Clarendon Press, 1999).

3   P. A. Stolypin, "Rech' P. A Stolypina vo II Gosudarstvennoi Dume 10 maia 1907g," in *Gosudarstvennaia duma. Vtoroi Sozyv. Sessiia vtoraia. Stenograficheskiie otchety* (St. Petersburg: Gosudarstvennaia tipografiia, 1907), 2: 433–445.

4   Osipova, *Rossiiskoe krestianstvo v revoliutsii i grazhdanskoi voine.*

5   Kornilov, *Kurs istorii Rossii XIX veka*, 337.

6   For more discussion about Russia in WWI, see Peter Gatrell, *Russia's First World War. A Social and Economic History* (Harlow: Pearson, 2005).

7   For further information on extensive revolutionary propaganda and activities at the fronts and throughout Russia, see M. S. Melancon, *The Socialist Revolutionaries and the Russian Anti-War Movement, 1914–1917* (Columbus, OH: Ohio State University, 1990).

8   For more discussion on this subject see Michael S. Melancon, "The Syntax of Soviet Power: The Resolutions of Local Soviets and Other Institutions, March-October 1917," *The Russian Review* 52.4 (1993): 486–505.

Chapter 12

1   Alec Nove, *An Economic History of the USSR* (London: Allen Lane/Penguin Press, 1969), 68–74.

2   Lenin, *Polnoe sobranie sochinnii*, 5th ed., vol. 50, 137.

3   Orlando Figes and Peasant Rassia, *Civil War: Volga Countryside in Revolution, 1917–1921* (Oxford: Clarendon Press, 1989), 250.

4   GARF, f. 393, op. 3, d. 44, ll. 172–173; idem, d. 160, ll. 91–95; idem, d. 210, l. 50.

5   For more discussion, see Michael Melançon, "The Expedition of Narkomzem to Orel Province, Fall 1918: The Development of the Grain Requisitioning Program," *Russian Review*.

6   GARF, f. 5207, op. 1, d. 48, l. 175.

7   James Hughes, *Stalin, Siberia and the Crisis of the NEP* (Cambridge: Cambridge University Press, 1991), 109.

Chapter 13

1 For more discussion about the Uralo-Siberian Method, see James Hughes, "Capturing the Russian Peasantry: Stalinist Grain Procurement Policy and the 'Ural-Siberian Method,'" *Slavic Review* 53.1 (Spring 1994): 76–103.

2 Merle Fainsod, *How Russia Is Ruled* (Cambridge, MA: Harvard University Press, 1970), 529.

3 James R. Millar, ed., *The Soviet Rural Community* (Chicago: University of Illinois Press, 1971), 27–28.

4 Sheila Fitzpatrick, *Stalin's Peasants: Resistance and Survival in the Russian Village after Collectivization* (Oxford: Oxford University Press, 1994), 67.

5 For more discussion about peasant resistance during collectivization, see Lynne Viola, *Peasant Rebels under Stalin: Collectivization and the Culture of Peasant Resistance* (New York: Oxford University Press, 1996) and Fitzpatrick, *Stalin's Peasants.*

6 *Pravda*, No. 6, March 2, 1930.

7 GARF, f. 5207, op. 3, d. 15, ll. 106, 107, 108.

Bibliography

Aleksandrov, V. A. "Semeino-imushchestvennye otnosheniia po obychnomy pravu v Russkoi krepostnoi derevne XVIII - nachala XIX v.," *Istoriia SSSR*, vol. 6 (1979).

Ascher, P. A. *Stolypin. The Search for Stability in Late Imperial Russia.* Stanford, 2001.

Bakhtin, Mikhail M. *Toward a Philosophy of Act.* Translated by Vadim Lopunov. Edited by Michael Holquist and Vadim Lapunov. Austin, 1993.

Baklanova, E. N. *Krest'ianskii dvor i obshchina na russkom Severe.* Moscow: Nauka, 1976.

Bartlett, Roger, ed. *Land Commune and Peasant Community in Russia: Communal Forms in Imperial and Early Soviet Society.* Macmillan: Basingstoke and London, 1990.

Belov, F. *The History of a Soviet Collective Farm.* New York: Praeger, 1955.

Benet, S., ed. *Village of Viriatino: An Ethnographic Study of a Russian Village.* New York: Anchor Books, 1970.

Black, Cyril, ed. *The Transformation of Russian Society: Aspects of Social Change since 1861.* Cambridge, MA: Harvard University Press, 1960.

Blackwell, William L. *The Beginnings of Russian Industrialization, 1800-1860.* Princeton, NJ: Princeton University Press, 1968.

Blackwell, William. *Russian Economic Development from Peter the Great to Stalin.* New York, 1974.

Blackwell, William, Olga Crisp, and Alfred Rieber, eds. *Merchants and Entrepreneurs in Imperial Russia.* Chapel Hill: University of North Carolina Press, 1982.

Blum, Jerome. *Lord and Peasant in Russia from the Ninth to the Nineteenth Century.* Princeton, NJ: Princeton University Press, 1961.

Boiarkin, N. "Vzgliad na selo Ivanovo," *Moskovskii telegraf*, vol. 17, part XI (Moscow, 1826): 114–115.

Bradley, Joseph. *Muzhik and Muscovite: Urbanization in Late Imperial Russia.* Berkeley: University of California Press, 1985.

Bradley, Joseph. "Subjects into Citizens: Societies, Civil Society, and Autocracy in Tsarist Russia," *The American Historical Review*, vol. 107, no. 4 (Oct. 2002): 1094–1123.

Brandenberger, David. *National Bolshevism: Stalinist Mass Culture and the Formation of Modern Russian National Identity, 1931-1956.* Cambridge, MA: Harvard University Press, 2002.

Brower, D. Estate, *Class, and Community: Urbanization in Late Tsarist Russia.* Pittsburgh: University of Pittsburg Press, 1983.

Brower, D. "Urbanization and Autocracy: Russian Urban Development in the First Half of the Nineteenth Century," *Russian Review*, no. 42 (1983): 377–402.

Brower, D. *The Russian City between Tradition and Modernity, 1850-1900*. Berkeley: University of California Press, 1990.

Burbank, Jane. *Russian Peasants Go to Court: Legal Culture in the Countryside, 1905-1917*. Bloomington: Indiana University Press, 2004.

Burbank, Jane, Mark Von Hagen, and Anatolii Remnyev, eds. *Russian Empire: Space, People, Power, 1700-1930*. Bloomington: Indiana University Press, 2007.

Burds, Jeffrey. *Peasant Dreams & Market Politics: Labor Migration and the Russian Village, 1861-1905*. Pittsburgh: University of Pittsburgh Press, 1998.

Burguière, A. "Pour une typologie des forms d'organisation de l'Europe moderne (XVI-XIX siècles)," *Annales ESC*, vol. 41 (1986): 639–655.

Bushnell, John. "Did Serf Owners Control Serf Marriage? Orlov Serfs and their Neighbors, 1773-1861," *Slavic Review*, vol. 52 (Fall 1993): 440–445.

Carr, Edward Hallett, Davies, Robert William. *A History of Soviet Russia: Foundations of a Planned Economy, 1926-1929: Volume 2*. London: Macmillan, 1971.

Chayanov, A. V. *The Theory of Peasant Economy*. University of Wisconsin Press, 1986.

Chebotarev, Kh. *Istoricheskoie i topograficheskoie opisaniie gorodov Moskovskoi gubernii s ikh uezdami*. Moscow, 1787.

Conquest, R., ed. *Agricultural Workers in the USSR*. New York, 1969.

Conquest, Robert. *The Harvest of Sorrow: Soviet Collectivisation and the Terror-Famine*. London: Hutchinson, 1986.

Cox, T. M. *Peasants, Class and Capitalism: The Rural Research of L.N. Kricman and His School*. Oxford, 1986.

Cox, T. M. *Rural Sociology in the Soviet Union*. London: Hurst, 1979.

Davies, Robert William. *The Industrialisation of Soviet Russia: Volume 1: The Socialist Offensive: The Collecitivisation of Soviet Agriculture, 1929-1930*. London: Macmillan, 1980.

Davies, Robert William. *The Industrialisation of Soviet Russia: Volume 2: The Soviet Collective Farm, 1929-1930*. London: Macmillan, 1980.

Dennison, T. K. *The Institutional Framework of Russian Serfdom*. London: Cambridge University Press, 2011.

Druzhinin, N. M. *Gosudarstvennye krest'iane i Reforma P. D. Kiseleva* 2 (Moscow, 1958): 296–390.

Easly, Roxane. *The Emancipation of the Serfs in Russia: Peace Arbitrators and the Development of Civil Society*. Routledge Series on Russian and East European Studies. Routledge: London and New York, 2009.

Ecloff, Ben. *Russian Peasant Schools: Officialdom, Village Culture, and Popular Pedagogy*. Berkeley: University of California Press, 1986.

Egerbladh, I. "From Complex to Simple Family Households in Northern Coastal Sweden, 1700-1900," *Journal of Family History*, vol. 14 (1989): 241–264.

Emmons, Terence. *The Russian Landed Gentry*. New York, NY: Cambridge University Press, 1968.

Engel, Barbara A. *Between the Fields and the City: Women, Work and the Family in Russia, 1861-1914*. Cambridge: Cambridge University Press, 1993.

Fedorov, V. A. *Krast'ianskoe dvizhenie v tsentral'noi Rossii, 1800-61*. Moscow: Izdatel'stvo Moskovskogo Universiteta, 1980.

Field, Daniel. *The End of Serfdom: Nobility and Bureaucracy in Russia, 1855-1861*. Cambridge, MA, 1976.

Figes, Orlando. *Peasant Russia, Civil War: The Volga Countryside in Revolution (1917 - 1921)*. Oxford: Clarendon Press, 1991.

Fitzpatrick, Anne L. *The Great Russian Fair: Nizhnii Novgorod, 1840-90*. New York, 1990.

Fitzpatrick, Sheila. *Stalin's Peasants: Resistance and Survival in the Russian Village after Collectivization*. New York: Oxford University Press, 1994.

Gatrell, Peter. *The Tsarist Economy, 1850-1917*. London, 1986.

Gorshkov, Boris B. "Serfs on the Move: Peasant Seasonal Migration in Pre-Reform Russia, 1800-1861," *Kritika*, vol. 1, no. 4 (Fall 2000).

Gorshkov, Boris B. "Democratizing Habermas: Peasant Public Sphere in Pre-Reform Russia," *Russian History/Histoire Russe*, vol. 31 (Winter 2004).

Gorshkov, Boris B. *A Life under Russian Serfdom: The Memoirs of Savva Dmitrievich Purlevskii, 1800-1868*. Budapest and New York: Central European University Press, 2005.

Gorshkov, Boris B. "Toward a Comprehensive Law: Tsarist Factory Labor Legislation in European Context, 1830-1914," in *Russia in the European Contest, 1789-1914: A Member of the Family*, Susan P. McCaffray and Michael Melancon, eds. New York: Palgrave MacMillan, 2005, pp. 49-70.

Gorshkov, Boris B. *Russia's Factory Children: State, Society and Law, 1800-1917*. Pittsburg: University of Pittsburg Press, 2009.

Gromyko, M. M. *Trudovye traditsii krest'ian Sibiri, XVIII - pervaia polovina XIX v.* Novosibirsk: Nauka, 1975.

Gromyko, M. M. *Traditsionnye normy povedeniia i formy obshcheniia russkikh krest'ian XIX veka*. Moscow: Nauka, 1986.

Gromyko, M. M. *Mir russkoi derevni*. Moscow: Molodaia gvardiia, 1991.

Habermas, Juergen. *The Structural Transformation of the Public Sphere: An Inquiry into a Category of Bourgeois Society*. Translated by Thomas Burger with assistance of Frederick Lawrence. Cambridge, MA: MIT Press, 1989.

Hoch, Steven. *Serfdom and Social Control in Russia: Petrovskoe, a Village in Tambov*. Chicago: University of Chicago Press, 1986.

Hughes, James. *Stalin, Siberia, and the Crisis of the New Economic Policy*. Cambridge; New York: Cambridge University Press, 1991.

Jannsens, A. "Industrialization without Family Change? The Extended Family and the Life Cycle in a Dutch Industrial Town, 1880-1920," *Journal of Family History*, vol. 11 (1986): 25–42.

Johnson, Robert E. *Peasant and Proletarian: The Working Class of Moscow in the Late Nineteenth Century*. New Brunswick, NJ: Rutgers University Press, 1979.

Kahan, Arcadius. *Russian Economic History: The Nineteenth Century*. Edited by Roger Weiss. Chicago: University of Chicago Press, 1985.

Kelly, Catriona. *Children's World : Growing Up in Russia, 1890-1991*. New Haven, CT; London : Yale University Press, 2007.

Kimerling Wirtschafter Elise. *From Serf to Russian Soldier*. Princeton, NJ: Princeton University Press, 1990.

Kimerling Wirtschafter Elise. *Social Identity in Imperial Russia*. Dekalb: University of Northern Illinois Press, 1997.

Kimerling Wirtschafter Elise. *Religion and Enlightenment in Catherinian Russia: The Teachings of Metropolitan Platon*. DeKalb: Northern Illinois University Press, 2013.

Kingston-Mann, Esther and Timothy Mixter, eds. *Peasant Economy, Culture, and Politics of European Russia, 1800-1921*. Edited by Princeton, NJ: Princeton University Press, 1991.

Kolchin, Peter. *Unfree Labor, American Slavery and Russian Serfdom*. Cambridge, MA: Harvard University Press, 1987.

Lenin, V. I. *Polnoe sobranie sochinnii*, 5th ed., vol. 50. Moscow: Politizdat, 1965.

Lewin, Moshe. *Russian Peasants and Soviet Power: A Study of Collectivization*. New York, 1975.

Male, D. J. *Russian Peasant Organization before Collectivization: A Study of the Commune and Gathering 1925 - 1930*. Cambridge: Cambridge University Press, 1971.

Malia, Martin. *Alexander Herzen and the Birth of Russian Socialism*. Cambridge, MA: Harvard University Press, 1961.

Melançon, Michael. "The Expedition of Narkomzem to Orel Province, Fall 1918: The Development of the Grain Requisitioning Program," *Russian Review*.

Melancon, Michael. "Popular Political Culture in Late Imperial Russia (1800-1917)," *Russian History/Histoire Russe*, vol. 31 (Winter 2004): 369–371.

Melancon, Michael. *The Lena Goldfields Massacre and the Crisis of the Late Tsarist State*. College Station, TX: A&M University Press, 2006.

Melancon, Michael. "Land Socialization in Soviet Russia: Theory and Practice: Guest Editor's Introduction," *Russian Studies in History*, vol. 52, no. 3 (2013): 3-10.

Melancon, Michael and Alice Pate, "Bakhtin Contra Marx and Lenin: A Polyphonic Approach to Russia's Labor and Revolutionary Movements," *Russian History/Histoire Russe*, vol. 31 (Winter 2004).

Millar, James R. "A Reformulation of A. V. Chayanov's Theory of the Peasant Economy," *Economic Development and Cultural Change*, vol. 18, no. 2 (Jan. 1970): 219–229.

Minenko, N. A. (Nina Adamovna), *Russkaia krest'ianskaia sem'ia v Zapadnoi Sibiri, XVIII - pervoi poloviny XIX v.* Novosibirsk: Nauka, 1979.

Moon, David. *The Russian Peasantry 1600-1930: The World the Peasants Made.* New York: Addison-Wesley, 1999.

Moon, David. "Peasant Migration, the Abolition of Serfdom, and the Internal Passport System in the Russian Empire, c. 1800–1914," in David Eltis, ed., *Coerced and Free Migration: Global Perspectives.* Stanford: Stanford University Press, 2002, pp. 324–357.

Morrison, Daniel. *"Trading Peasants" and Urbanization in Eighteenth-Century Russia: The Central Industrial Region.* New York: Garland Pub., 1987.

Osipova, T. V. *Rossiyskoye krest'yanstvo v Revoliutsii i Grazhdanskoi Voine.* Moskva: Izdatel'stvo Strelets, 2001.

Palli, H. "Estonian Households in the Seventeenth and Eighteenth Centuries," in R. Wall et al., eds. *Family Forms in Historic Europe.* Cambridge: Cambridge University Press, 1983.

Pallot, Judith. *Land Reform in Russia, 1906-1917.* Oxford: Clarendon Press, 1999.

Pipes, Richard. *Russia Under the Old Regime.* New York, 1974.

Pipes, Richard. *The Russian Revolution, 1899-1919.* London, 1990.

Plakans, A. "Interaction between the Household and the Kin Group in the Eastern European Past: Posing the Problem," *Journal of Family History*, vol. 12 (1987): 163–178.

Popkin, Samuel. *The Rational Peasant: The Political Economy of Rural Society in Vietnam.* Berkeley: University of California Press, 1979.

Retish, Aaron. *Russia's Peasants in Revolution and Civil War: Citizenship, Identity, and the Creation of the Soviet State, 1914-1922.* Cambridge University Press, 2008.

Robinson, G. T. *Rural Russia under the Old Regime.* New York, 1969.

Scott, James, C. *The Moral Economy of the Peasant: Subsistence and Rebellion in Southeast Asia.* Yale University Press, 1977.

Smith, Alison K. "Freed Serfs without Free People: Manumission in Imperial Russia," *AHR*, vol. 118, no. 4 (2013): 1029–1052.

Smith, R. E. F. *The Enserfment of the Russian Peasantry.* London: Cambridge University Press, 1968.

Thorniley, Daniel. *The Rise and Fall of the Soviet Rural Communist Party, 1927-39.* New York: St. Martin's Press, 1988.

Tugan-Baranovsky, M. I. *The Russian Factory in the Nineteenth Century.* Translated by Arthur and Claora S. Levin. Homewood, IL, 1970.

Viola, Lynne. *The Best Sons of the Fatherland: Workers in the Vanguard of Soviet Collectivization.* Oxford, England: Oxford University Press, 1987.

Viola, Lynne. *Peasant Rebels under Stalin: Collectivization and the Culture of Peasant Resistance.* Oxford: Oxford University Press, 1996.

Viola, Lynne, Danilov, V. P., Ivnitskii, N. A., and Kozlov, Denis, eds. *The War against the Peasantry, 1927-1930: The Tragedy of the Soviet Countryside.* Translated by Steven Shabad. New Haven, CT: Yale University Press, 2005.

Volin, Lazar. *A Century of Russian Agriculture. From Alexander II to Khrushchev.* Cambridge, MA: Harvard University Press, 1970.

Wade, Rex A. *The Russian Revolution, 1917.* Cambridge: Cambridge University Press, 2005.

Ward, Chris, ed. *The Stalinist Dictatorship.* London; New York: Arnold, 1998.

Wcislo, Frank, W. *Reforming Rural Russia: State, Local Society, and National Politics, 1855–1914.* Princeton, NJ: Princeton University Press, 1990.

Wildman, Alan. *The Defining Moment: Land Charters and the Post-Emancipation Agrarian Settlement in Russia, 1861-1863. The Carl Beck Papers in Russian and East European Studies.* No. 1205, September, 1996.

Wood, Alan. *The Origins of the Russian Revolution, 1861-1917.* London: Routledge, 1993.

Zelnik, Reginald E. *Labor and Society in Tsarist Russia: The Factory Workers of St. Petersburg, 1850-1870.* Stanford: Stanford University Press, 1971.

Index